T0294849

Praise for

Wiring the Winning Organization

"Having spent the majority of my thirty-five-year US Navy career and subsequent private industry career working in large, complex industrial organizations, what Kim and Spear have written with *Wiring the Winning Organization* completely resonates with me. I wish I had read this book decades ago; it would have helped me be a better leader."

—RADM Mark R. Whitney, US Navy (retired), USN Executive Director,
Hampton Roads Maritime Industrial Base Ecosystem

"In a world where complexity is the norm, *Wiring the Winning Organization* is the essential guide for those in need of a compass for the maze of today's business environment. With expert insights and practical strategies, Kim and Spear unravel the web of organizational structures and offer a blueprint for a more resilient and adaptive organization. This is more than a book—it's a toolkit for transforming your organization and rising to the challenges of our ever-changing landscape."

—David Silverman, CEO of CrossLead,
coauthor of *Team of Teams*

"*Wiring the Winning Organization* is an indispensable guide for modern leaders seeking to navigate the complexities of organizational success. With a keen focus on avoiding pitfalls and steering clear of the *danger zone*, this book provides actionable insights that propel a company into the *winning zone*. Drawing from a wealth of practical case studies, it equips leaders with the tools needed to lead effectively."

—Christopher Porter, SVP, CISO, Fannie Mae

"A great piece of work! By bringing together the conceptual frames of layers, *danger zone* vs. *winning zone*, and slowification/simplification/amplification, the authors not only provide an encompassing schema for those looking to drive performance by improving operations, but they also help take practices developed for particular industries and functions and generalize them across all contexts. The guidance they provide is outstanding."

—Joel Podolny, CEO, Honor Education,
former VP & Dean of Apple University

"In *Wiring the Winning Organization*, Kim and Spear have found fundamental mechanisms that allow you to rewire your organization's social circuitry, enabling people the time, resources, and capability to work together toward achieving seemingly impossible goals. This book is a must-read that deeply informs leaders on how to create great systems for outstanding performance and win."

—Jeffrey K. Liker, PhD, author of *The Toyota Way, 2nd Edition*

"As a longtime admirer of Gene Kim's groundbreaking work in DevOps and high-performing organizations, I had high expectations for *Wiring the Winning Organization*. Not only did the book meet them; it exceeded them in extraordinary ways. Gene and Steve's provocative assertion that common practices such as agile, DevOps, lean, the Toyota Production System, safety culture, resilience engineering, and more converge to form a larger, more meaningful whole deeply resonates. This insight transforms vague inklings into an elegant framework of slowification, simplification, and amplification, emphasizing the critical role of leadership in creating an environment for exceptional performance. With a compelling mix of carefully selected case studies from diverse industries and times, combined with actionable insights and reader prompts, *Wiring the Winning Organization* offers a unique blend of theory and practice. This book is an invaluable read for anyone seeking to create a winning organization—one where greatness can be achieved not by accident but because it is wired to do so."

—Adrienne Shulman, Founder, Tenger Ways

"It's a universal maxim in business that 'people problems are the hardest problems.' That maxim often precedes throwing our hands in the air and going on with business as usual, privately resigned to never understand how to address this 'hardest problem.' *Wiring the Winning Organization* illuminates the dynamics that drive organizations to success or failure. More importantly, the book condenses a century of disparate insights into a grand unified theory of management—simple enough for anyone to understand but profound enough to address the needs of the world's most high-stakes organizations. This book has the potential to equip generations of leaders with principles that are both effective and humane."

—Andrew Davis, author of *Mastering Salesforce DevOps*

"All organizations, large and small, public and private, are overwhelmed by complexity, multiple priorities, conflicting goals, shifting landscapes, and constrained resources. Gene and Steve lay out an amazing vision of the social circuitry for organizations to not only handle this but thrive while doing so."

—Phil Venables, Chief Information Security Officer, Google Cloud;
former Board Director, Goldman Sachs Bank

"Wiring the Winning Organization is a fabulous book that I highly recommend. I'm not aware of anyone who has put their finger on the fundamental truth that Kim and Spear have articulated so amazingly well: successful organizations flow from leaders who create the conditions in which many others thrive."

—Paul Gaffney, former CTO and head of technology,
The Home Depot, Kohl's, Dick's Sporting Goods

"All senior leaders should be wiring their organizations for the *winning zone*. I love the recommendation in this book that leaders need to start first, building their skills in slowification, simplification, and amplification, leading practical problem-solving and teaching. This will mean embracing what might seem like an anti-pattern when we are constantly getting pressure to move faster. This book clearly illustrates that you can apply these concepts; rewire your organization to move with focused, sustained urgency; and win!"

—Courtney Kissler, SVP Customer and
Retail Technology, Starbucks

"The framework in this book brings together the most useful insights I've learned over my thirty years of study and practice. Save yourself the time and start here."

—Jeffrey Fredrick, coauthor of *Agile Conversations*,
cohost of *Troubleshooting Agile* podcast

"Who hasn't been in an organization where everyone is super busy yet delivering value to customers is still super slow and requires vast amounts of perseverance and patience? Gene and Steve's book will guide you on how to move from that *danger zone* to a *winning zone* by improving the social circuitry which is present in all organizations but all too often neglected."

—Manuel Pais, coauthor of *Team Topologies*

"I was worried I might not be the target audience for the book, because it is so intentional about being geared toward people leaders, and I have been so adamant about my passion for the senior individual contributor role. Instead, I've found it inspiring. It has put into words, for me, the true role of the effective people leader and the importance of that role in complex problem-solving for an organization in a way that I've never understood before. For the first time in my career, it has me feeling a pull toward people leadership."

—Christina Yakomin, Senior Architect, Vanguard

"In their book *Wiring the Winning Organization*, Gene Kim and Steven J. Spear have made a clarion call to every organization in every industry sector around the world to refocus and 'rewire' internal communications and working practices to optimize for flow and outcomes. Through a coherent mix of new terminology, case studies, thought experiments, and guided reflections—all backed by sound research—the authors provide an irrefutable case for more deliberate, reflective communication and action as part of a winning organizational strategy. Highly recommended."

—Matthew Skelton, coauthor of *Team Topologies*
and founder at Conflux

Wiring the Winning Organization

LIBERATING OUR COLLECTIVE GREATNESS THROUGH
SLOWIFICATION, SIMPLIFICATION, AND AMPLIFICATION

Wiring the Winning Organization

GENE KIM and
STEVEN J. SPEAR

Foreword by ADM John Richardson, US Navy (Retired)
former Chief of Naval Operations

IT Revolution
Independent Publisher Since 2013
Portland, Oregon

25 NW 23rd Pl, Suite 6314

Portland, OR 97210

First Edition

Printed in the United States of America

29 28 27 26 25 24 23   1 2 3 4 5 6 7 8 9 10

Cover layout and book design by Devon Smith/D. Smith Creative, LLC.

Figures and Illustrations by Julianna Johnson and Kate Giambrone/

Bologna Sandwich, LLC.

Library of Congress Control Number 2023943083.

ISBN: 978-1950508426

eBook ISBN: 978-1942788874

Web PDF ISBN: 978-1942788898

Audiobook ISBN: 978-1942788904

For information about special discounts for bulk purchases or for information on booking authors for an event, please visit our website at www.ITRevolution.com.

WIRING THE WINNING ORGANIZATION

CONTENTS

LIST OF FIGURES

FOREWORD

By its own admission, *Wiring the Winning Organization* presents a theory of performance. In my experience, the best theories describe complex things in a way that is elegant and simple. The theory set out in this book meets these criteria, presenting the ideas of slowification, simplification, and amplification as mechanisms to consistently create superior performance. Gene and Steve provide a clear and accurate way of understanding the very complex problem of designing a successful architecture for success.

But "elegant and simple" does not necessarily translate to "easy." Often, it takes some dedicated effort to get the full value out of an important theory. Let me say three things about the theory presented in *Wiring the Winning Organization*:

1. I wish I had access to this book and theory at the beginning of my career because,
2. it absolutely works—as I read more, I found myself saying, "yes... that totally resonates...," and
3. it provides a simple and elegant framework and a vocabulary that I did not have when I was leading and teaching others to lead— something that is *so* valuable.

I would have been much more successful if I had known about and practiced the ideas that are put forward in *Wiring the Winning Organization*. I would have been more deliberate and efficient as a leader, and I would have been more clear and effective as a teacher and mentor for other leaders. All this is to say, it's worth every minute of your time to study and understand Gene and Steve's theory of performance. The payback is enormous.

Most of my professional experience is in the US Navy. I have led at every level, from a junior division officer (leading a team of about fifteen people on a submarine) up to the Chief of Naval Operations, the senior officer in the US Navy (leading a team of about six hundred thousand people deployed around the world). One of the most challenging and rewarding jobs I had was commanding the nuclear-powered attack submarine USS *Honolulu*.

The most challenging task for a submarine crew is to deploy at sea, far away from home, for six or more months. During such a deployment, a submarine spends about 85% of the time submerged, operating independently without any outside support, performing a wide array of missions in very stressful conditions, with severe consequences should a mistake be made.

The at-sea time is punctuated by visits to foreign ports, where the crew gets a chance to rest and relax. But even in these port visits, the sailors serve as ambassadors of the United States to the country they're visiting. So the mission never stops.

I think every reader can imagine the complexity of preparing for and successfully completing such a deployment. The material condition of the ship must be in absolute top condition. All of the logistics support for six months must be purchased, procured, received, and loaded in the submarine, which is already densely packed with equipment and people.

The crew must also be trained to do their jobs across a wide variety of disciplines. The engineers must keep the power plant and other equipment running. There are no windows on a submarine, so the ship senses its way through the ocean by sound. The sonar operators must be able to detect the faintest sound signals from among the myriad sounds of the ocean. The navigation team must plan and execute detailed plans for driving the ship submerged, weaving it through the topography of the sea floor and ocean currents. The communications team must be experts in the art of communicating in a way that is both predictable and undetectable. And the entire crew needs to do all of this while remaining unseen and always ready to defend themselves or press home an attack. And very importantly, the crew must be individually ready, healthy, and with all their personal affairs in order so that they and their families can succeed with the crew out of communication for long periods of time. It's focused and intense. And a mistake could mean the loss of the ship and everybody on board.

How did we go about preparing for such a mission? Let me describe the major steps we took as we moved through this challenge, and I think you'll see why I'm so excited about this book.

First, we got organized into teams: functional teams to maintain and supply the ship and operational teams to run the ship. Because space is so scarce on a submarine, every person in the crew serves on both types of teams—a functional team to supply and maintain the ship's material and personnel status in top condition and an operational team to drive the ship through the water, executing its mission 24/7/365. Our chiefs and junior officers (line leaders) ran these teams. We set up coordination meetings every day, sometimes twice a day, to coordinate resources, space, and time. As Captain of the boat, I partnered with my senior enlisted advisor, my Chief of the Boat, Master Chief Billy Cramer, who was the crew's representative directly to me.

We started by reviewing universal concepts valid for the general operation of a submarine. Then we specialized and focused on the specific places we'd go and the specialized missions we would be performing. We spent a tremendous amount of time optimizing the personnel in these teams to ensure we had the right talent in the right places. Eventually, all of these teams had to combine together into a "team of teams"—much like a football team is composed of offense, defense, and special teams—and those are further broken down into linesmen, backs, etc.

Little did I know then, but we were *simplifying* our task by modularizing—forming coherent teams that could train and perform their required tasks with little interference to or from adjacent teams. We linearized our approach into discrete work streams to prepare for extended operations. Then we incrementalized our tasks—first focusing on fundamentals and then learning the specific challenges for this specific mission.

That's just the first part—simplifying in time and space. Once that was done, we had to prepare for the mission. We had to ensure that we could safely operate the submarine: "rigging the submarine for dive" to operate submerged, being able to navigate into new places, being able to drive the ship among other ships, being able to operate the nuclear power plant within operational limits and recover from the unexpected to maintain propulsion. This was all just to go to sea safely! Then we needed to be able to "fight the ship," meaning to stealthily and effectively conduct high-end operations against an alerted adversary. This included, if necessary, being ready for combat operations. We were going to bring everybody home, no matter what happened.

We broke down complex tasks into basic training building blocks: first developing individual skills on personal computers, then bringing together small operational teams in more complex multi-operator simulators, and finally bringing the whole team together for at-sea training. At each step, we ensured that the challenge was representative of the tasks we would face. We trained in nominal and off-nominal situations. We simulated that various pieces of equipment failed, that the weather was terrible, and that some personnel were out of action. We stopped often to ensure we were learning as we went. As the saying goes, "Practice doesn't make perfect; perfect practice makes perfect!" We tried to make our practice perfect. At the end, we were certified for deployment by an inspection team.

What were we doing with all of that practice? We were *slowifying*! We moved the fast and complex job of operating a submarine at sea in combat into a slower, pace-controlled environment where we could get lots of "sets and reps," stopping and learning in between each one and escalating in difficulty over time. We tested our plans and execution with personal trainers, team trainers, and with the entire ship.

Now we were ready to deploy. We would spend more than 180 days away from home port, spending about 85% of our time underwater on mission. It's an unforgiving environment—the sea and the enemy are pressing in, and the slightest relaxation or the most minor problem could mean we lose the ship. It's so complex that we knew, despite all of our simplification and slowification, that we couldn't possibly anticipate every possibility. We had a vision of how things would go, but we needed to be alerted immediately when things—even the smallest things—departed from that vision. Small problems that aren't fixed combine to become big problems that will explode into catastrophes, often at the worst possible time. So we trained to become hypersensitive to finding and fixing small problems. We frequently held "alertness drills" to see if our teams were sensitive to finding, reporting, and swarming to solve small problems. In fact, we did this so much during our slowification that it had become part of our DNA. On USS *Honolulu*, we did not walk past small problems—we fixed them.

In the context of *Wiring the Winning Organization*, we were *amplifying*. We knew that we had to keep on learning and improving—during the training phases and also during performance. Learn and improve all the time through feedback and correction—through amplification.

We prepared and were certified. And then we deployed. We got stronger and better every day, even while we were operating far from any support for long periods of time. In fact, especially while we were operating far from any support for long periods of time. We didn't know it then, but we improved rapidly and sustained that growth by simplifying, slowifying, and amplifying. Or at least we came as close as we could on our own. If I had read *Wiring the Winning Organization* back then, we would have been much more focused. This theory of performance just truly—no kidding—works.

And the counterfactual is also true—neglecting these principles does not work. In addition to the many case studies and examples in the book, I have seen too many instances where the operational theory of performance was not thoughtfully and coherently employed, and the system failed, sometimes catastrophically.

The decay in performance usually starts with neglecting amplification—suppressing meaningful feedback in the interest of schedule or fiscal pressure. The team loses awareness of itself, of how dramatically performance is degrading. Small errors build up, shortcuts become the norm, and the system proceeds, relying on being lucky rather than being knowledgeable and rigorous. So feedback stops first.

Next, and very quickly, slowification gets sidelined. In the interest of time, all schedule and cost problems are often "paid for" by reducing training time and complexity. The team convinces themselves they are "good enough"—no training needed. After all, we've not seen or heard of any problems (because...you guessed it...no amplification). So proficiency degrades because slowification degrades. The degradation goes unnoticed because there's no amplification of feedback.

The last thing to go is simplification. You see, the three aspects of operational excellence—slowification, simplification, and amplification—all serve to reinforce one another. Once the first two go away, simplification, including its three techniques (modularization, linearization, incrementalization), just evaporates.

In the absence of the corrective forces of simplification, slowification, and amplification, low standards and luck become the norm, until luck runs out, disaster strikes, and the investigation uncovers the tragic timeline that shows how the team's wiring became frazzled and undone.

After my time in operational command was complete, I was assigned as a deputy squadron commander to help the submarines in our squadron, and then as the teacher for prospective submarine commanders. During those assignments, I would have treasured the clarity and vocabulary provided by *Wiring the Winning Organization*. Elegant and simple, it's a teacher's best companion—a lesson plan for teaching the theory of performance.

You have what I did not. You can learn the theory of operation and performance that *Wiring the Winning Organization* teaches. If you're just starting a new project with a new team—use the principles that Gene and Steve describe and design your approach to win. If you're inheriting a team in the middle of a project, take as much of a break as conditions allow and rewire your approach. You'll see the return on that investment almost immediately. And just to be clear, this must come from the top. Without clear prioritization and continual reinforcement by the boss and senior leaders (the C-suite!), it will fade into the background of day-to-day tactical priorities. If you are a new leader or a seasoned CEO, learn what this book teaches.

One last thing. During our time on the USS *Honolulu*, we established and met very high standards of performance for ourselves. But we worked smart; every minute was spent on achieving outcomes at the most decentralized level of capable performance. We understood and shared the mission, and we didn't waste time. Our morale showed it—we had terrific retention and promotion rates. Anybody who had a choice of which submarine to work with chose us. And when a member of our team left to go to another team, they instantly became a leader. High performance and high morale...that's magic.

We were performing at super-high levels of performance, and we were having a great time doing it. We were Wired to Win! Study this book, and you can be too.

—Admiral John Richardson, US Navy (retired)
31st Chief of Naval Operations
August 10th, 2023

Every day, people badge in, buzz in, swipe in, scan in, sign in, log in, or otherwise just walk into their places of work. From that common beginning, the differences in their experiences are vast.

For some, work is marked by drudgery or even danger. Their days are filled with frustration amid the regular confusion of figuring out what to do, when and how to do it, and even why it needs to be done. Too often, they're left cynical about what's going on around them and exhausted from trying to get meaningful things accomplished.

However, some people experience the opposite. They are well equipped and capable of succeeding at what they've been tasked to do; they are respected and appreciated for doing their work well; and they leave the workplace knowing they've added value for others and to their own lives.

We have observed that when people's days are miserable, the organization's performance is miserable too. On the other hand, when people's experiences are outstanding, the organization excels across all metrics: workplace safety, resilience, agility, time to market, quality, profitability, etc.

What's remarkable is that these vastly different outcomes don't require trade-offs; better experiences for individuals and their organizations are not bought at the cost of resources. People with the best experiences need fewer resources, less capital equipment, and less time to accomplish greater things.

We have observed this phenomenon regardless of the type of work being done or the products and services being generated and delivered. It is the management system that establishes the difference between whether work is miserable versus delightful, boring versus engaging, and whether individual experiences translate into an organization's failure or success.

Wiring the Winning Organization explains how leaders are responsible for enabling their people to work easily and well, generate and deliver valuable products and services that benefit society, and feel appreciated and treated with dignity.

The best leaders create, sustain, and improve their organizations' *social circuitry,** the overlay of the processes, procedures, routines, and norms that enable people to do their work easily and well. While individual specialists are focusing their attention on the problems immediately in front of them, this social circuitry establishes the patterns by which information, ideas, materials, and services flow, setting up people for success and integrating individual efforts for common purpose.

When that circuitry is well wired, the whole is greater than the sum of its parts. Conversely, when an organization is not well wired, people's efforts are squandered, and they are unable to put their full efforts toward achieving organizational goals. Too often, the parts don't come together into an effective whole, likely because leaders massively underestimate the difficulty of synchronizing disparate functional specialties toward a common purpose. It should be no surprise, then, why leaders of great organizations are so invested in creating outstanding processes and procedures. These leaders are rewarded with outsized performance benefits and tremendous competitive advantage.

Effective social circuitry is designed around the ingenuity and limitations of individual and collective human intellect. It allows people to repeatedly and persistently see and solve difficult problems and bring what they discover into practice quickly and well. In this way, the organization's

---

* We chose the term *social circuitry* (or *organizational wiring*) very carefully. Circuits exist to move a resource (e.g., electrical energy, pneumatic or hydraulic pressure, data) from where it is to where it is needed. Similarly, organizational circuits are the connections by which ideas, information, materials, services, resources, and support can flow from where they are to where they are needed so that effective collaboration, problem-solving, and value creation can occur. When an organization is wired to win, the movement of whatever is needed is accurate, fast, effective, and efficient. In contrast, when an organization is not wired to win, the organizational wiring is convoluted, which constricts, distracts, drains, diffuses, and saps energy from people, ensuring the systems that they are a part of perform badly.

resources are used to their best possible potential, and that potential continuously expands.

Wiring the Winning Organization is the culmination of a decade-long collaboration, to which we both bring our own perspectives and motivations. We'd like to take a moment to share a little about how we came to write this book and what we hope to achieve with it.

Gene

Many say the goal of science is to explain the most observable phenomena with the fewest number of principles, confirm deeply held intuitions, and reveal surprising insights. By doing so, we create robust and testable theories that can explain the world around us.

Scientists have been able to do this for the physical sciences, which has enabled so many of the modern miracles that we benefit from today. Many believe, as I do, that we are missing this same clarity when it comes to understanding how and why organizations work the way they do, both in the ideal and not ideal.

This motivated my study of high-performing technology organizations, which began in 1999. This was informed tremendously by working with Dr. Nicole Forsgren and Jez Humble on the State of DevOps research, a six-year, cross-population study that surveyed over thirty-six thousand technology professionals from 2013 to 2019.

This journey also led me to take a two-day executive education workshop from Steve Spear at MIT in 2014, which changed how I view the world. Personally, I attribute at least a one-year slip in the creation of *The DevOps Handbook* to this, as I tried to integrate what I had learned into the book.

I took the workshop because I had read Steve and Dr. H. Kent Bowen's famous *Harvard Business Review* article "Decoding the DNA of the Toyota Production System" in 2004 and read Steve's book *The High-Velocity Edge* when it was published in 2010.

What was so exciting about my interactions with Steve was a hint that there was something in common between agile, DevOps, lean, the Toyota Production System, safety culture, resilience engineering, and so much more—that they were all incomplete expressions of a far greater whole.

I am not exaggerating when I say that coauthoring this book has been the most intellectually challenging thing I've ever done.

There was a moment in the summer of 2022 when I almost gave up and considered abandoning the project. Steve and I had been struggling to create a simple scenario that would show the principles we were trying to explain, which we believed were the underlying mechanisms that have made great organizations great. After weeks of being unable to create a satisfactory example, I went for a walk on the beach, telling my wife that I wouldn't come back until I could explain to myself in a simple scenario what our theory was actually trying to say.

Six miles later, I was convinced that either I wasn't smart enough to understand what Steve was trying to explain to me, or I didn't understand software development well enough, or maybe even that our theory wasn't correct. Attempts to create a simple scenario using restaurant operations led me to conclude that I didn't understand restaurant operations well enough, or movie theater operations, or many others.

This is what led to a scenario based on the activities of moving furniture and painting a room. It was an extension of two vignettes we had created earlier in the year to explore the concept of coordination cost. I was so excited to share this idea with Steve and even more excited when he understood it within seconds.

We spent months debating and arguing what should and shouldn't be in the vignette. But I know all those deliberations were worth it. What resulted was a simple and concrete scenario that made it easy to determine what the essential concepts of our theory actually were. Furthermore, these debates often led to some of the largest "aha moments" of my career.

I am grateful for my collaboration with Steve, which is now a decade long, and I am certain that this book could come only from a collaboration like this. We share many common beliefs but come from very different research backgrounds and industry experiences. To massively oversimplify, my career has been in software, while Steve's career has been nearly everywhere outside of it. But I believe that this commonality and complementarity are what made this book possible—and this book is another example of what cross-functional problem-solving can achieve.

It is my fondest hope that the simple metaphors we use in the book—moving a couch as a metaphor for joint problem-solving and cognition, and moving furniture and painting an old Victorian hotel as a metaphor for how we integrate different functional specialties toward a common purpose—help clarify what leaders at all levels need to do to liberate everyone's ability to collaborate, use their full creativity, and solve ever more important and larger problems together.

Further, I hope that this work helps unify the language of how leaders manage systems, regardless of industry, domain of work, or the system being managed. As a consequence, I hope that those leaders are able to create immensely more value, both for the people they are responsible for, as well as the people who depend upon them.

Steve

The differences between well-managed organizations and those that are not are extraordinary. In organizations that are led best, all stakeholders benefit: employees invest their time to do work that is appreciated by others; investors gain returns on resources they provide; and the students, patients, customers, and others receive exceptional products and services in exchange for the trust they've placed in providers. In those less well managed, people's time is squandered, spirits are squashed, material resources are wasted, and societal needs are left unmet.

My awareness of the differences between the exemplars and their more ordinary peers started in the 1980s. At the time, once-storied American companies couldn't keep up with their Japanese counterparts. One by one, well-established firms—ranging from electronics to steel to automobiles—struggled, with some collapsing completely.

Many in my generation tried to grasp the causes of such differences and find solutions. In truth, many of us initially found the answers we were looking for. Those with a technical bent found fantastic tools, techniques, or algorithms. Those with a transactional mindset celebrated metrics and incentives that guaranteed, they thought, more commitment from the workforce to do the right thing.

The problem was, putting those ideas into practice didn't work. Each solution provided only a glimpse into what true superior performance might be. The technologists focused only on what people *used* to do their work; the transactionalists, on *how hard* they tried. They missed how management systems enhanced or inhibited people's ability to work together, in particular to solve difficult problems collectively and bring solutions into practice effectively.

Many practitioners and researchers came to appreciate just that point in the 1980s and 1990s. Following their leads, I saw how the "objective function" of the best leaders was creating such opportunities. My first deep dive on this was an immersive study of Toyota that informed "Decoding the DNA of the Toyota Production System" and *The High-Velocity Edge*.

Toyota had been an awful auto industry competitor in the late 1950s, emerging from the wreck of World War II. By the 1980s, though, it was the industry leader, a position it has expanded on in the forty years since.

This point was reinforced by working with Alcoa, which had become the safest employer in the country (despite the hazards of its industrial processes). Their safety success did not come with a trade-off. Alcoa was also a leader in quality, yield, and other competitive metrics.

The fact that the best lead by actively managing the design of the processes and procedures that comprise their social circuitry, regardless of competitive sector or technological domain, was validated by working with medical care providers. Some had simultaneously improved access, affordability, capacity, patient safety, and workforce experience.

Since then, experiences in a widening array of situations have validated the point: the common issue across all situations is creating conditions in which people's ingenuity can be liberated for its best possible use. Do that, and whatever resources are available will be put to great uses. Don't do that, and no matter how many resources are available, outcomes will be disappointing.

This book distills our research and experience to a few essential mechanisms that anyone responsible for coordinating the efforts of other people can use to generate greater outcomes quicker and easier than otherwise would have been possible. Scale doesn't matter: whether it's five, fifteen, forty-five, or five hundred people, there are ways to set them up for success (or not). This is regardless of whether they're doing esoteric, upstream research or are involved in the most basic production and delivery of goods and services. And it is regardless of the sector in which they work. There are better and worse ways to bring the parts into an outstanding whole.

This clarity was possible as a direct result of my decade-long collaboration and friendship with Gene and his background in fields in which I have little experience. It would have been easy to say, "Oh, that's a technology problem versus an industrial problem" and dismissively wave away commonalities in light of differences in products and services being designed, produced, and delivered or the science and technology used to create them. What has made this partnership work and enabled us to reach the conclusions presented here was a shared conviction that bona fide, testable science is better than simple, analogical reasoning.

One last thought before moving on. Each Sabbath, Miriam, our kids (Hannah, Eve, and Jesse), and I preface our lunch with a biblical declaration that we should be doing our work for six days and resting on the seventh. That's an admonition that life shouldn't be only toil; it should have dignity.

However, the declaration doesn't say that dignity is just for some people and not for others. Rather, for those who received this declaration, it is also for their sons, their daughters, their maids, their servants, the animals on which they depend for labor, and even the strangers who may have appeared at the city gates before the Sabbath commenced. Dignity is a universal right.

Our family is also blessed by living in "a nation, conceived in Liberty, and dedicated to the proposition that all men are created equal," as Lincoln said at Gettysburg. We aren't blind to gaps between people's lived reality and that espoused aspiration, but we take inspiration in knowing so many who actively close that gap for others each day. Miriam and I are proud our own children are crafting their lives to help close the gap between reality and aspiration too.

With sentiments like those in mind, Gene and I try to always write about people and the work they do with respect, appreciation, and admiration. If what we share here helps you bring more dignity and a sense of lived value to yourselves and those for whom you are responsible—whether that's five, fifteen, forty-five, or five thousand—then we will consider our own labors successful.

Conclusion

Our purpose in this book isn't to replace the major tools and processes that have been adopted by organizations to help them overcome hurdles, both small and large. Lean, agile, DevOps, and so forth are excellent approaches to problem-solving and value creation. However, these are concrete examples of the more general ideas we're introducing here.

A theme common across these various tools is that they recognize organizations as "platforms" through which people collaborate toward achieving common purposes. Focusing on the human element is consistent with Dr. Douglas McGregor's Theory Y, from *The Human Side of the Enterprise*, which emphasizes the positive motivations people have toward shared objectives, taking responsibility, and being creative and imaginative. It is also consistent with Dr. W. Edwards Deming's teachings on collaboration, systems thinking, and profound knowledge.[*] Deming also showed how management systems must fully engage people's ingenuity and motivation as active participants, to their benefit, that of the organization, and society more broadly.

We seek to make clear the specific mechanisms that are alluded to in these theories and that we've found and studied in many different organizations in a wide variety of industries that make the exceptional ones exceptional. We seek to create a way for leaders to take these, until now unknown, characteristics and apply them to their own organizations.

As you read, our hope is that you take away a deep understanding of the powerful mechanisms that can be used to wire your organization to win, an appreciation for the collective genius of the people who make all of your endeavors a reality, and a drive to achieve the greatness that is possible in all organizations.

—Gene Kim and Steve Spear, 2023

---

[*] For more on the lineage of ideas introduced in this book, please see Appendix A.

PART I

A New Theory of Performance Management

CHAPTER 1

The Pinnacles of Human Achievement and Why We Form Organizations

On July 20, 1969, masses crowded into Times Square, Central Park, Trafalgar Square, the city centers of the Soviet Union, North and South Vietnam, Hong Kong, and other places around the world. They gathered to watch *Apollo 11* astronauts Neil Armstrong and Buzz Aldrin start their descent to the lunar surface.[1] All told, 650 million people shared that experience,[2] watching and listening in theaters, taverns, airport and train terminals, and at home, in wonder and awe, as Armstrong stepped onto the Moon and declared, "That's one small step for man, one giant leap for mankind."

Armstrong's small step and mankind's giant leap were the culmination of three hundred thousand people's efforts, employed by twenty thousand industrial firms and universities, integrated into collective action for that common purpose.[3] In fact, just broadcasting Armstrong and Aldrin's landing and excursion required more than one hundred people, mostly young people in their early twenties,[4] who staffed tracking stations in Australia, receiving and processing the multiple signals being transmitted from 250,000 miles away, so those hundreds of millions could see and hear them wherever they were.[5]

All that was accomplished less than nine years after President John F. Kennedy addressed a congressional joint session in May 1961 and put forth the challenge "before this decade is out, of landing a man on the Moon and returning him safely to the Earth."[6]

This magic of collective human endeavor isn't just for the extraordinary; it can also be found in the seemingly mundane. Consider that right now, across the world, there are millions of people preparing their medication for the day. They are each shaking out a pill from a bottle and taking it with a glass of water. One of those millions might be taking medication to help relieve symptoms of her cardiac disease, helping her live a more fulfilling, healthier life, just as all the other medications being shaken out of all those other pill bottles right now will help all the other people live more fulfilling, healthier lives.

Those common medications, which convert diseases that were once horrific and terminal into conditions that can be managed if not cured, aren't simple or easy to create. They are made possible by thousands of person-years of work, spread across a decade, and performed by myriad specialists: chemists, biologists, pharmacologists, computational biologists, medicinal chemists, logisticians, clinical trial managers, doctors, nurses, computational chemists, data scientists, software engineers, and production experts. All their contributions are integrated and harmonized into the invention, production, and provision of that pill.

All that distributed genius—thousands of people working toward a common goal, inventing in parallel, with individual teams each working on their challenging problems and knowing that their efforts are important and fit into a larger goal—all that came together, be it in that small step on the moon or in that medication shaken out of a bottle. Both are pinnacle accomplishments that organizations achieved and that no single individual could have imagined doing alone.

Many of us have been lucky enough to work on projects like these once in our career—and it was likely the most rewarding experience of our life, not because the job was easy, but because the job was challenging and involved solving problems and conquering challenges much larger than ourselves.*

---

* For example, I (Steve) once mentioned to my Uncle Larry that I'd seen an SR-71 Blackbird spy plane on the deck of the *Intrepid* aircraft carrier museum. "That was the greatest program I was ever part of," he said. His comment surprised me. He and my aunt, Diane, had moved to California to work on that project when they were very young. He was a newly minted electrical engineer, and it was hard to imagine he had that much responsibility within such an enormous undertaking. But I'd missed the point. It wasn't his part that was great; it was the larger whole that gave the experience such meaning.

The sad and dismal reality is that too often daily work has little of this magic, regardless of the job, the industry, the importance of the mission, or even a person's seniority. In these situations, people are frustrated because they don't have what they need to succeed (e.g., information, approvals, requirements, time). In the absence of overwhelming clarity of purpose, people become exhausted from the heroics and politicking required to get even the smallest things done, and they are too often put in hazardous situations because obvious problems have not been resolved.

Over time, it's easy to understand how people in these situations become jaded, cynical, and bored, sometimes feeling that any effort is futile and that their dignity has been eroded away. Whatever potential someone thought they could bring to the job has been diminished, as they know they are unable to contribute to the larger goal.

But this is not a book about how leaders can make people feel inspired to work in these dismal conditions. Instead, this is a book that presents a *theory of performance* about how leaders can create the conditions so that people can do their work easily and well. By doing so, the part of the enterprise they are responsible for can succeed spectacularly.

This is the product of our thirty years (each) of studying organizations across almost every industry vertical* and across nearly every domain of work.† This combined work includes surveying over thirty-six thousand organizations to correlate practices with performance and gathering case studies from over five hundred organizations. We have also directly worked with or closely studied nearly one hundred organizations across nearly every industry vertical and in nearly every phase of value creation. Additionally, we have worked with leaders at nearly every level to help them achieve their organizational goals.

---

* The industries we have been able to study include airlines, automotive, banking, biotechnology, consulting, defense, enterprise software, entertainment and media, gaming, government agencies, healthcare, heavy industry, high tech, industrial production, insurance, manufacturing, military and intelligence agencies, oil and mineral exploration, pharma, retail, semiconductors, social services, software, sportswear, telecommunications, and universities.

† Domains of work studied include research and development, new product design, software development, factory design and construction, fabrication and production, and delivery and after-sales service.

Our research and combined experience have uncovered three surprisingly simple mechanisms that enable the magic that is found in the extraordinary and exemplary endeavors of the large number of organizations we have studied. With these three mechanisms, leaders can wire their organization for success instead of mediocrity.

We assert that greatness is created through three mechanisms, which create the difference between success and failure:

- slowification, to make solving problems easier to do,
- simplification, to make the problems themselves easier to solve,
- and amplification, to make it obvious that there are problems that demand attention and whether they've been seen and solved.

Our theory of performance explains many of the things we've seen in our respective and disparate journeys across industries and time. Many management concepts and methodologies already offer a glimpse into how greatness is achieved.

You may be familiar with agile, DevOps, Dr. W. Edwards Deming, the Toyota Production System, OODA (observe, orient, decide, act) loops, improvement katas, and Lean startup. Or you may have heard of system dynamics, learning organizations, double-loop learning, cognitive load, psychological safety, Westrum's organizational typology model, empowerment and participative management, enabling front-line workers, and normalization of deviance. And you may be using tools such as "gemba walks," Team Topologies, software architecture, Conway's Law, modularity, resilience engineering, and paying down technical debt.

All of these are *tools* for wiring the organization (the social circuitry of processes, procedures, policies, and routines by which individuals' efforts come together into a greater whole). Figure 1.1 shows how these different practices are examples of the three mechanisms of slowification, simplification, and amplification.

But none of the aforementioned methods or tools alone can wire your organization for success. (TPS and DevOps are arguably two of the most important changes in the management of organizations in the last fifty years, and they come the closest to wiring a winning organization.)

FIGURE 1.1 Venn Diagram of How Different Practices Slowify, Simplify, or Amplify

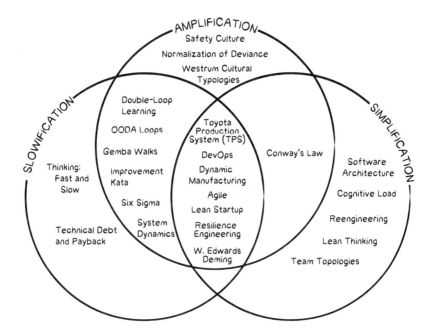

Before we dive deeper, let's take a brief step back and look at organizations broadly to better understand how these three mechanism can help you wire a winning organization.

Why We Join and Form Organizations

We create organizations for a variety of reasons, but certainly one of them is to accomplish seemingly common but actually audacious undertakings that one person cannot do alone. The goal may be as ambitious as sending a man to the moon or as common as providing a commercial product or service, such as running a restaurant, bakery, or hospital. Or the goal could be to help society by ensuring national security, educating children and adults, or providing places of worship or shelter for those in need.

Almost every organization has a mission or goal. And in all but the smallest organizations, these missions and goals require undertaking activities that are so vast, complex, difficult, specialized, or intricate that they are beyond the ability of any individual to fully comprehend, let alone execute, regardless of how smart, organized, strong, or dedicated they are.

What's exhilarating for some (those who pull it off) and frustrating for others (those who do not) are the enormous differences otherwise similar organizations have in fulfilling their aspirations.

The Paradox of Unlevel Performance on a Level Playing Field

It's been proposed that organizations gain competitive advantages largely by seizing opportunities that are unavailable to others. This concept, led by Dr. Michael Porter's "five forces" from his book *Competitive Strategy*,[7] asserts that organizations enjoy unfair returns by having made the playing field unlevel: by locking in customers (so they cannot consider alternative vendors), preventing suppliers from finding other outlets for their wares, or barring rivals from offering competitive products and services.

It would follow from such thinking that when the competitive environment is otherwise fair and free, enterprises would likely be unable to sustain advantage by large margins for long durations. After all, rivals compete for attention from the same customers; source the same capital equipment, IT systems, and raw materials from the same suppliers; are subject to the same rules, regulations, taxation systems; and so forth.

Yet, such predictions are refuted by reality. Even in sectors where the levelness of the playing field makes for free—even brutal—competition, some organizations create and sustain enormous advantages regardless of how they are measured: quality, affordability, availability, resilience, reliability, safety, security, responsiveness, speed, or agility. The best organizations generate more value in less time, at lower cost, and seemingly with less effort. They are simply "wired to win."

Obvious in Outcomes

Consistent and durable winners dominate their industry, sometimes for decades, by large margins, and across many metrics and dimensions, whereas mediocre organizations are unable to.* The winners are better by a lot and for a long time.†

Let's explore what this means, whether it's through cross-sectional or longitudinal comparisons.

- Toyota has led in design and production in the auto industry for some fifty years. Despite being woefully uncompetitive in the late 1950s, it gained advantages through superior quality and productivity (and hence affordability).[8] It built on those leads by cutting in half the time required for major model upgrades,[9] by cutting from weeks to minutes the time to convert plants from one model year to the next, and by being incredibly fast to introduce whole new products and invent whole new technologies.[10] (Learn more in the exemplar case study in Chapter 10.)

- In 2007, Apple released the groundbreaking iPhone, with only dozens of software developers creating its applications and user interface libraries. The resulting product redefined what consumers expect from mobile devices. As a result, they were able to dethrone Nokia's dominance in the smartphone market and beat them, and the rest of the industry, in terms of profitability, market share, etc. (Learn more in the Apple/Nokia case study in Chapter 8.)

Similarly, longitudinal comparisons show how organizations were able to massively improve their performance when leaders changed the organizational wiring:

- Toyota rewired an organization with its joint venture with General Motors in Fremont, California (New United Motor Manufacturing, Inc., or NUMMI).[11] Within two years, what had been one of the worst

---

* Imagine two sports teams with nearly identical players. The only thing different is the coach. Yet one team consistently beats the other team. When they switch coaches, the other team consistently wins. Here we can conclude that the decisive factor of performance is who is coaching the team. (Indeed, this is what happened in numerous case studies we present in the book, such as at NUMMI.)

† Prolonged mediocrity will inevitably lead to failure and losing.

facilities in the country became one of the best. This was achieved by changing the management system in the facility. The result was that the same people who'd been so unproductive when working for General Motors achieved world-class outcomes when working with Toyota leadership.

- In manufacturing microprocessors, the differences between the leaders and the rest are huge in terms of throughput times, quality, yield, and sustained product variety within a single plant, etc. What's encouraging is that such performance is replicable. One plant cut its throughput times by two-thirds, increased yield, reduced scrap, and otherwise made it far easier for engineers and technicians to use the sophisticated capital equipment they had. The benefits were enormous: $10 million per month in additional profitability.[12]

- In 2002, Amazon struggled to upgrade its e-commerce software, able to make only twenty software changes (deployments) per year because of the high risk of outages and the difficulty of coordinating across hundreds or even thousands of software engineers. In 2014, however, Amazon was making some 136,000 deployments every day, quickly and safely. This didn't just make their online retailing more competitive. It became the basis for the cloud computing market. By 2020, this generated $80 billion in revenue for Amazon, 75% of its overall profits.[13] (Learn more in the Amazon case study in Chapter 8.)

- The US Joint Special Operations Command (JSOC) was struggling to dismantle Al Queda in Iraq, despite "a huge advantage in numbers, equipment, and training." A "team of teams" rewiring allowed JSOC to reduce its response times, increase its operational tempo, and dismantle the terrorist network.[14] (Learn more in the Team of Teams case study in Chapter 8.)

- Organizations such as Allegheny General Hospital (AGH) and Western Pennsylvania Hospital have improved safety, access, and affordability—better care, for more people, at less cost—while reducing overburden on staff. For instance, AGH completely eliminated deaths due to CLAB* infections from nineteen in 2003 to zero

---

* Central line–associated bloodstream infections.

in 2006, which was replicated by University of Pittsburgh Medical Center, Monongahela.[15]

These are just a fraction of the examples that show how some organizations are better at accomplishing great things across sectors—planes, trains, automobiles, tech, high tech, biotech, education, medical care and health services, heavy industry, national defense, public sector services, and so on.

Obvious in Experience

Differences between exceptional and ordinary performance aren't just obvious in aggregated, lagging measures of performance. They're obvious by observing the experiences of people doing their work. When people have difficulty doing their work easily and well, despite investing their best time and energy to support the larger effort, we shouldn't expect the enterprise as a whole to perform well either. This is an organization that has not been wired to win.

Conversely, if the organizational wiring regularly sets people up for success, it shouldn't be surprising that the enterprise as a whole succeeds outstandingly. You find this connection between individuals and the organization in the list of organizations in the previous section.

Consider the transformation of an emergency department. It started as a place where it was difficult to be a clinician and frustrating to be a patient. After leaders rewired the organization, the emergency department became a very different place, one where clinicians could do their work easily and well, and where patients appreciated the fantastic care they received. Plus, care was available to more patients because of all the liberated capacity of people and place.

Initially, patients and their family members were crowded in a waiting area, many anxious to get a clinician's attention. That's probably familiar to those who've needed emergency care. Patients started with registration and triage but found themselves waiting after each step in the experience: in exam rooms, on chairs, or on gurneys in hallways. Their frustration didn't end there, even after waiting an hour or more for clinicians' attention. Nurses were often distracted from providing care because they had to track down missing information, equipment, or supplies that weren't readily available. Doctors were invariably tethered to computer monitors, trying to navigate medical systems instead of examining and treating people in need. One young resident was seen to throw her hands up in frustration and mutter, "I didn't go to medical school to do this!"

Now consider the same emergency department after it rewired its social circuitry to better integrate everyone's individual effort toward a common goal. The waiting area was nearly empty, despite patients constantly arriving for care. This was because they changed the registration process. Instead of all the extended waits, patients signed in, were registered almost immediately, and triaged. Within eighteen minutes, they were being examined by a doctor, nurse practitioner, or physician assistant.

Getting patients through sign-in to examination more quickly had tremendous impact. Nearly three-quarters of the patients could be discharged with a prescription or referral right away. Another 10%–15% were in serious enough condition to be admitted directly to the hospital. Only a few patients had to be held in the emergency department for observation, pending more advanced imaging and monitoring. The emergency department became a better place for both patient and caregiver.

The new social circuitry enabled moving patients gracefully, capably, and respectfully through the department. This meant space was no longer occupied by the many patients stuck somewhere mid-process. The space was repurposed for better uses: Imaging equipment was brought in to save time on having to transport patients to the imaging department. Space was set aside for residents to study collaboratively, to become more skillful in their specialties, and to otherwise have a quiet space for an interlude between often urgent and demanding cases.

What caused the transformation? The department leaders, the medical director (the head doctor) and the unit manager (the head nurse), changed how problems of processes, procedures, norms, and routines were addressed. Rather than having their colleagues struggle with the same obstructions, inconveniences, and obstacles that plagued them every day, the leaders amplified problems and devoted time to solving them, creating solutions that could be systematized.

For instance, registration had required reconciling names, IDs, SSNs, and medical record numbers; staff figured out how to get patients into the system faster and more reliably, even with limited information. Exam rooms had been stocked and equipped somewhat haphazardly; staff methodically identified exactly what was needed, where and when, and created a reliable restocking system. The result was that everything was on hand. Similarly, they methodically figured out how to get the right information where and when it was needed and in the right format. Doctors and nurses no longer wasted their time, energy, and creativity searching and foraging for items. Instead, they could examine, diagnose, and treat patients.

By rewiring the organization, leaders helped clinicians and administrators do great work for patients. They spared themselves from always firefighting and expediting for people and resources. Instead, they could lend their own expertise to solve difficult medical problems.

What they experienced is what we observe in all organizations that are wired to win: It's easier to work. Collaboration seems choreographed. Performance is graceful. And beneficiaries are grateful. Hopefully, you've had reason to be the source and the subject of such feelings.

The Three Layers Where We Create Value

All organizations are sociotechnical systems, people working with other people, engaging (sometimes complex) technology to accomplish what they are collaborating on. This was certainly true for the clinicians mentioned in the example above; the professionals working at Toyota to develop, design, produce, and deliver vehicles; the software developers at Apple; and the engineers and technicians in the microprocessor plants. Regardless of domain, collaborative problem-solving occurs on three distinct layers, where people focus their attention and express their experience, training, and creativity:

> Layer 1 contains the technical objects being worked on. These are the technical, scientific, and engineered objects that people are trying to study, create, or manipulate. These may be molecules in drug development, code in software development, physical parts in manufacturing,

or patient injuries or illnesses in medical care. For people in Layer 1, their expertise is around these technical objects (i.e., their structure and behavior), and their work is expressed through designing, analyzing, fabricating, fixing, repairing, transforming, creating, and so forth.

Layer 2 contains the tools and instrumentation. These are the scientific, technical, or engineered tools and instrumentation through which people work on Layer 1 objects. These may be the devices that synthesize medicinal compounds in drug development, the development tools and operational platforms in software development, technologies that transform materials in manufacturing, or the technologies to diagnose and treat patients' illnesses and injuries. Layer 2 capabilities include the operation, maintenance, and improvement of these tools and instruments. These first two layers are the "technical" part of a sociotechnical system.

Layer 3 contains the social circuitry. This is the overlay of processes, procedures, norms, and routines, the means by which individual efforts are expressed and integrated through collaboration toward a common purpose. This is the "socio" part of a sociotechnical system.

When leaders wire their Layer 3 (social circuitry) well, the people for whom they are responsible have what they need, when they need it, and in the format they need it.* Problems have been redefined so that they are easier, safer, and faster to solve. As a result, people can invest their full creative energies and focus on solving their problems, either in Layer 1 (the work object) or Layer 2 (the tools or instruments to do their work). Their collective efforts flow together as a team, gracefully, as if precisely choreographed.

---

* Again, this explains why we very deliberately chose the term *social circuitry*. Circuits exist to move a resource (e.g., electrical energy, pneumatic or hydraulic pressure, data) from where it is to where it is needed. Similarly, organizational circuits are the connections by which ideas, information, services, resources, and support can flow from where they are to where they are needed so that effective collaboration, problem-solving, and value creation can occur.

In contrast, consider when the wiring in Layer 3 is inadequate. People doing work are unable to do that work easily or well. They must spend their energy, effort, and cognitive capacity to get what they need, coping and compensating for Layer 3 problems. They are unable to generate and deliver value that others will appreciate. This is because Layer 3 was either overlooked or misaligned with the needs of people working in Layers 1 and 2.

FIGURE 1.2 The Three Layers

LAYER 3
SOCIAL CIRCUITRY
FOR FLOW OF IDEAS
AND INFORMATION

LAYER 2
TOOLS AND
INSTRUMENTATION

Person doing
Layer 2 work;
maintaining
tooling.

LAYER 1
TECHNICAL OBJECT

Person doing
Layer 1 work.

Danger Zones and *Winning Zones* for Solving Really Difficult Problems

Leaders manage the social circuitry (Layer 3) that determines whether their organizations get dismal or great outcomes. How this circuitry is designed and operated dictates the conditions in which people can solve difficult problems, continually generate great and new ideas, and put them into impactful practice. Certain conditions make it more difficult to solve problems or generate new and useful ideas. We call that the *danger zone*. Other conditions make getting good answers easier. We call that the *winning zone*. The *danger zone* and *winning zone* differ across five dimensions, as outlined in Table 1.1.

TABLE 1.1 *Danger Zone* vs. *Winning Zone*

DIMENSIONS	DANGER ZONE	WINNING ZONE
Nature of problems.	⚠ Complex problems with many highly intertwined factors.	✓ Simplified problems that are well bounded, have fewer factors, and can be addressed by smaller teams.
Hazards and risks.	⚠ Dangerous and risky.	✓ Less hazardous and less costly failures.
Speed of environment in which we're trying to solve problems.	⚠ Fast moving and not controllable.	✓ Slower moving with the opportunity to control pace and introduce pauses.
Opportunities to learn by experience or experimentation.	⚠ Experiences are singular or "one-off" so feedback may be missing and learning loops may not exist.	✓ Experiences can be repeated to gain experiential and experimental learning, and knowledge can be captured for recurring use.
Clarity about where and when to focus our problem-solving efforts.	⚠ It is not obvious that problems are even occurring, so they get neither contained nor resolved.	✓ It is obvious when problems are occurring, so attention is given to containing and solving them; and it's obvious whether the problems have been contained and resolved or not.

In the *danger zone*, problems are complex, with many factors affecting the system at once, and their relationships are highly intertwined. Hazards are many and severe, risks of failure are high, and costs of failure can be catastrophic. Systems in the *danger zone* are difficult to control, and there are limited, if any, opportunities to repeat experiences, so feedback-based learning is difficult if not outright impossible.

In contrast, leaders enable much more advantageous conditions in the *winning zone*. Problems have been reframed so they are simpler to address. The hazards and risks have been reduced so failures are less costly, especially during design, development, testing, and practice. Problem-solving has been shifted into slower-moving situations, where the pace of experiences can be better controlled. Opportunities to learn by experience or experimentation are increased to allow more iteration. And finally, there is much more clarity about where and when to focus problem-solving efforts, because it is obvious when problems are occurring, so attention is given to containing and solving them.

When we leave ourselves and our colleagues in the *danger zone*, it becomes extremely difficult to develop and design products and services and to develop and operate systems through which we collaborate and by which we coordinate. In fact, in such conditions, given the complexity and pace of the environment, it's often difficult to even recognize that significant problems are occurring and that they must be addressed to avert disaster.

In contrast, when we change our experiences so they happen in the *winning zone*, generating good answers to difficult problems is much easier, because people are better able to put their capabilities to best use. We can move ourselves from the *danger zone* to the *winning zone* using the three mechanisms of slowification, simplification, and amplification.

Let's take a closer look at defining each of these mechanisms:

Slowification makes it easier to solve problems by pulling problem-solving out of the fast-paced and often unforgiving realm of performance (i.e., operations or execution). Instead, solve problems this in the more controllable, forgiving, lower-cost, less-demanding, and repeatable realms of planning and practice.* This shifting of Layer 3

---

* Examples of slowification practices: using mock-ups, prototypes, simulations, scale model tests, offline problem-solving, land-based models, etc.

problem-solving into planning and practice allows people to engage in deliberative, reflective, experientially, and experimentally-informed reasoning rather than having to constantly react with whatever habits, routines, and legacy approaches have already been ingrained.

Simplification makes the problems themselves easier to solve by reshaping them. Large problems are deliberately broken down into smaller, simpler ones through a combination of three techniques: incrementalization, modularization, and linearization. By doing so, we partition complex problems with many interacting factors into many smaller problems. These problems have fewer interacting factors, making them easier to solve. Furthermore, Layer 1 (technical object) problem-solving can be done in parallel, with less need for Layer 3 coordination, increasing independence of action.*

Amplification makes it obvious there are problems, and makes it clear whether those problems have been seen and solved. Mechanisms are built into Layer 3 (social circuitry) to amplify that little things are amiss, drawing attention to them early and often. This focuses attention on containing and resolving small and local glitches before they have a chance to become large and systemically disruptive.†

Ideally, an organization will have the latitude to do all three: slow things down to make problem-solving easier; partition big problems into smaller ones that are simpler to solve, and amplify problems so they're addressed sooner and more often. Even if we cannot do all three, doing two or even one still brings us closer to the *winning zone*, making it easier for us to take situations about which we know too little and can do too little and convert them into situations in which we know enough and can do enough.

Figure 1.3 shows the *danger zone* in the upper right-hand corner and the *winning zone* in the lower left-hand corner. Slowification, which makes

---

* Examples of simplification practices: simple workflows, agile software development, modularization, just-in-time, pull systems, etc.

† Examples of amplification practices: stress tests, andon cords, smoke detectors, etc. to flag problems sooner rather than later.

problem-solving easier to do, moves us from right to left. Simplification, which reformulates problems so they are easier to solve, moves us from the top to the bottom. Note the small signal symbol in the upper right-hand corner, which denotes a lack of amplification, while the larger signal symbol in the lower left-hand corner denotes high amplification.

FIGURE 1.3 Moving from the *Danger Zone* to the *Winning Zone* through Slowification, Simplification, and Amplification

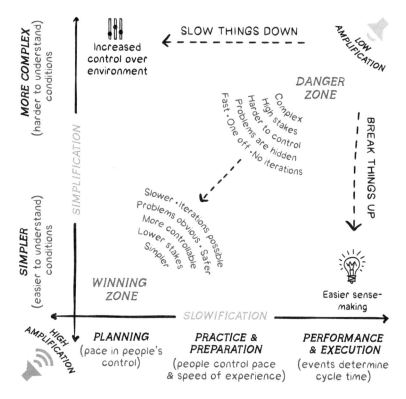

Leadership and the Circuitry They Create

There has been much written on the difference between leaders and managers.[*] In this book, we use the terms interchangeably and define leaders as

---

[*] See for instance "Managers and Leaders: Are They Different" by Dr. Abraham Zaleznik or "How Managers Become Leaders" by Dr. Michael D. Watkins.

those tasked with creating the conditions in which the people whom they manage can achieve the goals or complete the missions for which they are responsible. In all but the smallest endeavors, a leader's primary contribution is not doing the work required to achieve the goal. Instead, they are responsible for everything required to enable that work to be done easily and well. This is achieved through the social circuitry by which people's collaborative efforts are easily coordinated and integrated.

Much has also been written on change being driven from the "bottom up" versus the "top down." The first suggests that the change is a grassroots initiative driven by lower- to mid-level leaders, while the second suggests that the change is being driven by the highest-level leadership.

What we have found is that in winning organizations, leaders are deliberate about ensuring that Layer 3 (social circuitry) is supportive of people's efforts in solving Layer 1 (technical object) and Layer 2 (tools) problems. Their role is less supervisory, in the characterized fashion of directive leadership or command and control (e.g., "I say; you do" "compliance without question"). Rather, it is more supportive, continuously monitoring the conditions in which people are working and then adapting and adjusting so those conditions are most conducive to success.

This might remind some of the concepts of servant leadership or frontline empowerment, but this is more than that. It is an emphasis on leaders actively engineering the social circuitry of their organization, so when people for whom they are responsible badge in, buzz in, and otherwise arrive to do work, they walk into situations that are constructed to be the most conducive for success.

What to Expect in This Book and How to Read It

This book is organized into four parts. Here in Part I, we present all of the key concepts and terms needed to explain the theory and show their application through two vignettes. We designed these vignettes as simple models to introduce fundamental concepts, stripped of real-world complexity. Consider these the equivalent of using pendulums to illustrate Newtonian mechanics in physics or using supply and demand of widgets to illustrate the basics of economics.

Understanding more complex situations doesn't depend on adding new concepts. It depends on using the same ones but with more sophistication. For instance, the more advanced case might be a pendulum that bounces into a spring, swinging through a viscous fluid. Supply and demand might be for a product with imperfect markets. By the time you finish reading Part I, you should understand the main ideas of this book.

In the next three parts, we go into more detail on the three mechanisms of slowification, simplification, and amplification. Each part starts with an illustrative case study, showing the mechanism in action to help readers understand the high-level concept. That is followed by an explanation of the theory underpinning the mechanism, with references back to the introductory case study to highlight key points.

Next, we present a number of case studies of that mechanism at work, drawn from numerous and varied situations. The quantity and variety of cases is to make a point: the same Layer 3 mechanisms apply, from small scale to large (from an individual artist or small design team up to enormous undertakings), across industry sectors (planes, tech, education, healthcare), and at different phases of value creation (R&D, design, production). These case studies also help generalize the principles so you can better recognize the problems you encounter in your organization and more easily generate useful solutions.

Finally, each part concludes with an exemplar case study, which shows the mechanism being used in a consequential and significant situation to create an advantage. You'll likely have heard of these exemplars. Our goal is to interpret what happened through the lens of the three mechanisms so it's clear how using them makes great outcomes possible.

Although we wrote the book to be read from the beginning to the end, there are alternatives. You might want to focus on the theory (the "why"), before diving into the details (the "what" and "how"). If this sounds like you, you might skip over the case study chapters (5 and 8).

Or, you might want to see these mechanisms in pinnacle use. If so, make sure you read the exemplar case studies in Chapters 6, 9, and 10.

Or, you might love reading a lot of stories about people accomplishing great things. If this is you, you'll likely love reading the case study chapters and perhaps skimming the theory chapters.

No matter your personal style, if you are reading this book, we assume you are someone who is responsible for leading a group of people to achieve something important. This is something that can be achieved only through collaborative effort, requiring a considerable amount of problem-solving, ideally by everyone, every day, and about most things.

Regardless of how you read this book—whether start-to-finish, theory first, details first, or reading what the world's best do—our goal remains the same: that after reading this book, you're equipped with ideas and examples that make you more effective at making your colleagues outstandingly successful.

A Call to Action

The preface began with the observation that everyday people badge in, buzz in, swipe in, scan in, sign in, log in, or otherwise just walk into their places of work. From that common beginning, the differences in their experiences are vast. For some, they can regularly say that they've been able to succeed, that their work was appreciated, and that they added value to their own lives. For too many, they faced regular impediments, felt unrecognized, and had to do work discordantly with what they otherwise value. Either way, those individual experiences are tightly associated with how well the organizations—of which people are a part—perform.

Our hope is that we provide enough theory and examples and offer enough detail and clarity to help you reshape the experiences of those for whom you are directly responsible, improve on your own experiences as a leader, and, in doing so, change in some positive way the fortunes of the organization of which you are part.

CHAPTER 2

Navigating from *Danger Zones*
to *Winning Zones*

In this chapter, we present two vignettes to introduce the key concepts of wiring an organization to move from the *danger zone* to the *winning zone* through the mechanisms of slowification, simplification, and amplification. These two vignettes are simple models to illustrate fundamental concepts. We will use the same concepts to explain far more complex situations, such as the case studies in Chapters 4 through 10.

This mirrors how many topics are taught, and for good reason. In many fields, expertise does not depend on juggling ever more concepts. Rather, mastery is acquired by practicing some few concepts, first in simple situations and then gradually gaining facility using them expertly in extremely challenging ones.

For instance, in physics, Newtonian mechanics (i.e., $F=ma$) is introduced with examples like single forces on point masses or with calculations of the period of a pendulum. Eventually, the same concepts are used to understand the flight path of interstellar space probes, as well as the structural designs of the probes themselves. Similarly, in finance, the time-value-of-money is introduced with an intuitive understanding of why getting paid a dollar today is better than getting paid the same dollar tomorrow. The same concept is applied to multi-period cash flows, with payment and discount rate uncertainty added on, eventually becoming the tools by which complex transactions can be constructed.

Following the same approach, the first vignette is about two people moving a couch. It reveals that even "brawn work" involves significant "brain work." Even two people moving a couch requires joint problem-solving and cognition. This is to help leaders recognize that everyone is doing "knowledge work" of some form, regardless of the nature of their work in Layers 1 and 2.

We will show how leaders can help or hinder knowledge work by the decisions they make in Layer 3 (the social circuitry). It is insufficient to focus primarily on the flow of materials or information through machines, with people merely as bystanders. Rather, leaders must shape the social circuitry so that people can best engage their ingenuity and problem-solving capabilities.

In the first vignette, we use the act of moving a couch to describe how the boundary of a group solving problems must be large enough that it is coherent, having all the people and resources needed to solve the problem. However, the boundary must also be small enough to not require large amounts of coordination. We also show how leaders must ensure the communication channels are sufficiently direct and have sufficient bandwidth to support joint problem-solving.

The second vignette is about two people managing the refurbishment of an old Victorian hotel. This requires three interdependent steps from two functional specialties: movers must first remove furniture from the room, painters must prep and paint the room, at which point, the movers return the furniture back into the room.

We will show how the social circuitry (Layer 3) that leaders create has direct and profound impact on how well people can work and use their professional expertise in Layer 1 (technical object) and Layer 2 (tools and instrumentation). And we'll show how leaders can use the three mechanisms to rewire the social circuitry of their organization to dramatically improve the conditions for people to do their work easily and well. But first we will show how decisions leaders make in Layer 3 can create spectacularly bad outcomes for even this simple scenario. This will provide insight on how to manage far more complex situations in the real world, spanning different sectors and across different phases of value creation.

As you read the vignettes, you might notice familiar concepts from industry practices such as agile software development, DevOps, lean, Toyota Production System, cross-functional teams, organizational topologies, safety culture, or software architecture. The mechanisms are not replacements for sound practice. Rather, those sound practices are specific examples of the slowification, simplification, and amplification mechanisms in practice.*

Vignette One: **Moving a Couch, Together**

Gene and Steve are trying to move a couch. This may seem like a problem that involves physical labor only. However, in order to succeed, they must collaborate to solve many important problems. These include: Where should they place their hands to lift the couch? How do they keep the couch balanced when they move? To get through a narrow doorway, do they orient the couch vertically or horizontally? To get down a narrow and winding staircase, who should go first? And should they face forward or backward?

Gene and Steve don't need to conduct elaborate studies to answer these questions. They assess the couch and the room it's in, lift it to get a feel for its weight and balance, and work together so their efforts are coordinated. Through trial and error and fast feedback, as well as by communicating and coordinating, Gene and Steve are able to generate the information they need to solve their problems.

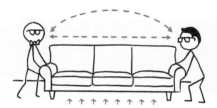

As they go, there are unforeseen problems, such as balance, positioning, and pace. They resolve some issues by talking, but some are communicated by gestures—nodding in which direction to move, shifting a grip, vocalizing when the effort is too great. Regardless of how problem-solving occurs, it must be a team effort. Gene can't just change his grip without risking Steve losing his. And Steve can't speed up the stairs without putting Gene at risk.

Of course, their ability to collaborate can be compromised. When the sun sets, the room where they are working gets darker. Because Gene and Steve are no longer able to see and sense what's around them, everything takes

---

* For a deeper dive on that point, readers are invited to review the Appendix.

more time. Furthermore, someone may trip over something on the floor, or someone's finger might get pinched.

Their work may also become even more difficult when a fire alarm goes off or a car alarm starts blaring outside. This is because they are no longer able to hear each other's concerns and corrections, reducing their ability to communicate and coordinate.

It is important to note that the added noise does not make the task at hand more difficult, unlike with the loss of light. In this situation, it is Gene and Steve's inability to communicate that makes it more difficult to solve problems and complete their task.

Yet another way for their work to become more difficult is if an intermediary is introduced. Let's say a friend tries to help, relaying messages between Gene and Steve, telling them what's going on, what to do, how to do it, and why. Despite their best efforts, the friend may actually make matters worse. This is because the friend cannot convey information with nearly the frequency, speed, detail, or accuracy as compared with when Gene and Steve communicate directly.

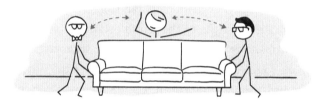

Key Concepts

Two people moving a couch together is different from two people each moving a chair. When moving the chairs, the two people can work independently. However, two people moving a couch is collaborative, requiring communication, coordination, and interaction. And when their ability to collaborate degrades (e.g., the room becomes too dark to see, too noisy to hear, or the friend intermediates their communication), their task becomes increasingly difficult.

In the beginning, Gene and Steve worked together in a *coherent* environment. The conditions for doing the brain work were hospitable, which enabled them to succeed in the brawn work. Conversely, when the conditions became incoherent, the brain work was more difficult, and so too was the brawn work.

By *coherent*, we mean having the quality of a unified whole. The elements that interact frequently and intensely (e.g., Gene and Steve) are in the same group, and they can communicate directly and with needed frequency, speed, accuracy, and detail. This is necessary for the performance of the whole to be logical and consistent. In this case, a well-lit, relatively quiet room meant Gene and Steve could solve problems as they arose. On the other hand, a poorly lit and noisy room with an intermediary degraded that coherence, which made moving the couch much more difficult.

For now, let us state that leaders make many Layer 3 decisions about the social circuitry of their organization that create or destroy coherence. For Gene and Steve, diminishment in lighting, increase in noise, and intermediation in communications were all arbitrary events. However, in more complex situations, leaders often make decisions that deliberately or accidentally improve or impede people's ability to make sense of their situation (e.g., the lighting), to exchange information (e.g., the noise), or communicate and collaborate directly (e.g., the intermediating friend).

Related to coherence, we'll introduce another term: *coupling*. Elements in a system are coupled when changes in one affect the other. Gene and Steve are coupled through the couch. Gene's actions affect not just the couch but Steve as well, and vice versa. For instance, if Gene twists his end of the couch, Steve has to adjust to compensate.

How much coupling there is determines how much coherence leaders must create so that people can collaborate. Two people moving a couch are coupled; two people each moving a chair are not (unless, of course, they have to go through the same narrow door at the same time).

Depending on conditions, even people in the same situations can have different degrees of coupling, necessitating a different drawing of the boundaries to maintain coherence. For example, during normal flight operations, air traffic controllers and flight crews are loosely coupled. There can be less concern for defining a small, coherent working group. Controllers need to know the location, direction, and speed of aircraft in the space for which they are responsible. Flight crews have to manage their aircrafts' controls to control their flight paths.

Because of this precise division of responsibility, communication between the controller and pilot can be terse and coded. In the following transcript from the Dallas/Fort Worth Airport tower, note the consistent wording between the tower and pilots, and how pilots repeat the controller's instructions to confirm they understand, reducing the likelihood of a misinterpretation going unnoticed:[1]

> *Pilot:* "Good Morning DFW Tower, American 121, visual for one-eight right."
> *Tower:* "American 121, DFW Tower, cleared to land one-eight right, winds one eight zero at seven."
> *Pilot:* "Cleared to land, one-eight right, American 121."

> *Pilot:* "Regional approach, American 71, one-zero thousand for eight thousand, requesting direct NETEE."
> *Tower:* "American 71, regional approach, regional altimeter three zero zero six, cleared as requested. Descend and maintain six-thousand."
> *Pilot:* "Cleared direct NETEE, down to six-thousand, American 71."

From the air traffic control perspective, pilots are just a flight number, and from the pilot's perspective, controllers are just the tower. Flight crews can choose whether it's the captain or first officer on the radio without the approval of the tower. Similarly, the controllers can pass responsibility for a flight to another controller without approval from the flight crew. Both sides have independence of action.

This is an example of loose coupling. In these situations, there can be a protocol, like in the example above, that is agreed upon by both sides, of what information to exchange, how, when, with what frequency, and in what format.* What is important can be communicated in the message; it is not dependent on the messenger.

In contrast, in an emergency, pilots and air traffic controllers will do many things to increase coherence because they must be more tightly coupled. To communicate with greater frequency, intensity, and clarity, they may dedicate a controller to the pilot and move other flights to another radio frequency. That way, the pilot and controller can focus on the emergency together, without distractions from other flights.[2]

---

* Standards as set by the International Civil Aviation Organization.

Consider how, in 2018, Maggie Taraska, a seventeen-year-old solo student pilot, was guided to a safe landing by the controller after the landing gear fell off her plane during takeoff.

> *Tower:* "Warrior 2496X...your right main is now missing from the airplane. It's fallen off the airplane. Say your intentions."
> *Pilot:* "Can I circle back to land?"
> *Tower:* "Warrior 96X, affirmative. Are you a solo, ma'am?"
> *Pilot:* "I'm a student pilot solo, yes."
> *Tower:* "Okay. It'll be okay. Just go ahead and circle the airport for now. Make a right turn to circle. We're going to get some people out to help you, okay?"[3]

This communication was more casual, not the highly coded talk of normal operations. The tower used simple terms, such as "circle the airport for now" and "make a right turn to circle." This calmed everyone involved in the situation and made it easier for the student pilot to understand what was needed. Once the situation stabilized, the controller found the student's instructor, summoned him to the tower, and they all worked the problem.

> *Tower (Instructor):* "You're doing a great job flying the airplane. Keep doing what you're doing. They're going to stage the equipment [emergency crews, fire trucks] just in case anything is needed...We've got plenty of time; we've got plenty of fuel; we've got plenty of daylight. So, try to relax and [you've] always heard me say 'go back to the basics.' So, we're gonna work the basics here as much as possible... I can see you turning at altitude lining up the runway, so continue down like you normally do. What I'm thinking is just have you fly down the length of 09* like you're doing right now, and then, when you're comfortable, I'm [going] to have you turn to the left, enter a downwind on 09. Would that work for you?"

---

* "09" refers to the runway number, named after the compass bearing of the runway orientations.

Pilot: "Yeah, that works."

Tower (Instructor): "...[I'll keep] my eye on you and maybe suggest when you might want to start to turn crosswind and downwind...Okay, I know it's hard to say this, but treat it as much like a normal landing as you can. So, the power setting will be all the way down, the pitch, the airspeed, keep everything as normal as you can."

Pilot: "Alright."[4]

They created a small, coherent working unit to solve the problem. Together, the controller, the pilot, and her instructor landed the plane safely, with the instructor saying, "You did a beautiful job, Maggie. You've got a bunch of people clapping for you up here."[5]

This was made possible by switching from loosely coupled elements (people in planes and control towers) to tightly coupled elements in a well-defined, coherent working group (Maggie, her instructor, and a flight controller on their own frequency).

Leaders must appreciate that all the work they are managing is knowledge work. At times, some of this work is loosely coupled, while at other times, it is tightly coupled. It is not arbitrary. Instead, it depends on how much coherence has to be provided to whom, in which working groups, and the type of problem they are trying to solve. This, in turn, determines how leaders must configure the social circuitry of their organization (Layer 3). This includes the design of roles, routines, processes, and procedures. For instance, the social circuitry to support normal air traffic control operations is different from the circuitry needed to ensure the safe landing by a student pilot in a damaged aircraft.

Coupling and coherence are important, not just for Gene and Steve trying to move a couch or Maggie Taraska landing safely. Look around your own work environment and assess whether you are wired to win or not. Have many people have been placed into the same group arbitrarily, when the problems they're dealing with are not tightly coupled? If so, this is likely a couch team that is actually moving chairs. This social circuitry design error creates the predictable consequence of people being drawn into situations where they are not needed and for which they will not be affected by the outcomes. This creates more meetings, memos, status updates, and the like, which adds work and time but does not add value.

Conversely, as you look around your work environment, are there people who are responsible for some portion of a larger problem scattered around the organization, not taking into account how coupled their work is? If so, this is likely because a couch problem is being solved by multiple chair teams. People who should be solving problems together can't. Collaboration should be frequent, fast, and rich but becomes occasional, slow, and imprecise. Instead of conversation, there are forms, work orders, tickets, intermittent meetings, and convoluted reporting channels.

Wired this way, people with tightly coupled work are not in a coherent working group. They don't have everything they need to do their work easily and well, which includes people, skills, resources, decision rights, and so forth. This makes it more difficult to find solutions, and those solutions are worse than they otherwise would have been. This is also a social circuitry design error, one of breaking things into such small pieces that coherence is lost. That's both coherence of completeness and coherence in terms of being able to act logically and reliably.

In the first case, the system was over coupled and under partitioned. In the second case, the system was under coupled and over partitioned. Later in the book, we'll describe how leaders can address both of these situations to be wired to win.

This first vignette demonstrated the effects of cohesion and coupling to make it easier or more difficult to jointly solve a problem. In the second vignette, we'll illustrate how management systems can make it easier or more difficult to integrate different functional specialties to achieve a common goal, what can go wrong, and what we can do about it.

QUESTIONS FOR THE READER

1. What interactions within your organization are "over couched?" These are situations where there's been too little partitioning of groups around the problems you have to solve. How can you better partition a

problem, thereby returning time to people to solve Layer 1 and Layer 2 because they are no longer burdened by Layer 3 problems?

2. What interactions within your organization are "under couched?" These are situations where the contributions of people necessary to help solve problems and get things done are not within a coherent unit. What might be done to increase the coherence across those boundaries and enable better joint problem-solving, so Layer 1 and Layer 2 issues can be addressed more effectively?

Vignette Two: **Moving Furniture and Painting an Old Victorian Hotel**

Due to their splendid sense of aesthetics and design, Margueritte Kim and Miriam Tropp Spear have been asked by their friend to help refurbish an old Victorian hotel in a remote part of rural Maine. The friend's idea is to turn it into a not-for-profit center for children who've undergone trauma.

Because of its remote location and the fact that it'll be a charity undertaking, professional general contractors, who might otherwise hire the necessary tradespeople and manage their work, aren't readily available to do the work that is needed.

Given the tight deadlines to open the center, Margueritte and Miriam need to focus their time on design and help their friend with opening the center. So they ask their respective spouses, Gene and Steve, to hire people to clear the rooms of furniture, do all the necessary prepping and repainting, and return the furniture to where it belongs. Gene and Steve assure Margueritte and Miriam that they can complete this.

Steve takes responsibility for hiring and scheduling movers, while Gene takes responsibility for hiring and scheduling the painters. They pick a date to get started, thinking, "What could go wrong?"

Right after Gene and Steve assure their spouses that all will go well, everything goes wrong. Painters are calling Gene to say the rooms haven't been fully emptied, so they can't set up and do their work. Movers are complaining to Steve that they emptied the rooms but there's no sign of the painters, so they don't know when to put the furniture back. Some movers and painters are trying to work in the same place at the same time, tripping over each other.

Gene and Steve are surprised when they discover that the movers and painters started at opposite ends of the hotel. The movers wanted to do the top floors first, before they got tired. The painters wanted to start on the bottom floors so they wouldn't have to haul all their supplies up the stairs. As a result, many rooms had been started but few had been completed. Furthermore, movers and painters were getting in each other's way, either in the hallways and staircases or within the rooms they were working in.

To try to better synchronize everyone, Gene and Steve create a single moving-and-painting schedule in a spreadsheet. This assigns times for the movers to remove the furniture, the painters to paint, and the movers to return the furniture. Gene and Steve figure the schedule will ensure everyone is where they need to be, when they need to be there. However, Gene and Steve are amazed by how quickly the situation devolves into disarray. Movers show up while painters are still painting, and painters show up to rooms that haven't yet been cleared.

It turns out that Gene and Steve's estimates for the time to remove furniture is nearly always wrong—every room has a different mix of chairs, tables, bureaus, and so forth, with different sizes and weights, which require different times to move.

Their painting estimates are just as inaccurate. There are a variety of surfaces throughout the rooms, so the time required for each is different. After all, this is an old Victorian; each room has a different floor plan. As for the finishes, sometimes there is drywall and sometimes there is an older form of plastering. Sometimes there is crown molding that needs to be stained. Sometimes the crown molding needs to be replaced. And occasionally, some rooms have lead paint that needs to be managed according to code.

Because Gene and Steve's schedule did not account for these factors, tasks rarely start or finish as expected. Cajoling and hectoring from Gene and Steve don't help. Everyone is in everyone else's way. Painters are frustrated with movers, movers with painters, and everyone is rightly frustrated with Gene and Steve.

To try to get the movers and painters where they need to be, Gene and Steve do two things. First, they try to create a more accurate schedule by getting better information. They start interrupting people while they're working, asking for more accurate estimates of how long their work will take. But they discover that even these estimates are still not accurate enough. Movers and painters keep showing up too early or too late. Worse, everyone grows increasingly irritated by Steve and Gene's constant requests for status updates, especially when there is no obvious improvement.

Gene and Steve also start expediting. When a room becomes "critical," they demand that movers and painters drop their work mid-task to go work on that room. Expediting requires a lot of time and effort from Gene and

Steve, and the constant stopping and starting of tasks is even more disruptive to movers and painters trying to get work done.

When Gene and Steve propose measuring the movers on "number of pieces of furniture moved" and painters on "number of walls painted" and "percentage of wall paintings started on time," many of the movers and painters threaten to quit. Several painters, frustrated with waiting for the movers, start moving the furniture themselves. Tensions keep escalating as movers and painters start blaming each other for their inability to achieve their goals.

It gets worse. When Margueritte and Miriam return to the hotel, they are flabbergasted and mortified at how badly things are going, with so few rooms actually completed and absolutely no one proud of the work that has been done. Everyone agrees that the center cannot open in its current state, despite promises made to the community, donors, and the families of the children.

Reflections and Key Concepts

The problems that Gene and Steve are grappling with in this vignette are likely familiar to anyone who has ever worked in a functionally oriented organization—where people are divided based on their specialties. Leaders in these organizations often assume things will naturally self-organize or that schedules can always integrate those specialties toward a common purpose. They often neglect, as Gene and Steve did, the careful design of their organizational wiring (Layer 3).

One potential result is the system is over partitioned, so no part in the system is coherent. In other words, no part of the system can work independently, requiring massive coordination effort to do anything at all.

Unfortunately, this is a common problem. For instance, Steve and Miriam took their eight-year old daughter, Eve, to the emergency department after she fell in a playground and jammed her wrist. At every step in the experience—registration, triage, examination, imaging, diagnosis (to determine that the "jam" was actually a buckle fracture), treatment (to cast her arm), and scheduling for follow-up—they found clinicians who seemed deeply concerned with providing sympathetic and quality care.

However, each step in the process was disconnected from the whole: registration took all of Eve's information correctly (Steve and Miriam saw the printout), but that printout didn't accurately make it to the triage nurse. The triage nurse slotted Eve into the orthopedic track, but Steve and Miriam sat in an exam room until they finally lost patience and went to find the physician assistant, who responded, "Oh, I didn't know you were waiting."

When they got to imaging, the technician had the sites aligned on Eve's forearm, not her wrist, because the instructions he received weren't clear enough as to where the injury was. When Eve was finally casted (which turned out to be plaster instead of the preferred, more kid-friendly and waterproof fiberglass, because of a disconnect with the supply department), Steve and Miriam tried to schedule a follow-up appointment, which they couldn't do from the emergency department. They had to call an external phone number, which they had to locate on their own.

Yes, the pieces finally came together, but only because of Steve and Miriam's repeated interventions to make it happen.

Gene had the same type of experience when his father suffered a stroke. It was left to Gene and Margueritte to get all the specialties to coordinate across multiple days in the trauma center.

After his father was transferred from the neurological intensive care unit to the neurological care unit, he was seen by various specialists during the daily rounds, which included neurologists, nurses, case managers, etc. On the first daily round, a decision had to be made about whether to put Gene's father on blood thinners. They deferred making a decision until they could examine the brain MRI images, which would be available the next day. Overhearing this, Gene showed them a picture he had taken of the brain scans the neurologist studied the day before. They huddled around Gene's phone and decided to prescribe blood thinners that day.

This is another example of Layer 3 design errors causing people to not have what they need when they need it to do their work easily and well. The different functions were poorly integrated, much as we saw in the chaotic emergency department that treated Eve's fracture. In effect, in the absence of well-designed social circuitry (Layer 3) to integrate across the different medical professions, the coordination function is often a concerned family member, with no medical training, to ensure their loved one receives timely care.

Such problems are not unique to healthcare. Consider an oil refinery that has to repair valves, pumps, and motors that help move fluids throughout the facility. In the repair department, there is a valve that has been waiting for months to be repaired. Why? Mechanics had taken the device apart to inspect and assess it. The valve required certain parts to be sent to machinists for refurbishing, while another part had to be sent to the hydraulics shop to be fixed by the specialists there. The machinists had completed their work, but the mechanics in the hydraulics shop were still waiting on some sign-offs from engineering, which is in yet another department.

Making the problem worse, mechanics who were waiting for "paperwork" from engineering or parts from other functions were idle. So, they looked for other work to do. This increased the number of open and active jobs that had to be tracked (e.g., what part was in what location and in what stage of processing). This increased even further the information needs of the system.

Repairing the valve should have been a simple, linear sequence of work. Instead, the valve became "stuck," just like Miriam and Steve's daughter in the emergency department or Gene's father in the neurological care unit. Each was seemingly lost in all of the Layer 3 coordination required because of the insufficient coherence between functional departments.

And what happened to that valve in the repair department? It was not repaired in time. As a result, those doing maintenance on the larger system had to scavenge another valve to get things back up and running, adding even more people, machines, material, and information that needed to be coordinated and expedited.

Here's another example: Consider the complex and sprawling software systems that run the operations of a mobile phone service provider. Leadership wants to present a checkbox on their website to enable their customers to subscribe to a $4.95 monthly service, such as to watch movies or get email. Implementing this capability requires changes from over forty teams—ten parts of various applications (e.g., web front end, middleware, back end, notifications,), across every channel to the customer (e.g., retail, digital, customer support), as well as billing, collections, and so forth. Implementing the seemingly simple checkbox requires scores of project managers, near CEO-level sponsorship, and over one year to complete—delaying a new revenue stream that would bring in tens of millions of dollars every month.

Requiring one year to add this simple checkbox is not because it is technically challenging at Layer 1 (the object being worked on) or Layer 2 (the tools and instrumentation). Quite the opposite. Instead, the checkbox had become "stuck" because of the inadequate Layer 3 (social circuitry) that leaders created among the forty teams. Each team operated independently of each other. They had their own priorities, budgets, operating plans, schedules, and so forth. The checkbox was "stuck" in just the same way as the other three examples.

This is nearly the same situation that Gene and Steve created in the old Victorian hotel, where rooms became "stuck" in terms of progress not being made because the efforts of the movers and painters were not coordinated. Before we explain what Gene and Steve did to get things right, let's first analyze and reflect on what they did to get things so badly wrong. How did they miswire their Layer 3 so dismally?

When Schedules Fail as an Effective Integrating Mechanism

At first, Gene and Steve did not coordinate the efforts of the movers and painters at all, resulting in their starting at opposite ends of the building. Next, they tried to use a schedule as the coordination and integration mechanism but were still unable to get the movers and painters where they needed to be when they needed to be there.

What Gene and Steve did not appreciate is that scheduling a project of this complexity, let alone one of even greater complexity, is nearly impossible. They were unable to get sufficiently accurate forecasts of how much time the movers and painters needed to complete their work, nor were they ever able to get adequately complete and timely information from everyone in their system to tell people where to go.

But even if they had all that information, creating an accurate schedule is still hopeless. It was mathematically proven over fifty years ago that it is often impossible to compute a correct and optimal scheduling solution in finite time for schedules of any significant size.* Gene and Steve created the best schedule they could in their spreadsheet, based on insufficient detail, guaranteeing a poor schedule and their dismal outcomes.

FIGURE 2.1: Example of Production Control

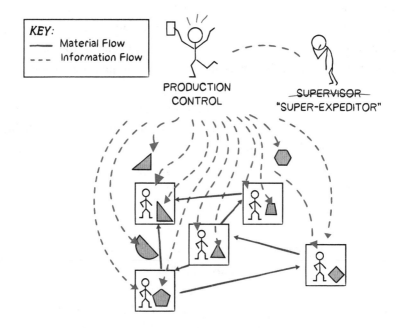

---

* In computer science, "job-shop scheduling" is known to be "NP-Hard," a category of problem that requires exhaustive search. Because the time required to solve these problems can grow polynomially based on its input size, some are not computable in finite time. Another well-known NP-Hard problem is cryptography, which depends upon having the key to decrypt a message. Later in this book, we will discuss why scheduling is so difficult.

Expediting Adds To, Doesn't Diminish, the Chaos

Gene and Steve also tried expediting, having movers and painters drop whatever they were doing to do something "more urgent." The resulting chaos they experienced is not an exaggeration.

In settings where there is a daily production schedule, such as in manufacturing or IT operations, many of us have experienced morning production control meetings, daily review meetings, and so forth. After schedules have been released, managers start generating hot lists (the list of urgent schedule changes), super hot lists, and extra hot lists, all while shop floor supervisors are running about trying to expedite, firefight, and reroute workflows* for "blocking" of upstream work by downstream work and "starving" of downstream work by upstream work.

Furthermore, notice how their system couples everyone to everyone else—if any mover or painter runs late, they quickly cause other rooms to become late, and the lateness spreads like a contagion. In this system, small problems quickly become large problems. As a result, expediting may provide some immediate gratification but actually makes matters worse.

As they did in scheduling, Gene and Steve ran into another theoretical limitation, this time for control systems. Their ability to see and solve problems was not able to keep up with the frequency, speed, or detail of the work of the movers and painters they were trying to coordinate and control.†

---

* We use the following terms interchangeably: workflows, value streams, flows of work, etc.

† Control system overlays must be faster and more reliable than the underlying systems being controlled. The Nyquist-Shannon Sampling Theorem, first introduced in 1928, explains why. A receiver (sensor) must sample at least twice the rate of the sender (the thing being monitored and controlled) to accurately measure and control a system. This theorem forms the basis of all things digital, including telecommunications, medical imaging systems, astronomy, and more. In reality, to control a complex engineered or biological system, the receiver and controller must be much faster to maintain resilience and agility. This has stark implications for top-down management. For instance, if reports are generated and reviewed once a week, they can be used to control (manage) only situations that change no faster or more frequently than every two weeks. Anything faster moving may not be detected or is not controllable. This explains why exemplary organizations are typically characterized by overlays of people in supportive roles that are uncharacteristic of their lower-performing peers. That is not "overhead" but absolutely necessary bandwidth for sustaining high performance of fast-moving, complex, dynamic systems. Just such an example is described in Part IV: Amplification.

Gene and Steve created the best schedule they could in their spreadsheet, based on insufficient detail, guaranteeing a poor schedule and their dismal outcomes.

Parochial Performance Measures

Note how any isolated performance measure, such as "number of pieces of furniture moved" or "number of walls painted," did not improve overall performance—and may likely make things worse. For instance, to meet the furniture-moving goals, movers may start moving rooms before they are needed, jeopardizing the rooms that actually need moving. One can even imagine a situation where they "over produce" and run out of space to store the furniture.*

Lack of Isomorphism between Layer 3 and Layers 1 and 2

At this point, we have illustrated how Gene and Steve's social circuitry (Layer 3) was profoundly unsuited for the work of the movers and painters (Layers 1 and 2). In mathematics, there is a term for this: *isomorphism*. Isomorphism is the quality of related items having similar structures. In the simplest case, the work of refurbishing a room requires movers to clear out the furniture, which signals the painters to begin their work, who, upon completion, signal the movers to bring the furniture back in when the paint is dry to the touch.

But consider how the information travels in Gene and Steve's Layer 3 wiring, which did not flow in anything like this pattern. Instead, information traveled from painters and movers when they completed their work to Gene and Steve, who would determine what people should actually be doing

---

* One could interpret Gene and Steve's actions so far as a "transactional" view of leadership—they believed they merely had to hire the right people; tell them exactly what to do, as well as when and where; and then measure and hector (and maybe even penalize and reward) their performance in ways that do not improve overall performance. Also, this would motivate "hiring lowest cost resources," instead of "rank and yank" practices to rank all employees and fire the bottom-performing 20%.

rather than what they were doing. Then, they sent instructions (information) back to the movers and painters.

The work, in effect, was flowing linearly through time, whereas the information had to be moved (with great effort) vertically, up and down silos. The "structural" problem was that the people who really needed to be in direct communication with each other were not. All information had to be processed through Gene and Steve as opposed to flowing directly between the movers and painters. The resulting problem (dynamics) was as described: scheduling and expediting occurred with a frequency, speed, and detail completely inadequate for the frequency, speed, and detail with which work was being done.

It is clear that Gene and Steve created organizational wiring that was incongruent, or not isomorphic, to the work being done. (We will explore this in more detail in Part III: Simplification.)*

Summary of Gene and Steve's Problems

Gene and Steve created Layer 3 wiring that resulted in a system where movers and painters were working in nothing remotely resembling a unified and coherent whole. The functional silos divided the people who needed to coordinate and collaborate frequently and intensely. The only mechanism their system gave them to coordinate was escalating to Steve and Gene.

Let us marvel for just a moment at how thoroughly we can screw up even this relatively simple system, placing Gene and Steve very much in the *danger zone*. Of course, the consequences are graver in situations that are more complex, across all the dimensions of frequency, complexity, variety, consequence, speed, information density, the number of functional specialties, and so forth, such as the healthcare, oil refinery, and telco software examples.

Let's return to Gene and Steve's story to see what they do to rewire the system to move them into the *winning zone*.

---

* People in software engineering may be correctly reminded of Conway's Law, which is commonly stated as "If you have four groups working on a compiler, you'll get a 4-pass compiler." (Credited to Eric S. Raymond.) We will discuss in Part IV: Amplification.

A Better Way

As the implications sink in of how poorly things have gone, Gene and Steve listen to the considerable frustration of the painters and movers and begin to appreciate just how much coordination has to occur between them for their work to get done. They also see the futility of trying to coordinate people through schedules and expediting.

They realize they should partition the whole project into smaller pieces, organizing people into individual "room teams," so the work in one room is less coupled to the work in other rooms. As we'll see, this is an approach of ensuring each team is coherent and less coupled to other teams. This is the opposite of what they had before: low coherence and high coupling.

Each room team includes both movers and painters who have all the supplies, materials, and decision rights necessary to start and finish renovating a room on their own. Gene and Steve assign each team a group of rooms, which the team will complete, one after another.

Each team can now work independently because they are a coherent whole. By spreading the teams across the hotel, teams are also less likely to interfere with each other. In other words, the distance between teams reduces interference and coupling, which reduces the need to coordinate.

The work within each room becomes easier to complete too. Each room team needs to worry only about coordinating the efforts of the movers and painters within that team. They are not dependent on any other room teams to do their work, and vice versa. This one change significantly reduces the amount of friction and interference between room teams.

Now some room teams are able to partition even more, reducing interference within their own teams, specifically between the movers and painters. To do this, the movers and painters of a room team discuss with one another how to make it easier for the other group to do what they need to do. For instance, the painters explain to the movers that they don't need everything cleared from the rooms—very large furniture can be left behind, so long as it is moved away from the walls. Painters can do their work behind the furniture and cover it to prevent paint spatter. These explicit handoffs make it more obvious what each person needs to accomplish to achieve the system goals and how to get it done.

FIGURE 2.2 Partitioning into Room Teams

Creating flows within phases stages.

HIGH CHAOS / HIGH COUPLING   LOW CHAOS / LOW COUPLING

Similarly, the team agrees that movers should return the furniture only after all the paint surfaces are dry to the touch and after all the fumes have left the room, preventing the movers from marring the paint and ensuring health and safety.

This creates immediate benefits for the movers and painters. By more clearly defining their boundaries and handoffs, they further partitioned their work and simplified their system. Everyone has fewer people they need to interact with and everyone is able to stay productive with fewer things to worry about. Movers and painters can work more independently of each other, and they've reduced opportunities for error.

FIGURE 2.3 Further Partitioning within Room Teams

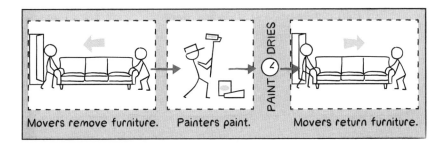

Movers remove furniture.   Painters paint.   Movers return furniture.

Note how within the room teams, movers and painters are able to continually redefine how they interact with each other. There is no risk of impacting those outside of their team. This liberates movers and painters to fix their own problems and solve their own frustrations, with no need to coordinate with anyone outside their team. In effect, by changing Layer 3 (the social circuitry), Gene and Steve made it much easier for the people for whom they were responsible (the movers and painters) to do outstanding work in Layer 1 and Layer 2.

However, the movers and painters still encounter problems that have to be solved. For instance, painters are occasionally frustrated that they need more time to find the right mix of stain for the wood in the rooms. This is time consuming to get right, meaning those rooms take longer to finish.

Instead of trying to solve these problems in the moment, while the movers are waiting for them, the painters decide to solve these problems "offline." The painters finish their day by experimenting on wood samples to test different formulations for absorption and coloration. When they discover that some paneling is oak and other paneling is elm, which stain differently, they pass this knowledge on as "standards" for the other teams, which makes these operations easier and faster to complete in the future. They've used slowification to solve difficult problems ahead of time, during planning and preparation, so they are spared surprises during performance.

In another complication, Steve notices movers struggle with furniture through a dimly lit, narrow staircase that has a loose tread. He installs extra lighting and temporarily reaffixes the tread. Rather than "being more careful" or "working around the problem," they *solved* the actual problem. By amplifying the signal of problems and fixing them offline, work is quicker, easier, and safer.

With both the stain and the staircase, Gene and Steve helped make it easier for movers and painters to do their jobs easily and well. The workers were able focus on their work and stay "locked in," without having to keep pausing to figure out how to work around some problem.

So far, the movers and painters have created advantages for themselves by creating room teams (simplification), sequencing their work within the teams (simplification again), solving more difficult problems offline (amplification and slowification), and capturing their best-known approaches as "standards" for getting each room done (simplification again).

FIGURE 2.4 The Three Mechanisms at Work

However, despite everything, the movers and painters still run into unforeseen problems that make their work difficult. For instance, painters were still sometimes surprised by how much primer the old plaster absorbed before it was ready to be painted. Movers occasionally had to deal with large, awkward items, such as a large, delicate giraffe statue, which was very difficult to carry and navigate through the hallways.

To deal with these periodic glitches, Gene and Steve first try to help by finding a mover or painter in a nearby room who doesn't seem too busy at that moment. However, to their surprise, this makes matters much worse. What they didn't realize was this caused problems to cascade out further. This is because the team from which the person was "borrowed" is now shorthanded and requires help too. In trying to be helpful, Gene and Steve inadvertently "coupled" the two rooms together, creating a problem in the social circuitry (Layer 3).

They now had two problems instead of one: the room with the original problem and the room that was now understaffed. And, of course, coupling was exactly what they were trying to reduce when they created independent room teams in the first place.

To avoid this, Gene and Steve decide to keep a few movers and painters in reserve, not assigned to any of the room teams. They choose people who are particularly good at dealing with trickier issues. Their job is to help teams deal with especially challenging situations as they arise. By doing this, problems are contained and stabilized. That is, problems in one room don't "escape," disrupting the teams around them.

This Layer 3 mechanism ensures that room teams quickly get the help they need, instead of struggling with their problem alone—and it does so without impacting the other room teams. The effect is that problems are quickly and reliably contained, teams are able to do their work better, and work becomes smoother than ever.

FIGURE 2.5 Example of Coupling and Decoupling

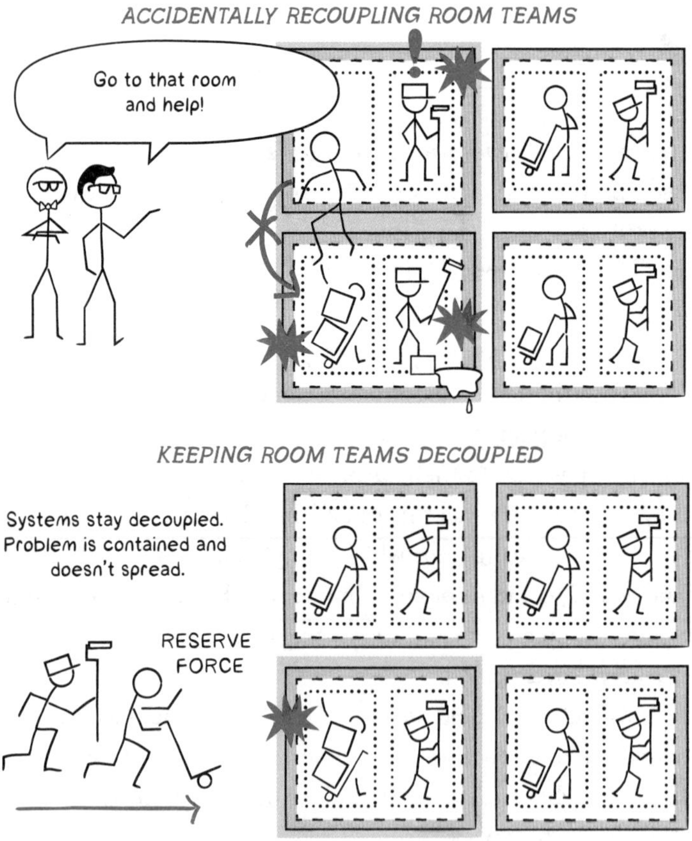

What's astonishing is that this new system quickly becomes self-synchronizing. The room teams know what they need to do next merely by examining the room, without the need for a schedule to tell them. The teams clearly define all the steps that need to be performed, as well as how each step is supposed to be done. It is now easy to tell how far along work actually is, without tedious or time-consuming reporting. It is quick and easy to call for help, and small problems stay small (and local), as opposed to having a large or lasting effect.

FIGURE 2.6 Self-Synchronized Teams

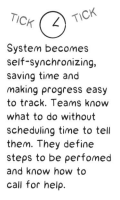

System becomes self-synchronizing, saving time and making progress easy to track. Teams know what to do without scheduling time to tell them. They define steps to be perfomed and know how to call for help.

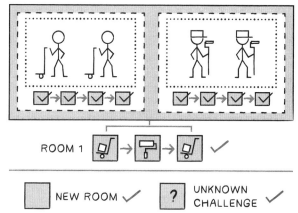

This is all achieved without Gene and Steve having to do anything reactive, impulsive, or interruptive. Instead of having to constantly fight fires (without actually creating enduring solutions), Gene and Steve are able to assess the system's performance and help with things the movers and painters can't do alone.

Gene and Steve look around, marveling at the differences in experience and performance between when they started and now. Work is getting done quickly and beautifully. Everyone is proud of the work they are doing, as the teams keep getting better at every aspect of their work. Instead of being mired in coordination, people are able to collaborate around moving and painting with harmony. They are actively improving how they work within teams and between teams.

By changing Layer 3's social circuitry, Gene and Steve helped create conditions in which it was much easier for the movers and painters to solve the problems they faced, liberating their collective ingenuity and professional capability to push the frontiers of their performance.*

More importantly, Gene and Steve are finally able to report to Miriam and Margueritte that the hotel rooms have been refurbished. Everyone is delighted by how beautifully the rooms have been painted and restored. They all take pride in their work and their role in helping this not-for-profit center open their doors to serve children in need.

Conclusion

In this chapter, we presented two vignettes: one with a couch as a metaphor for joint problem-solving, and another with moving furniture and painting rooms in a hotel as an example of how we integrate two functional specialties toward solving a common objective. In these vignettes, we showed good and bad characteristics, classifying them as the *danger zone* and *winning zone* respectively.

Next, we'll further explore the moving-and-painting vignette through the perspective of the three mechanisms to wire a winning organization: slowification, simplification, and amplification.

---

* These are not exaggerations. Every study comparing outstanding organizations with those less well-managed found productivity differences of several multiples, quality differences of several orders of magnitude, and differences in reliability and workplace safety, also in the hundreds if not thousands of times better. See, for instance, State of DevOps Research by Forsgren, Humble, and Kim, 2019; Garvin's 1983 "Quality on the Line"; Krafcik's 1988 "Triumph of the Lean Production System"; Ward, Sobek, and Liker's 1993 "The Second Toyota Paradox"; and *Dynamic Manufacturing* by Clark, Hayes, and Wheelwright.

CHAPTER 3

Winning Based
on Liberating Ingenuity

In Chapter 1, we described the change in experiences for both patients and staff at a hospital's emergency department. Modifying the emergency department's social circuitry (Layer 3) made it easier for clinicians to deliver outstanding care easily and well.

The same thing happened in Chapter 2 with Gene and Steve's efforts to help refurbish the old Victorian hotel. They were able to make the work of movers and painters easier by changing how they wired the social circuitry. The basic nature of the work at Layer 1 (technical object) and Layer 2 (tools and instrumentation) did not change. Movers still used carts, dollys, and hoists to relocate furniture. Painters still used sanders, scrapers, and brushes to paint and prep each of the rooms. It was changing Layer 3 that made the difference. Ultimately, Gene and Steve helped move their teams out of the *danger zone* and into the *winning zone*.

People working in the *danger zone* are unlikely to be able to fully use their ingenuity, to solve difficult problems individually and collaboratively, and to bring new and useful insights into practice effectively. In the *danger zone,* conditions are complex, fast changing, and unforgiving. It's hard to exercise control and the stakes are high. Learning from experience is challenging in this space.

On the other hand, when leaders put those same people in the *winning zone,* conditions are simpler and slower moving. Control can be exercised and the stakes are lower. Learning from experience is possible. And people are capable of inventing wildly innovative and useful solutions to challenging problems.

Leaders can help their organizations move from the *danger zone* to the *winning zone* by changing how they wire their organization's social circuitry

(Layer 3). This is achieved through some combination of three mechanisms—slowification, simplification, and amplification (see Figure 3.1). Slowification makes solving problems easier to do, simplification makes difficult problems easier to solve, and amplification makes it obvious that there are problems that demand attention and whether or not they've been adequately addressed.

FIGURE 3.1 Moving from the *Danger Zone* to the *Winning Zone* through Slowification, Simplification, and Amplification

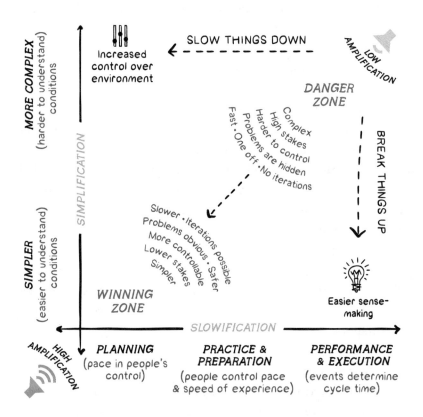

In this chapter, we will explain the moving-and-painting vignette through the perspective of these three mechanisms, which gives us insight into how to succeed in complex real-world situations.

Interpreting the Narrative: Navigating from the *Danger Zone* to the *Winning Zone*

In the moving-and-painting vignette, the jobs of moving and painting were improved by slowification, simplification, and amplification, which helped everyone move from the *danger zone* to the *winning zone* (Figure 3.2).

FIGURE 3.2 Hotel Refurbishment: Moving from the *Danger Zone* to the *Winning Zone*

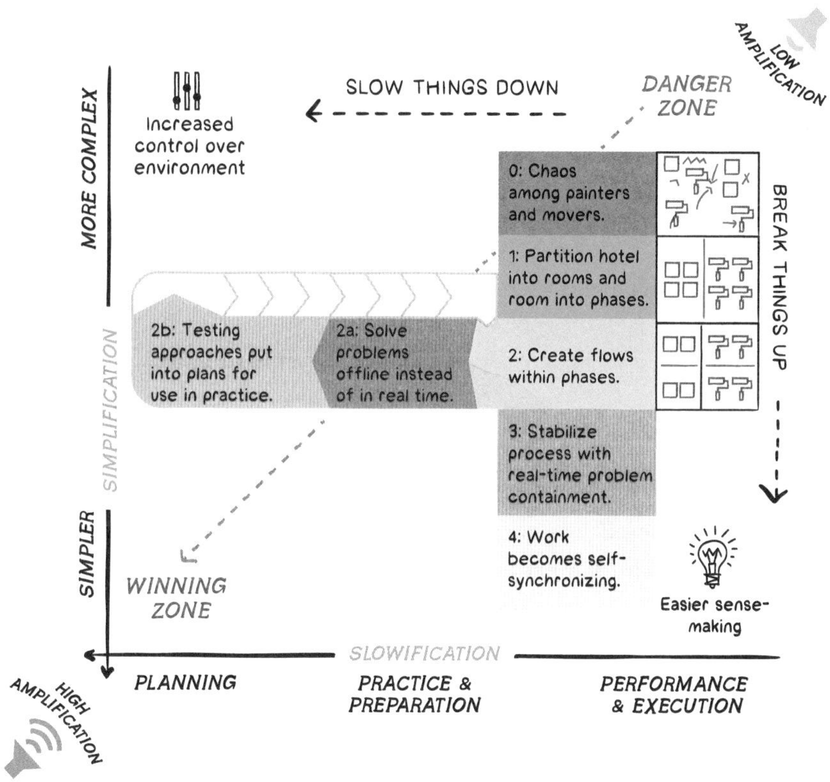

Slowification in Action

Slowification changed how and when problem-solving occurred, so people could be more deliberate and creative in solving problems. It was essential to first slowify before they could simplify, because people needed opportunities to figure out how to decouple their work (as we'll see in the next section). But slowification showed up in many more places.

In the beginning, movers and painters were forced to solve challenging problems in the production environment, solving problems as the work was being done. That's in the *danger zone*, the wrong time to solve such problems.

Fortunately, Gene and Steve had enough sense to pause. Instead of expecting teams to solve these problems in the production environment, teams were able to shift their problem-solving into the more forgiving environments of planning and preparation.

Later, Steve, freed from having to "supervise," as he and Gene had done with scheduling and expediting, supported movers by setting up extra lighting in the dimly lit stairs and installing a temporary tread on a questionable step. Painters set up "laboratories," with Gene's help, to test and try out stains. And, movers worked out how to handle particularly awkward pieces of furniture before actually committing to moving through halls, in and out of doorways, and up and down stairs.

These acts of slowification created opportunities to capture knowledge of local discoveries and then share the new insights across all the room teams. All this was made possible by deliberateness and time being committed to slowification by Gene and Steve.

To slowify or not is a choice that leaders make. Gene and Steve could have stuck to their (doomed) plan and insisted on "getting the work done," doubling down by setting objectives such as "number of walls painted." They got lucky that the movers and painters—using their brains, talents, and experiences—were able to help them create better ways of working by slowifying.

Simplification in Action

Simplification helped move the situation out of the *danger zone* by making the problems themselves easier to solve. In the beginning, the entirety of the refurbishment project was the only coherent unit. No portion of the system could start and complete a room independently. Instead, Gene and

Steve allocated movers and painters to rooms through schedules and expediting, which was completely inadequate.

This changed when they partitioned the whole project into individual room teams, an example of modularization, which is one of the three techniques of simplification. Each room team had all the resources needed to refurbish a room independently, with no need to coordinate with anyone outside of the team. This made things simpler, because everyone had fewer people they needed to interact with.

Later, the room teams further partitioned their work by defining the handoffs between movers and painters (i.e., the conditions created by removing furniture, painting the room, and returning furniture to it). This created even more opportunity for independent problem-solving, meaning more people's ingenuity was being put to good use at the same time. They could solve more problems simultaneously.

This recursive nesting of modules (i.e., from the entire hotel to room team to stages to steps, while still protecting coherence) enabled easier, clearer, faster problem-solving between the people doing the work. Work was increasingly able to be performed and improved in parallel. Collectively, this helped fully unleash the movers' and painters' skills, expertise, and ingenuity to better use, all without Gene and Steve having to do anything, let alone constantly interfering.

Modularization, the first technique of simplification, is a concept that is used heavily in computer science. It refers to partitioning large systems into smaller ones, which are each coherent. They connect to each other through pre-established interfaces (just as air traffic controllers and flight crews followed a terse and coded protocol during normal operations in Chapter 2). This property allows modules to hide internal complexities, which is called "information hiding."

The goal of information hiding is not duplicity or deception. Rather, it enables modules on either side of an interface to operate together (e.g., exchange information, goods, or services) without having to know how the work is actually performed inside the other module.

For instance, an air traffic controller does not need to know how the flight crew set their flaps and rudders. The controllers have confidence that the flight crew can control the plane and can proceed in the direction and altitude instructed. Changes can be made inside the module without having to get permission or coordinate with people on the other side of the interface

There is another required property of modularity: problems inside the module are contained, as opposed to escaping outside of the module. Initially, when room teams ran into trouble, Gene and Steve stole movers and painters from other room teams. This inadvertently coupled the room teams together, causing local problems to spread.

To solve this, they created a reserve team who helped room teams in trouble. In this way, the problems were contained. The more frequent and severe the problems, the more people need to be held in reserve.

The enormous differences in performance in the moving-and-painting vignette were not achieved in one step or as a grand mandate from Gene and Steve, prescribing exactly what the end state should look like and how it was to be achieved. Instead, it emerged through *incrementalization*, the second technique of simplification. Rather than changing everything all at once, what was known was kept intact and novelty was added bit by bit.

For instance, there was the iterative (incremental) approach to partitioning the project into rooms, rooms into phases, and phases into steps. Then, within these modules, there were small iterations and experiments that the room teams performed to deal with difficulties as they emerged. It was not someone trying to outline in advance every possible issue they could imagine occurring, and then designing and implementing those solutions all at once.

Within the room teams, once the movers and painters defined their handoffs, they linearized their work. *Linearization* is the third technique of simplification. This made it more obvious what work was being done and what had to occur next, further enabling independence of action. (Linearization does for sequential processes what modularization does for parallel processes.)

As we'll see in Part III, simplification, through the techniques of modularization, incrementalization, and linearization, makes it far easier to engage large numbers of people in managing and mastering large, complex, and otherwise unwieldy situations.

Amplification in Action

Amplification makes it more obvious, earlier and more often, that problems exist for which people's ingenuity is needed to create solutions. Also, the continued existence of problems makes it evident that these problems have not been seen and successfully solved. Amplification is the opposite of suppressing signals that something is amiss, thereby letting problems persist or even cascade into larger problems.

In the beginning of the vignette, due to the high coupling within the system, there were problems everywhere, all the time. Gene and Steve were so overwhelmed worrying about which movers and painters were in what rooms that they couldn't help solve other problems, like loose stair treads or difficult-to-stain trim. There were signals of problems everywhere, but they couldn't respond to any.

As the teams became increasingly able to focus on moving and painting problems in Layers 1 and 2, rather than the problems of sense-making and coordination in Layer 3, amplification played an ever-larger role in triggering further improvement. When painters struggled with unpredictable stains, and when movers struggled with furniture that could be surprisingly hard to handle, these both triggered a pause. The result was assigning some movers and painters to a "stabilizing" role, so they could help teams before problems spiraled out of control.

By increasingly specifying ahead of time what the work was, how it should be performed, and how it should be handed off, movers and painters could generate signals earlier and more frequently when things were not going as planned. Each of these helped trigger more improvements and helped everyone push the frontiers of performance.

Further Considerations for Leaders

Winston Churchill said, "We shape our buildings and afterwards our buildings shape us." Similarly, we shape the architecture of our organizations (how they are wired), which then shapes the behavior of the people within them.

How we wire our organizations dictates whom we interact with, what we interact about, when we interact, and how we are allowed to interact. In an ideal situation, to get what we need done, we are talking to only the right people, on the right teams, at the right time, in the right way, about the right things.

However, all too often, organizations have flawed wiring (Layer 3), which means we spend all our time and energy talking to the wrong people, at the wrong time, in the wrong way, and often about the wrong things. Under these conditions, it is no wonder that doing even small things requires heroics.

Our organizational wiring also dictates the type of feedback that is generated. Ideally, everyone gets direct and fast feedback on the work they do, so they can see the effects of their actions, which can be used to stabilize systems and improve. After all, in any complex, adaptive system, there are unexpected events and a general tendency toward entropy. We need fast and frequent feedback to keep our systems under control.

As a leader, you are responsible for the achievement of your organization's goals and for creating the organizational and management systems that everyone in that organization uses to contribute to those goals. Thus, it is your professional and moral responsibility to create the conditions so that people can contribute to those organizational goals and create value for both the customers that depend on your organization and the colleagues who depend on them. In particular, this requires you to adopt a developmental mindset, one oriented around designing, sustaining, and improving the social circuitry that lets people do great work easily and well. This, as we show throughout this book, is antithetical to a transactional mindset, reflecting an assumption that leadership is largely a matter of giving instructions and determining who is doing what, when, where, and with what resources.

Building Your Model Line

Through creating great management systems, leadership creates great value. However, when done poorly, leadership destroys value or, at least, squanders it. Exercised well, leadership can be the reason work is meaningful to those who do it. It can be the reason why products and services are a source of delight for those who receive them. In turn, work is done well because the conditions in which it is performed are managed well. This results in excellent financial and operational metrics that reflect how effectively or efficiently resources were utilized.

Success is enabled by changing the structure (i.e., organizational wiring) and the resulting dynamics of the processes by which people's efforts are integrated through collective action toward a common purpose. Those structures and dynamics are brought into effect through slowification, simplification, and amplification.

This is where the *model line* as a transformative tool comes in, which is a segment of the larger enterprise where new approaches can be tested, tried, and "modeled." It's an opportunity for people to feel what it is like to change their behaviors, which is a precursor for changing their beliefs.

The very first thing a leader has to do to make that transformation is to literally carve out a piece of their larger enterprise and learn to manage it using the mechanisms of slowification, simplification, and amplification. They and their colleagues use this platform to learn while doing, and their colleagues can use the platform to teach others to do the same.

In the moving-and-painting vignette, a model-line approach might have designated one room or a small set of rooms as the platform for the model-line team. However, in that case, the undertaking was such an abject failure, time pressures were so great, and the scale of the work was small enough that transitioning through a model line might not have been a reasonable approach.

The model line is a microcosmic set of processes relative to the enterprise as a whole. While model lines are small, they are still coherent. There's a natural boundary around these model lines with natural beginnings and ends and obvious starts and stops. It's in the model line that people can practice applying and mastering slowification, simplification, and amplification.

A model line usually starts with relatively few people. With fewer people, you can accelerate learning through faster problem-solving because you're concerned with a smaller set of activities. Likewise, the development of capabilities is accelerated because the people dedicated to the model line have the chance to test ideas and practice new concepts with frequent and fast iterations.

After all, when we talk about rewiring the organization, we're really talking about rewiring people's behaviors and beliefs. Dr. Jerry Sternin, of the Harvard Business School, explained how important it was to focus on changing behaviors in order to change beliefs: "It's easier to act your way into a new way of thinking than think your way into a new way of acting."[1]

The model line is a small, unobtrusive, "safe" environment to introduce and reinforce new behaviors, the positive results of which convince people to believe in a new way of managing the situations for which they are responsible.

FIGURE 3.3 Implementation of a Model Line

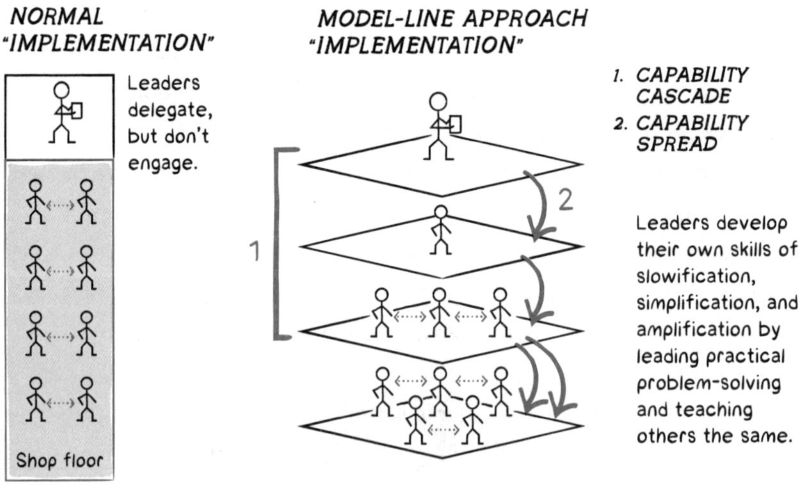

Creating a model line creates the conditions in which everyone, including leaders, learn to behave differently in order to get different outcomes. Within the model line, everyone performs experiments together, learning what works and what doesn't, and the causal mechanisms that result from those outcomes.

Of course, once the model line is up and running, the chance for spreading greatness is created. Other colleagues can experience firsthand what it feels like to work in slowified, simplified, and amplified conditions. Those who've learned how to slowify, simplify, and amplify can be envoys into adjacent areas, meaning that everyone can be less overburdened on coordination problems (Layer 3) and can be more engaged with practical problems (Layers 1 and 2). We will be revisiting the model-line concept throughout the book to demonstrate how it can be used effectively in an organization to practice slowification, simplification, and amplification.

Conclusion

In this chapter, we described the three mechanisms of slowification, simplification, and amplification that leaders can use to rewire their organization so they are configured to win, albeit in the simplified example of refurbishing an old Victorian hotel. In the following chapters, we will describe each of these mechanisms in more detail, providing more information about the underpinning theories on which they are based, as well as case studies of their usage in examples far more complex and consequential.

QUESTIONS FOR THE READER

The three mechanisms of well-wired organizations move us from the *danger zone* to the *winning zone*. Slowification makes problem-solving easier, simplification makes the problems themselves easier to solve, and amplification makes it more obvious when there are problems so they can be seen and solved.

As a leader, consider a challenging situation for which you have responsibility: it could be the design of something novel and complex, or it could be the operations of something complex and dynamic. Then rate yourself on the following:

1. *Slowification: On a scale of 1–10 (1 is not at all, 10 is completely), to what extent have you allocated dedicated time for your people to solve difficult problems in a deliberative and rigorous fashion, during offline planning and practice, instead of expecting people to solve those problems while performing their work?*
2. *Simplification: On the same scale, to what extent have you taken your large programs, projects, or processes and deliberately broken them into smaller, coherent pieces, so that smaller groups of people can solve simpler problems simultaneously?*
3. *Amplification: And finally, using the same scale, to what extent have you created opportunities for fast, detailed, and accurate feedback into the experiences people are having, so that it's immediately obvious when and where problems are occurring that need to be quickly contained and resolved?*

KEY CONCEPTS AND TERMS

In Chapter 1, we promised that by the end of Part I, you would have an introduction to all the concepts and terms to explain organizations that are wired to win or not. The ideas and mechanisms listed below are sufficient to explain success and failure in designing, operating, and improving the wiring (Layer 3) of complex technical systems and organizations, to assess existing designs and improve on them, and to predict success and failure.

Amplification: The act of calling out problems consistently so help is generated and swarms the problem to contain it and investigate, so causes can be found and corrective actions created to prevent recurrence.

Coherence: The quality of having a unified whole, which requires that elements that interact frequently and intensely are included in the same grouping so their interactions can be well managed, and that those that are not are excluded. This is necessary for the behavior of the whole to be logical and consistent.

Control system characteristics: In control theory, the control system (in our case, the management system) must have a frequency, speed, accuracy, and detail of control greater than the underlying system being controlled (as per the Nyquist-Shannon Theorem). Otherwise, the system being controlled will tend to instability or even chaos. (In system dynamics parlance, the structure is the extent to which there is isomorphism among Layers 1, 2, and 3, and the dynamics are the stability or instability of the system.)

Coupled: Two entities are coupled when a change in the state of one changes the state (the condition) of the other.

Decoupled: Two entities are decoupled when a change in the state of one does not change the state (the condition) of the other.

Functionally organized: In functional organizations, experts are responsible for ensuring people within that function can do work according to the standards expected of that profession. However, when functional managers also try to determine the timing of work, they risk interference between functions that haven't been adequately synchronized.

Incrementalization: A technique within simplification of partitioning a large problem-solving effort (a great leap) into small, incremental steps. This involves establishing a stable base and then iterating and testing changes in a few factors at a time as opposed to testing the effect of changing many factors all at once.

Isomorphism: The quality of related items having similar structures so they can fit and operate together (e.g., "hand in glove"). In our context, we use *isomorphic* most frequently to describe to what extent the Layer 3 social circuitry supports and enables the work being done in Layer 1 (technical object) and Layer 2 (tooling and instrumentation). When Layer 3 is not sufficiently isomorphic, the organization is in the *danger zone*. (Isomorphism can also apply to other layers. An example of Layers 1 and 2 not being isomorphic: the tools aren't available at the right time for work to occur. An example of Layers 2 and 3 not being isomorphic: parts, materials, information, etc. are not in the right place at the right time for work to occur.)

Joint problem-solving: The activity where solving a problem requires two or more people to identify, describe, characterize, investigate, and resolve, who must actively exchange ideas, information, perspectives, etc. in a real-time, nuanced, noncoded fashion. (See also: *Moving a couch*.)

Knowledge capture and knowledge sharing: The deliberate commitment to (a) codify what's discovered when problems are seen and solved, so similar experiences don't recur locally and (b) share what has been discovered, so similar experiences can be avoided elsewhere throughout the system. How knowledge can be usefully shared varies, depending on what has to be conveyed from whom to whom, and about what. It could be as visually simple as directions on assembling an IKEA® cabinet; more complex instructions like in a cookbook; more elaborate like in a journal article, a physical part such as a jig, or code or automated tests in software; all the way to the sophistication of a simulation or virtualization, or recreated, shared problem-solving experience.[*]

Layer 1 problem: A problem with the object on which work is being done (e.g., "I don't understand the design or the function of this thing.").

Layer 2 problem: A problem with the instrumentation or equipment used in the work (e.g., "I'm having problems with the equipment needed to make the part.").

Layer 3 problem: A problem with the social circuitry or organizational wiring (e.g., "I don't even know what part I'm supposed to be making right now.").

Linearization: A technique within simplification of *sequencing* tasks associated with completing a larger set of work so that they flow successively, like a baton being passed from one person to the next. What follows is *standardization* for those sequences, for exchanges at partition boundaries, and for how individual tasks are performed. This creates opportunities to introduce *stabilization*, so when a problem occurs, that triggers a reaction that contains the problem and prevents it from enduring and from its effects spreading. Those allow for *self-synchronization*, so the system is self-pacing without top-down monitoring and direction.

---

[*] See, for instance, Chapter 8 in *The High-Velocity Edge*.

Limitations of expediting: A reaction to a failed schedule when someone attempts to, on the fly, redirect people and products and reassign
processes to "keep things moving." For large, complex, fast-moving
systems, expeditors cannot keep pace. The problem is, they're making
decisions that seem to make sense immediately and locally but might
actually make matters worse—like Gene and Steve pulling a "spare
painter or mover" from one room to help in another, only to realize
they've now got compromises in both.

Limitations of scheduling: In a system that is too scheduled, it is assumed
that the antidote for failures of a functionally managed system is building complex schedules that determine who does what, when, and
where. The failure mode for that is trying to arrive at a "solution" that is
comprehensive across all the work and all the workers. It turns out that
arriving at a solution requires so many computations and calculations
that it borders on impossible to generate. So, even with the best of
intentions to adhere to a schedule, generating a schedule that is precise enough to solve the coordination problem often cannot be done.[*]

Modularization: A technique within simplification of partitioning a system that is unwieldy in its size, complexity, and inter-wiredness of
relationships among its many component pieces into more, smaller,
simpler, coherent pieces.

Moving a couch: An example of a situation in which those tasked with
solving a problem and completing a task are coupled in their undertaking and have to engage in joint problem-solving and so must be
grouped in a coherent fashion. (See also: *Joint problem-solving*.)

Moving-and-painting: An example of a situation that starts out poorly
managed, with a chaotic and frustrating experience for the participants, resulting in a disappointing performance. The scarce and
precious resource of the participants' time and creativity is exhausted
on figuring out what to do, when to do it, and with whom coordination has to occur (organizational wiring issues in Layer 3), leaving too
little of those resources left to solve the actual problems of moving
furniture and painting rooms (Layers 1 and 2 of technical objects and

---

[*] This is because "job-shop scheduling" is an NP-Hard problem in computer science, as
described in the previous chapter.

tooling and instrumentation). However, the systematic application of slowification, simplification, and amplification mechanisms reduces the distractions of figuring out how to fit into the larger enterprise and makes it quicker and easier to solve practical problems and do the actual work for which people have been engaged.

Simplification: Reducing the number of interactions one component of the system has with other components of the same system (e.g., technical interactions between component parts in an engineered system or among people in a working group). Simplification contains three techniques: incrementalization, modularization, and linearization.

Slowification: Shifting problem-solving from performance (operation, execution) back to practice (preparation) and planning with forceful backup, stress testing, and other deliberate ways of finding flaws in thinking before they become flaws in doing.

Social circuitry (organizational wiring): The connections by which ideas, information, services, and support can flow from where they are to where they are needed so that effective, collaborative problem-solving and value creation can occur. It is the overlay of processes, procedures, routines, and norms by which individual efforts are integrated through collective action toward a common purpose.

PART II

Slowification

CHAPTER 4

Slowification:
A Theory Overview

I n 1968, United States Navy pilots were suffering during air-to-air combat in Vietnam, with a win-to-loss ratio of only two to one. In a single seventeen-day span, eleven US aviators were killed.[1] Navy leadership appointed Captain Frank Ault, a World War II veteran who had been a surface ship and aviation unit commander, to figure out why and what to do.[2]

The resulting *Ault Report* highlighted several issues, but a key one showed the Navy was overly dependent on on-the-job learning.[3] Aerial combat is fast-moving and wildly hazardous. The costs of a bad outcome is catastrophic, and there is limited opportunity to control the situation. There is also no opportunity during combat to repeat events and then iteratively converge on an effective solution. Pilots were having to learn in the *danger zone*, literally.

Among other things, the *Ault Report* recommended creating the Navy Fighter Weapons School, which was established at the Naval Air Station Miramar in 1969. It is broadly known as Top Gun. The four-week program involved some classroom instruction, but the highlight was advanced in-flight training and simulated combat.

The Top Gun environment was fast paced. Pilots flew advanced fighter jets against other pilots also flying sophisticated jets. Instructors used tactics and planes similar to those of North Vietnamese pilots.[4] However, the pilots were no longer in the *danger zone*. This was "mock combat." If situations threatened to get out of control, they could be paused. Between flights, there was time to reflect and develop new approaches. And those new approaches could be tested with colleagues to find flaws in thinking before they became flaws in doing.

When these Top Gun pilots returned to their units, they also integrated what they had learned into their squadron's training. By 1973, the shoot-down ratio was thirteen to one.[5]

The US Navy's Top Gun program is an example of *slowification*. Instead of expecting pilots to learn life-and-death lessons in the middle of air combat (during what we call performance), they could learn and hone their skills before entering combat (in what we call planning and practice). Flaws in their performance could be spotted and coached by instructors in a slower classroom environment.

Slowification is the first of the three mechanisms that move organizations out of the *danger zone* and into the *winning zone*. There are many maxims that convey a similar idea: go slow to go fast, pause to sharpen the ax, and so forth. Yet there's no single English word that conveys the duality of the idea that going faster often depends on going slower. In the absence of such a word, we opted to make one up: *slowification.*[*]

Slowification is applied in one of two ways. The first involves slowing *ourselves* down so we can be more deliberate and self-reflective. An example of this is the Crew Resource Management approach used by United Airlines Flight 232, which we'll present in Chapter 5. The second involves slowing down the *environment* (i.e., pausing work). This involves moving work into the planning or practice phases,[†] as in the Top Gun example, so

---

[*] Words that we considered but discarded because they did not fully express the concept included *deceleration*, *optimization*, *progress*, and *to mature*. Interestingly, the Germans do have a word for slowification: *verbesserung*, emphasizing improvement through slowing down.

[†] Throughout this book, we refer to planning, practice, and performance phases and sometimes to environments. That's because some things progress steadily across phases as ideas and concepts mature. For instance, when creating new medications, work progresses from upstream discovery through development onto research and design and so forth. Those are phases. Other times, the relationship between planning, practice, and performance is less linear and more cyclic. For instance, a sports team might have periods of planning plays, practicing plays, and actually performing them in games. But even within games, there's sometimes a shift from performance to new planning and new practice during time-outs, at halftime, etc.

we accomplish our more difficult problem-solving in slower-moving, more controllable environments. When we have more time, lower stakes, and less fear, our creativity can flourish. And it is our creativity that lets us generate fantastic novel solutions to new and old problems.

Fast Thinking vs. Slow Thinking

All around us, we see the modern miracles that have been enabled by the incredible problem-solving capability of the human mind. Dr. Daniel Kahneman, 2002 Nobel Laureate in Economic Sciences, and his colleague, the late Dr. Amos Tversky, distinguished between two thinking modes: System 1 (or fast thinking) and System 2 (or slow thinking).*

When we're under pressure, due to time or other factors, we are forced to depend on fast thinking (System 1) to generate answers quickly, these are our already-established heuristics, habits, preexisting routines, etc. (i.e., muscle memory).

We often use these established solutions when we are faced with Layer 1 and Layer 2 problems. In these situations, we depend on our prior experiences to understand the new problem or task in front of us (e.g., an injury being examined by a clinician, a material failure being examined by a technician).

We also use these fast-thinking habits and routines to quickly resolve Layer 3 (social circuitry) problems: What do we do? Where do we draw support from? Whom do we depend on? When and how do we escalate a problem for attention?

But there's a downside to relying solely on fast thinking: it makes us more susceptible to poor decision-making. When we are thinking quickly, we are using only what we *already* know. Fast thinking doesn't encourage or allow time to *improve* our thinking. This muscle memory works in

---

* The concept of fast thinking aligns with *single-loop learning* versus *double-loop learning* from Dr. Chris Argyris and Dr. Donald Schön. In single-loop learning (like fast thinking) our routines are not altered by feedback. Double-loop learning (slow thinking) allows us to study the problem, be informed by feedback, and create new understandings. This creates new fast-thinking routines and capabilities that we can use during future performance.

situations for which we've practiced,* but it fails us in situations that are
unfamiliar (see Table 4.1).

TABLE 4.1 Advantages and Disadvantages of Fast and Slow Thinking

	STRENGTHS	LIMITATIONS
Fast thinking	Speed: Heuristics give us quick, reliable answers to familiar problems and situations.	Inaccuracy: Heuristics and their attendant biases may give us inaccurate answers to unfamiliar problems or situations that are framed poorly.
Slow thinking	Flexibility: Allows us to improve our understanding of familiar situations or add to our understanding of new ones.	Slowness: Requires time, patience, and openness of mind that we may be lacking in the moment.

For instance, when driving conditions are favorable, most of us can
drive safely with relatively little thought. We make minor steering and
speed adjustments almost automatically because our habits and preexisting routines are reliable. This frees up our brains to have conversations with
our passengers, listen attentively to the radio or a podcast, or sing along
with our favorite music.

But these fast-thinking skills were acquired over time. When we first
learned to drive, everything had to be slow and deliberate. A more experienced driver showed us how to start the car, pull away from the curb,
accelerate, and stop. And we likely learned to drive in an empty parking lot
or street (a slower-moving, safer environment) where we could practice basic
skills in a controlled, incremental, and instructed fashion. During practice,
our skills progress until we are sufficiently competent in performance.

---

* This is consistent with the findings of cognitive psychologist Dr. Gary Klein, who
  studied decision-making in data-limited, high-stress environments and highlighted
  the role of intuition and expertise. Klein demonstrated how seasoned experts use
  their extensive experience to make swift and effective decisions, which he attributed
  to a combination of fast reflexes and honed skills.[6]

However, even with decades of experience, when driving conditions are not favorable, our fast-thinking habits and routines are less adequate. Suppose it's dark and begins to rain, then pour. We can't see how deep the puddles or potholes are. Even worse, what if the temperature drops, the rain turns to snow, and the road starts freezing over. In this situation, we can no longer drive on autopilot. To drive safely, we must slow down and turn off distractions. This helps us stay focused on navigating the increasingly difficult and treacherous driving conditions.

Of course, there are some people who can seemingly drive just fine in hazardous conditions, for example, stunt drivers, Formula 1 racers, and so forth. But this is a learned skill. Stunt drivers develop their exemplary capabilities over time in risk-controlled, repeatable, lower-stakes circumstances before filming the car chase or crash. Likewise, F1 racers develop their skills in their own planning and practice phases, where slow thinking can occur. This allows them to progress their capabilities so they are be able to perform at a higher level in a fast-thinking way.

Cognitive Biases

Even if we're in familiar situations, our heuristics and habits can still fail us because we are prone to *cognitive biases*, as Kahneman and Tversky discovered in the 1970s and 1980s.[7]

Biases show up everywhere, including in how we perceive individuals. When we meet someone new, for instance, we make quick judgments and assessments influenced by our own personal background, experiences, memories, and cultural environment, often entirely subconsciously and subtly.[8] In the military, it might be the quick signals of uniform and rank and unit insignia. In a hospital, it might be the nuances of a white lab coat's length or ornamentation or the color of someone's scrubs. All that might be fine for quick assessments, but it is also problematic to make snap decisions about people.

These biases can often appear in surprising ways. For instance, people tend to rely more heavily on information they receive first (known as an anchoring bias). If several people are given the same list of numbers to multiply in their head within a short time frame (say, five seconds), their best guess depends on the order in which those numbers are shown.

Table 4.2 shows the dramatic differences in guesses (based on Kahneman and Tversky), depending on whether the smallest or largest number was presented first. When given a time constraint, most people multiply only the first few numbers. Those anchoring on larger first numbers get a larger (but incorrect) result, and those anchoring on smaller first numbers get a smaller (but also incorrect) result.[9]

TABLE 4.2 Example of Anchoring Bias

When presented this...	...the typical guess is...
8 x 7 x 6 x 5 x 4 x 3 x 2 x 1	2,250
1 x 2 x 3 x 4 x 5 x 6 x 7 x 8	512

Note: The actual answer is 40,320.

Similarly, we also have trouble comparing situations that are framed as certain (which we tend to overweight) versus probabilistic (we which tend to underweight or discount).[10] We'll see the costs of discounting risk in the next chapter in case studies on preparations for the Battle of Midway in 1942 and in how NASA's Space Shuttle program was managed.*

The Three Ps

Because of the limitations of fast thinking, in many situations we want to employ slow thinking. We want to create opportunities in which we can be more deliberate, contemplative, self-reflective, and inquisitive. In this unrushed, lower-risk environment, we can deliberately challenge our pre-

---

* Kahneman and Tversky demonstrated that we use a different decision-making heuristic based on whether there is the possibility of gain or loss. In their famous paper where they present prospect theory, they observed that "losses loom larger than gains."[11] In other words, people are more willing to take a risk to avoid a loss than to make a gain. This theory won Dr. Kahneman the Nobel Prize.

existing mental models and update them based on additional experiences and experimentation. This is essential if we are to get to new and useful outcomes and discover great things.*

Leaders must make time for slowification, which creates opportunities for slow thinking during the three phases of work: planning, practice, and performance. Slowifying during the planning and practice phases, allows us to hone our understanding and capabilities. Thus, when we have to perform, we are well equipped. We know what to do and we are able to do it (see Figure 4.1). Each of the phases of planning, practice, and performance also has a corresponding environment.

FIGURE 4.1 The Three Ps: Planning, Practice, and Performance

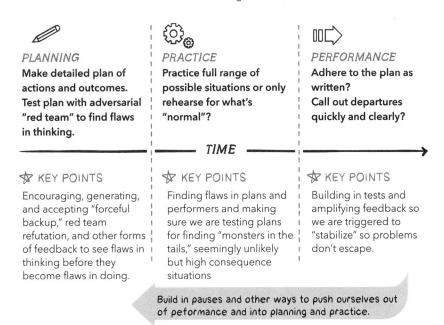

PLANNING
Make detailed plan of actions and outcomes. Test plan with adversarial "red team" to find flaws in thinking.

PRACTICE
Practice full range of possible situations or only rehearse for what's "normal"?

PERFORMANCE
Adhere to the plan as written? Call out departures quickly and clearly?

— TIME —→

✦ KEY POINTS
Encouraging, generating, and accepting "forceful backup," red team refutation, and other forms of feedback to see flaws in thinking before they become flaws in doing.

✦ KEY POINTS
Finding flaws in plans and performers and making sure we are testing plans for finding "monsters in the tails," seemingly unlikely but high consequence situations

✦ KEY POINTS
Building in tests and amplifying feedback so we are triggered to "stabilize" so problems don't escape.

Build in pauses and other ways to push ourselves out of peformance and into planning and practice.

The *planning environment* (e.g., design or development) is the slowest-moving, lowest-cost, safest environment in which to develop and test

---

* In other words, we are too often stuck in single-loop learning, as described by Argyris and Schön, when we don't adjust our fast-thinking routines. Double-loop learning allows us to slow down, to study the problem, to experiment with potential new methods, and to practice them, developing new fast-thinking routines.

ideas. Here, ideas are literally or figuratively words and drawings penciled on paper, so the cost of expressing and capturing them is low. Ideas can be tested many times (e.g., through mock-ups, simulations, thought experiments). The low cost also allows running iterative experiments toward ever-improving solutions. This is the fastest, quickest, easiest environment in which to find flaws in thinking before they become flaws in doing.

The *practice environment* (e.g., preproduction, testing, offline problem-solving) is a more demanding environment than planning because ideas are being put into action. However, actions are taken in a safer and more controllable environment. In practice, we can control the pace and the (incremental) complexity of what is occurring so we are not overwhelmed. We can also build multiple learning cycles into the experience, which allows us to keep adjusting what we are doing and how we are doing it.

In the practice environment, feedback is used to improve our plans and improve our abilities to execute those plans. Feedback also makes sure we've developed capabilities to address the most likely scenarios and the less likely but highly consequential scenarios. By doing this, we find the "monsters in the tails."* Instead of investing the most energy in planning and preparing for the most likely events (often due to fast-thinking cognitive biases), we take care to examine less likely scenarios, which, if mismanaged, will have monstrous consequences.

FIGURE 4.2 The Monsters in the Tails

MONSTERS
IN THE TAILS

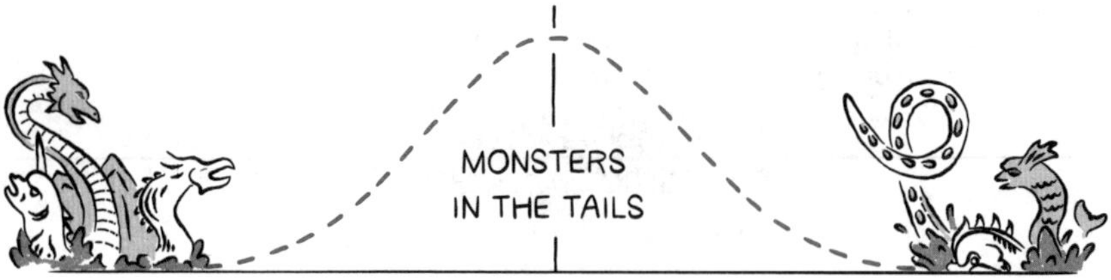

* "Monsters" refers to potentially catastrophic but often overlooked, dismissed, or unconsidered problems that might attack us in performance. "Tails" refers to how we think about the likelihood of events spread out over a distribution, like a bell curve.

The *performance* environment (e.g., operations, execution) is the most unforgiving environment. It controls the pace of the experience, forcing us to depend almost exclusively on already-developed routines, skills, and habits. We likely have limited ability to redo or otherwise correct our actions in this environment. Performance is the last place we can learn, but only if we recognize that our situation is different from expected or needed. This is also what enables us to swarm problems, limit their duration, contain their spread, and solve them. It also enables us to share and systematize what we've learned so the problem doesn't reoccur.

In the driving example, the *performance environment* includes all the conditions that affect a driver as they are driving, such as the car, the other occupants, the road, other cars, and the weather and lighting. Changes to those conditions (the performance environment) affect what the driver should do and why it should be done.

The performance environment is also bounded. That is, changes in conditions to the performance environment affect only the people working inside it. For instance, cars on a distant road that never intersects the highway the driver is on are not in that driver's performance environment. Similarly, mistakes can be safely made in planning and practice without adversely affecting the performance environment.

How Do We Slowify?

Think of *slowification* as the "bullet time" special effect in *The Matrix*, where the main character slows or pauses time entirely, allowing them to dodge bullets or defeat their nearly frozen opponents. We *slowify* by decelerating our performance environment (e.g., slowing down the car in hazardous conditions) or finding slower-moving conditions in which we can build skill and understanding (e.g., the conditions in driving school).

When we cannot slow down the environment, we create triggers to slow down our fast-thinking processes. This signals that we need to be more

---

* We use the terms *production* and *performance* interchangeably. We will typically use the term *production* for commercial or industrial contexts and *performance* for spaceflight or military contexts.

deliberative and creative rather than impulsive and dependent on preexisting routines. Slowification helps us to shift from the *danger zone* to the *winning zone*, as shown in Figure 4.3.

In the moving-and-painting vignette, slowification helped improve Gene and Steve's outcomes. The painters worked offline to figure out the best formulas for stain. The movers analyzed how best to move awkward pieces of furniture. And the movers and painters paused their work to better partition and define handoffs between their tasks. These are all examples of shifting more complex problem-solving from the difficult-to-control performance environment into the more controllable environments of planning and practice.

FIGURE 4.3 Using Slowification to Move from
the *Danger Zone* to the *Winning Zone*

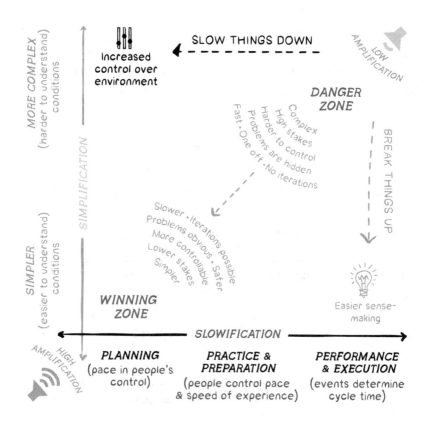

When we slowify, we first make plans and find flaws before committing time and other resources and before using the plan in performance (e.g., tabletop exercises, mock-ups, thought experiments, simulations, minimally viable versions, virtualizations).

Practice is not only a time to coach those who'll be responsible for performing the plan, but also a time to find flaws in the plan's design. This can be achieved through rehearsals and dress rehearsals, red teaming, scale models, pilots, prototypes, and so forth. Practice also gives us a chance to build our playbook, both for the most likely scenarios and the less likely but high-risk scenarios (monsters in the tails). As we perform, we ensure we call out early and often what went wrong, identify where our fast-thinking routines were not sufficient, and bring those issues back to practice or maybe even planning. This is the source of our immediate stability and resilience and our continuous progress: feedback-rich, slow-thinking learning that occurs throughout the three environments.

Slowification vs. the Tyranny of Maintaining Operating Tempo

Slowification helps us create better approaches to situations instead of repeatedly exercising old habits and routines. A common objection to slowification is that maintaining operational tempo is the highest, even overwhelming, priority. But, as is warned in Ecclesiastes 10:10, "If the ax becomes dull and he has not whetted the edge, he must exert more strength. Thus, the advantage of skill [depends on the exercise of] prudence."[12] Leaders must make time for slowification in order to "sharpen the ax" and avoid the (sometimes enormous) penalties of not pausing performance long enough to solve real problems and systematize new solutions.

Sports teams conduct practice sessions and call time-outs mid-game to quickly review what's going wrong and introduce modified approaches. This is true even in sports that don't allow breaks. In rowing, for instance, a coxswain might call on a crew to focus on a particular aspect of their technique for five or ten strokes to recover their timing. A basketball point guard might dribble a few seconds off the shot clock while shouting directions to her teammates so they can regroup.

Similarly, leaders must reserve time for slowification. Toyota, studied for their organizational learning and outstanding performance, routinely puts breaks between shifts so leaders can run problem-solving and improvement activities before production resumes. When production is interrupted, downtime is often used as a slowification opportunity. (Read more in Chapter 10.)

In software development, engineers are often pressured to deliver features instead of fixing defects, addressing reliability issues, or working on internal improvement projects. As a result, so called "technical debt"* adds up, leading to more complex problems that are increasingly difficult to solve. Consequently, Marty Cagan, a product expert who has trained generations of product leaders on building software products that customers love, stresses the importance for product and engineering leaders to allocate at least 20% of engineering's time to proactively fix issues before they snowball into catastrophic ones, such as having to "rewrite the entire codebase from scratch."[14]

Knowledge Capture for Reuse

In all phases and environments, the common element to slowification is feedback. During planning, feedback helps us find gaps between what we are thinking of doing and what we want to happen. In practice, feedback shows us gaps between our preparations and our intentions. And in performance, feedback sheds light on what is happening versus what should be happening.

When we are using slowification well, feedback triggers and informs modifications and improvements in our thinking and our actions. This newfound knowledge should then be fed into subsequent cycles of planning, practice, and performance.

Conclusion

Slowification helps leaders wire our organizations to move from the *danger zone* to the *winning zone*. It helps us create better conditions to solve complex,

---

* This term was coined by Ward Cunningham in the 1992 OOPSLA experience report.[13]

difficult problems. We do this by shifting where problem-solving occurs, moving it from the faster-moving performance environment to one that is slower-moving and more forgiving, such as planning or practice. This enables us to switch from depending on established habits, routines, and muscle memory to being more deliberative, self-reflective, and self-correcting. It also builds our understanding of what to do and why to do it, and grows our capabilities to get things done.

In the case studies in the next chapter, we will present scenarios where people were able to shift difficult or complex problems from the performance environment into the planning and practice environments so they could progress their capabilities and improve their performance and outcomes. For many of the slowification case studies, we also present a similar case study in which no slowifying mechanism was employed, resulting in the opposite dynamic—no progress was made and performance wasn't improved, causing more dismal outcomes.

QUESTIONS FOR THE READER

1. As a leader responsible for the social circuitry (Layer 3) of your organization or team, to what extent have you created an environment where problem-solving is easier?

2. Are you solving your most challenging problems in the fast and unforgiving performance environment, or are you pausing performance so problems can be solved in the slower, safer, feedback-rich environments of planning and practice?

3. Are you asking your people to solve their most difficult problems extemporaneously in the performance environment (i.e., on the fly, by the seat of their pants)? Or, are you allowing, encouraging, or even insisting that they define challenges in the performance environment and then take the time to create effective responses and test them in the planning or practice environment?

CHAPTER 5

Slowification: Case Studies in Planning, Practice, and Performance

In this chapter, we present several detailed case studies of how slowification helps improve real-world problems at organizations from several industries. To further illustrate the importance of slowification, we will also follow most of the case studies with a counter example in a similar setting where no slowification was used and the outcome was different. If you're a fan of details and examples, then keep reading. But if you if you dislike a lot of detail, go ahead and skip to Chapter 6, where we provide a single exemplar case study of slowification.

Pausing Performance vs. Maintaining Operating Tempo

The following two case studies show two extremes of problem-solving. In the first, leaders punctuated performance with pauses when the team encountered problems. Problems were solved and then solutions were deployed into performance. In the second, leaders just keep working as normal, even though problems were discovered.

Case Study: MIT Sloan School Sailing Team: Pausing Performance for Rapid Learning[1]

In the summer of 2013, Adam Traina and David Hume joined a small cohort of graduate students in MIT's Leaders for Global Operations program. Experienced sailors (Adam had some two decades of racing experience;

David had been in the Merchant Marines before graduate school), the pair wanted to keep competing. They secured a spot in a regatta on the Italian Riviera. Teams of eight sailors from more than twenty leading business schools would race identical boats on a buoy-marked course.

But there were obstacles. First, the regatta was only a few weeks into the fall semester, so there wasn't much time to prepare. Adam and David were in an intense graduate program, so there wasn't much time to practice. Their team included fellow students, most of whom had little or no experience, so a lot of practice would be required.

They had a plan based on what they'd learned in class about high-velocity learning and operations in outstanding organizations. When a problem occurred, they planned to deliberately step out of the *danger zone* of fast-paced, hurried competition and enter, if just briefly, the slower-moving, more controllable *winning zone*.

First, they formed a team and taught the novices as much as they could in the time they had before the competition. Most of this practice was on land. This was hardly adequate, but it was a start. The most important element of their strategy was creating a dynamic of pausing even when small problems occurred, so solutions could be developed and practiced before racing resumed. Since each heat of the regatta was two laps around the buoyed course, they literally stopped after the first lap to review what had gone wrong and make adjustments to solve those problems. They were then able to bring this new understanding to the second lap. In effect, they rejected the idea of "maintaining operational tempo." Instead, they created and accelerated their learning tempo. They even stopped mid-race—not just between laps—to develop and rehearse new routines before resuming racing.

One can imagine how this looked. As other boats tacked and jibed around the course's buoys, the MIT Sloan team bobbed along as they paused to resolve issues. Maybe not surprisingly, they finished dead last in the first heat, and in the second, too, but by a smaller margin. However, by the third and fourth races, their strategy started to pay off. The Sloanies led the pack and won.

Their victory was due to two factors: (1) slowification had allowed the MIT Sloan team to learn and get better; and (2) their rivals fell apart, squabbling about who was doing what wrong on their own boats.

While the MIT Sloan crew did not advance to the 2013 finals (they'd fallen too far behind by cumulative time in the first two races), the second year's competition was a different matter. To protect themselves from the effects of attrition (half the crew had graduated), Adam, David, and their teammates captured the lessons learned in a diagrammed playbook.

The 2014 crew used the same strategy: race using your best-known methods (what was in the lessons-learned playbook) but pause performance (slowify) when you see a problem. Then, use the better understandings and capabilities learned from deliberative, slow thinking.* The core strategy remained a problem-solving/learning one, powered by fast, frequent shifting between performance and (re)planning and practice. In 2014 the MIT team won in the heats, advanced to the finals, captured the title, and went home with prize watches and trophies.

The third year added additional complications. Adam and David had graduated, so now a new crew *and* new captains would compete. But the 2015 crew started with even better lessons learned and an ethos of pausing in performance. They took home the trophy and the watches yet again.

FIGURE 5.1 MIT Sloan Team Results using Slowification

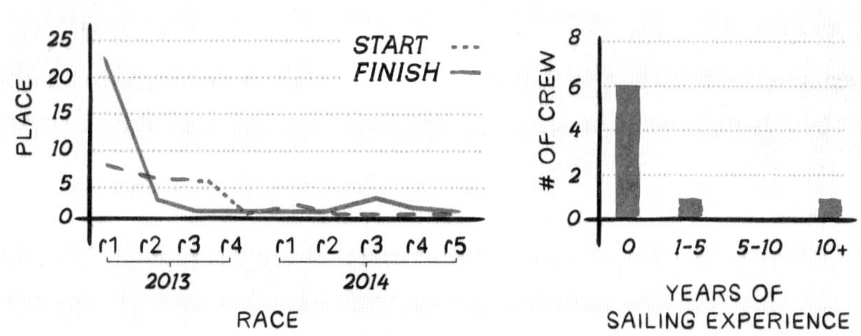

(Left) Chart showing improvement within a race (difference between start and finish) and improvement race to race.
(Right) Chart showing experience of crew members.

---

* In *The High-Velocity Edge*, pausing in performance is referred to as "see a problem, solve a problem, share what you've learned." "Pausing during performance" is akin to "seeing problems" and "solving problems with immediacy and rigor." Taking new lessons learned out of (re)planning and new practice is akin to "sharing" and "systematizing."

Case Study: **Mrs. Morris/Ms. Morrison: When We Don't Pause Performance**

In contrast to the phenomenal learning dynamic created by slowification in the previous case study, consider the dire consequences that can result when leaders do not pause performance when signals of problems emerge. The *Annals of Internal Medicine* published a series of cases that described how patients were harmed during hospitalizations. In each case, clinicians had great intentions and technical skills, but poorly designed social circuitry systems (Layer 3) compromised their best efforts and inadvertently caused harm. Because these problems were caused by Layer 3 problems, not medical ones, they were inherently avoidable.

Consider the case of Mrs. Morris versus Ms. Morrison. Mrs. Morris had been admitted for a brain procedure (cerebral angiogram).[*] Instead, she was mistakenly given an invasive heart procedure (electrophysiological cardiac procedure) that was meant for Ms. Morrison. This was despite Mrs. Morris objecting to the procedure, knowing that it was not intended for her. Leading up to the incorrect procedure being performed, there were seventeen errors involving incorrect patient identification and problematic information exchanges (shown in Figure 5.2). Here's how the event transpired:

Early in the day, a registered nurse (RN1) was looking for Ms. Morrison. The nurse was initially told that her patient had been transferred to another unit (she hadn't been). When she called that unit, she was told the patient was there (she wasn't—it was Mrs. Morris).

As a result, the wrong patient, Mrs. Morris, was taken to the electrophysiology laboratory at 6:45 despite her objections, presumably because "patients don't always know what is going on". Furthermore, there was no consent form in the chart ("consent forms get lost all of the time"), none of the nurses in Mrs. Morris's unit knew the procedure was planned, and the neurosurgery resident didn't know why he hadn't been told about his patient ("no one ever tells me anything").

---

[*] A cerebral angiography is a procedure that uses a special dye (contrast material) and x-rays to see how blood flows through the brain.

FIGURE 5.2 Diagram of Wrong Patient Event

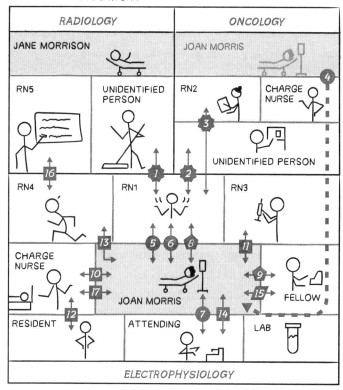

Diagram of the fifteen miscommunications that led to the incorrect procedure.

Later, when the team started catheterization, a wound from the previous day's procedure was obvious. Rather than asking why the patient had already undergone a procedure, the team found another location to insert the probe. These were all mixed with multiple missed opportunities to verify Mrs. Morris's actual identity.

The procedure was performed despite many obvious signs that something might be amiss. These were failures in social circuitry (Layer 3) that hospital leaders had created. Leadership had crafted a system that was not conducive to pausing performance when problems occurred. Thus, doctors, nurses, etc. did not use problems as an opportunity to pause, reflect, and correct, before resume performance.

There were many Layer 3 problems. First, clinicians began their work without a shared clarity of how to integrate the work of one person with another, such as how to communicate the details of a patient consistently throughout that patient's stay. Compounding this was persistent denial of obvious problems (e.g., "consent forms are always lost"; "no one ever tells me anything").[2] This combination of poor clarity coupled with working around problems to maintain operational tempo is a failure in Layer 3 (social circuitry) and created grave risks for patients and staff.

Unlike the MIT sailing team, in this case people didn't pause as the situation deteriorated. They didn't get into a slow-thinking mode and get recentered with better approaches. Rather, they pushed harder and harder while the situation got worse and worse.

Such breakdowns are avoidable. For instance, at Allegheny General in Pittsburgh, Pennsylvania, Dr. Rick Shannon, director of cardiac critical care, and his colleagues were alarmed by the number of patients who suffered central line–associated bloodstream infections (CLABs).*

Leaders initiated slowification by asking nurses, physicians, and residents to pause each time there was confusion about inserting a line or maintaining a wound site. Learnings from each pause informed what eventually became forty-two small solutions.[3] Within a year, there was a nearly perfect elimination of CLABs.[4] This same discipline helped eliminate ventilator-associated pneumonia and other complications.[5]

In a fortunate coincidence, one of the people supporting these efforts in Pittsburgh hospitals shared what he was learning with his partner. She, in turn, shared those lessons with the leadership at the Women's Center and Shelter of Greater Pittsburgh (WS&C), whose mission is to provide safety, shelter, support, and guidance to all survivors of domestic violence.

Among their services is a hotline for women seeking help. However, turnaround times were a problem. Securing housing, legal representation, medical care, and other help required counselors to navigate several dozen

---

* A central line is a catheter, placed into a vein at the neck line or in the crotch, to deliver medication quickly.

agencies and could take up to four days. Learning how long it would take, many callers hung up, terrified they'd be caught trying to get away.

The center's leaders didn't give up. They set a norm. If counselors couldn't quickly and easily arrange services, such as safe housing, they would trigger slowification. The center would work with the agency to create a better approach.

Like Dr. Shannon and his colleagues, the team kept pausing performance to generate dozens of small solutions. The result was awesome. Turnaround times were reduced from four days to four hours. Victims could extricate themselves from terrible situations quickly. A counselor could take an address, promise a car within minutes, and assure the caller that in a few hours housing, medical care, legal representation, restraining orders, food, clothing, school re-enrollment for kids, and so forth would be in place.[6] These changes allowed the center to better fulfill upon its mission.*

Lessons and Guidance

There's an obvious contrast between how the MIT Sloan sailing team, the practitioners in some Pittsburgh hospitals, and staff at the Women's Center improved social circuitry compared with the Mrs. Morris/Ms. Morrison case. First, leaders must learn to allow for pauses in performance to study and reflect. This is what the MIT Sloan sailing team did, even pausing in the middle of a race to study what was going wrong and develop new routines to use in performance. This is what outstanding operators routinely do.

Many will note that Dr. W. Edwards Deming's learning cycle of Plan-Do-Study-Act (PDSA) is a tool to encourage slowification. Following the PDSA loop, teams develop a "Plan" that captures whatever is best known about a situation, "Do" according to that plan, and then "Study" the experience for differences between what happened and what was predicted to happen. Then, they further study the situation to develop a better understanding of what to do, why, and how to do it. Finally, they "Act."

---

* Steve worked on this project, and it was among the most rewarding professional experiences in his career. Not only did it validate concepts informed by Toyota and Alcoa being introduced into healthcare, but it also had great impact in an organization, the work of which was far afield from where the ideas originated. Most significant, though, is the number of people whose lives were improved through this collaborative effort.

Second, leaders must capture the lessons learned to create an ever-improving baseline. Sailing on the team was predicated on being a student at the MIT Sloan School of Management, and the longest anyone could be a team member was one or two years before they got "cut" by graduation. Adam and his teammates were aware that this made the team's tacit knowledge "perishable"—it would disappear as teammates graduated. Therefore, they deliberately captured lessons learned, not only race to race but season to season. They built a diagrammed playbook of what to do, how to do it, and when it would be necessary. They also created land-based and boat-based exercises to convey those skills quickly and easily.

In doing so, they captured the logic behind "standard work." When done well, it's a way to capture the best-known approaches, make them available for repeated use, and use them as the basis for further improvement (a topic we'll return to in Part III: Simplification).

If the sailing, central line, and victim hotline examples are inspirations, the invasive procedure performed on Mrs. Morris poses a warning. For whatever reason, the hospital's leadership didn't receive or respond to feedback. They didn't create a "pause time" culture to figure out what the problems were when other nurses, doctors, and technicians had gotten confused before.

As a leader, this should leave you with the following questions about your own organization and social circuitry: In performance, are difficulties, glitches, deviations, and departures called out once seen, swarmed to be contained (stabilized), and solved? And are the lessons learned shared and otherwise systematized for future use? (These techniques are explored further in Part IV: Amplification.)

How Planning and Practice Determined Success and Failure at NASA

In the previous case studies, we saw the power of pausing during performance and the consequences of not doing so. The next two case studies show another aspect of slowification: when planning and practice are even more critical because the task has never been performed before and there is only one shot to get it right.

When preparing for a novel scenario, we often make our best guess about what will be required, but our best guess may well be wrong. We must also prepare for scenarios that might seem less likely but would still be consequential (i.e., finding the "monsters in the tails"). NASA's storied history provides examples where preparing for the "monsters in the tails" brought great reward and when not doing so had terrible consequences.

Case Study: *Apollo 11*, the First Lunar Landing (1969)

On July 16, 1969, *Apollo 11* astronauts Neil Armstrong and Buzz Aldrin were less than an hour away from fulfilling President Kennedy's 1961 challenge of "achieving the goal, before this decade is out, of landing a man on the Moon and returning him safely to the Earth." However, in the moments before Armstrong uttered his famous words "The Eagle has landed," the mission's outcome was in peril.

Many issues arose during the sixty-mile descent to the lunar surface. Armstrong discovered that they had begun their descent two to three seconds too early. As a result, they were traveling too fast, putting them on a course to land miles west of their target. Then, six thousand feet from the surface, the lunar guidance computer started generating "1201 program alarms,"[7] signaling that it couldn't process all the computations in real time. Finally, within a minute of landing, Armstrong saw that the landing zone was strewn with boulders and was on the edge of a three-hundred-foot-wide crater, making it risky to land.[8]

These complications, as well as many others, could have forced them to abort the landing. However, the *Apollo 11* crew and mission controllers had created well-practiced contingency plans. They had spent endless hours challenging simulations to find holes in their approaches and to figure out how to plug those holes.

Gene Kranz, who was NASA's chief flight director for the Mercury, Gemini, and Apollo space programs, explained why he put such a high value on developing and testing procedures:

> During a mission countdown, or even a flight test, so many things would be happening so fast that you did not have any time for second

thoughts or arguments. You wanted the debate behind you. So, before the mission, you held meetings to decide what to do if anything went wrong…There was no room in the process for emotion, no space for fear or doubt, no time to stop and think things over.[9]

To prepare to pilot for lunar descent, astronauts trained in the lunar module simulator at the Kennedy Space Center, outfitted with the same computers, controls, and screens that were on the real lunar module that the astronauts would pilot during their actual mission. During landing simulations, the astronauts would see realistic displays of the landing site projected from physical models. In addition, they built lunar landing training vehicles, which astronauts also flew during training.

FIGURE 5.3 Stages of Development for Lunar Landing Module

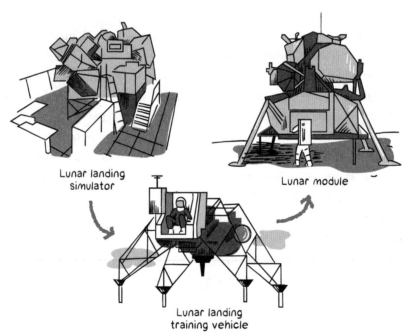

Lunar landing
simulator

Lunar module

Lunar landing
training vehicle

Planning and practice weren't just for the astronauts. They were also for Mission Control, the nexus of the tens of thousands of people on the ground whose work enabled the mission. Kranz described how the simulation team was constantly "studying the controllers, crews, and mission strategy, looking for the holes and developing new training runs to exploit the perceived holes."[10]

Weeks before the scheduled launch of *Apollo 11*, the simulation team kept proving that astronauts and controllers still had not figured out key elements of the mission. Kranz described one training session: "...[in the simulation,] the crew was splattered across the Sea of Tranquility [the intended landing zone]. This was our first crash, the result of a few seconds' delay in our communication and decision process."[11]

During this period, to help find more problems and generate better answers, the *Apollo 12* team kept training and practicing to improve the *Apollo 11* procedures. During the final practice simulation, Kranz and the controllers were in Mission Control. The guidance officer (GUIDO) peered at his display, trying to make sense of a sudden lunar module "1201 alarm code," indicating computer restart.[12] After consulting the computer expert, the GUIDO told Kranz, "Something is wrong in the computer...Abort the landing!"[13] Kranz agreed.

Afterward, the simulation supervisor told Kranz that he had made the wrong call, that according to their defined procedures, aborting requires two indications to abort, and Kranz had done so with only one. Realizing his error, Kranz used this feedback to reinforce to everyone what was required to abort, accounting for these types of situations. Kranz wrote, "A single busted training run is abysmal; a busted run on the final day of training is unacceptable."[14] They scheduled four more hours of training on program alarms the following day.[15]

All their hard work and aggressive preparation paid off. During the last few minutes of Armstrong's and Aldrin's descent to the lunar surface, Mission Control knew that the 1201 alarm code alone was not a reason to abort the landing. Similarly, Armstrong had already trained extensively on taking manual control of the lander and finding a new landing site, having studied the lunar terrain from the high-fidelity maps in the simulator.

Each one of these complications presented a potentially mission-ending problem. However, the aggressiveness of feedback during practice forced the astronauts and controllers to confront these problems in advance, so they could develop the necessary plans, backup plans, habits, and routines that they could execute in performance. As a result, the lunar module was piloted successfully to the surface, confirmed by Armstrong's line "The Eagle has landed."

Case Study: The *Columbia* Space Shuttle Disaster (2003)

In contrast to the feedback-rich dynamic in planning and practice for *Apollo 11*, let us consider the catastrophe of the space shuttle *Columbia*. This tragedy was caused, in part, by the absence of the forceful learning dynamic and practice of preparing for the "monsters in the tails" that was common under the Apollo missions. While both missions were overseen by NASA, they took place during different eras, and the respective leaders organized the social circuitry in different ways.

Two days after *Columbia's* launch, controllers had observed on a routine video review that a twenty-one-inch piece of foam had broken off the external fuel tank and struck the reinforced carbon-carbon (RCC) thermal protection panels on the left wing.[16] After much study and consideration, NASA leadership concluded that there was no risk to the shuttle or its crew. The decision was made to proceed with the landing.

At 8:10 a.m. on February 1, 2003, the seven astronauts aboard *Columbia* began reentry to Earth. Shortly afterward, there were reports of debris being shed over the Southwestern US, a loss of signal, and cameras showing the shuttle breaking up in the sky. All seven astronauts were lost.

There are two key issues with the social circuitry of NASA that we feel helped lead to this tragedy. First, foam had shed from external fuel tanks, collided with shuttles, and broken thermal protection panels on previous flights. But that deviance (departure from the original engineering design) was normalized (treated as a non-deviance). Consequently, no solution was developed. Moreover, panels breaking because of foam strikes were not treated as a critical risk, so no backup plan was developed. This is in direct contrast to the planning and practice routines we saw with *Apollo 11*.

This was among the many questions explored by the Columbia Accident Investigation Board (CAIB): If safe reentry was known to be impossible, could the astronauts have been rescued?*

---

* The rescue plans appear in the CAIB report as Appendix D.13, showing scenarios that assume that a decision to repair or rescue the *Columbia* crew was made.

An anonymous engineer who was involved in creating this plan for future flights wrote, "It took 18 months of planning to develop the procedures, modify the tools, test and simulate the GN&C, EVA, and robotics choreography, and prepare all the paperwork to satisfy everyone that it was a safe plan for both orbiters and the crew."[17] They continued, "The only hope that this plan would have ever had would have been if the plan had already been in place prior to *Columbia*'s launch, as there is no way on this Earth that NASA would have approved a flight with untested procedures that could destroy both orbiters."[18]

In other words, for such a plan to be useful, it must have already been written and tested. No plan could be developed "on the fly." Had it existed, though, it "could have been NASA's finest hour," as written by Lee Hutchinson, senior technical editor at *Ars Technica*.[19]

Instead, the *Columbia* disaster took the lives of astronauts and cost the careers of NASA leaders.[20]

Lessons and Guidance

In preparation for the fast-moving, unforgiving experience of landing on the moon, NASA set its astronauts up for success. They kept stress-testing their systems during practice sessions to find the "monsters in the tails." Then they created exercises, simulations, and other opportunities in which the astronauts and flight controllers could develop and master plans and backup plans. This way, if those monsters revealed themselves, the team would be ready.

This was a demonstration of slowification (pulling problem-solving back from the unforgiving performance environment to the planning and practice environments) coupled with rich and aggressive feedback. The crew was challenged with demanding simulations, which helped them define and refine their mindsets, procedures, and decision-making processes during practice and preparation. This set them up for success in performance.

In order for Kranz to lead such a complex series of undertakings as the Mercury, Gemini, and Apollo missions, one might imagine that his most important gift was an ability to solve challenging technical problems (Layer 1) or an understanding of the instrumentation through which people work (Layer 2). Without a doubt, Kranz was capable of both. But accomplishing something as ambitious, high profile, high risk, and cutting edge as going to the moon and returning safely to Earth requires extraordinary Layer 3 capabilities.

Kranz and his colleagues created the conditions (the social circuitry) for a vast number of people in a sprawling enterprise to see and solve problems, and deploy useful solutions reliably and quickly. As a result, when they found themselves in a dangerous situation, Armstrong and Aldrin had prevalidated methods for figuring out what to do and how to do it.

In contrast to the *Apollo* mission, which was known to be high risk and experimental, the *Columbia* and the missions it supported were framed differently. During the 1970s, the space shuttles were pitched to Congress as cheap and reusable spacecraft that could deliver safe, frequent, and economical access to space.[21] NASA leaders then set their operating tempo accordingly, and parts of this promise were fulfilled. The space shuttle program did provide repeatability. After all, *Columbia* had completed twenty-seven successful missions before it's tragic end.[22]

The failure of *Columbia* was partly due to a combination of maintaining operational tempo and "normalization of deviance."[23]* Of the seventy-nine shuttle launches that had imagery, foam strikes occurred on sixty-five (including two potentially serious events where the foam struck a shuttle wing) but did not result in problems.[24] As such, the deviances (foam strikes) became normalized (i.e., had become accepted as safe).†

In fact, NASA flight director Steve Sitch sent an email that included the following: "We have seen this same phenomenon [foam strikes] on several other flights and there is absolutely no concern for entry."[25]

Shuttle managers had gotten used to not worrying about the "monsters in the tails." The tragedy, of course, is that the monsters had not gone away; they had just been waiting.

Kranz's experience provides a positive example of how to craft successful social circuitry. As a leader, ask yourself: Of the things you are currently

---

* This term, coined by Dr. Diane Vaughan, describes a situation where an unsafe practice comes to be considered normal if it does not immediately cause a catastrophe, such as foam breaking off the external fuel tank and striking the spacecraft.

† Normalization of deviances will be explored much more in Part IV: Amplification.

planning, are you humble and open-minded enough to expose your best ideas to aggressive testing? When those tests find flaws, will you be receptive enough to recognize that your best ideas have been refuted? And once those ideas are refuted, will you be creative enough? Will you solicit the contributions of others to generate new ideas that can be tested?

Similarly, the failures of NASA with *Columbia* offer warnings. As a leader, when you think about the initiatives you're leading right now, are you presenting and characterizing initiatives as "operational" (e.g., reliable, repeatable, dependable, safe) when, in fact, they're still developmental and in need of feedback-informed improvement? When things go wrong in the earliest stages of performance, do you dismiss that as a transitory or an inconsequential aberration (i.e., do you "normalize the deviance")? Or, do you seize the feedback and recognize that there is something in the system that needs correction?

As a leader, you set the operational tempo. But ask yourself: Do you also reserve enough time to find the "monsters in the tails"?

Compliance Leadership vs. Learning Leadership before the Battle of Midway

The previous case studies showed that important capabilities can be developed if feedback is generated during planning and practice. Doing so has a significant impact on outcomes, as can be seen in our next case study. It shows how two adversaries managed planning and practice, resulting in victory for one and defeat for the other at the Battle of Midway.

Case Study: The Imperial Japanese Navy and Command, Control, and Compliance Leadership

Summer 1942 should have been celebratory for the Imperial Japanese Navy (IJN). They had launched a surprise attack on Pearl Harbor in December 1941 and immediately added victories in the Philippines, Singapore, and Guam. June 1942 was supposed to be the coup de grâce. A Japanese fleet was directed to Midway Island to draw the US into a decisive battle. Victory seemed certain because the US Navy wouldn't have battleships. The ruins of the US Navy marked the bottom of Pearl Harbor. Plus, the Japanese fleet had more ships, more sailors, more planes, and more pilots than the US.

Contrary to the IJN's plans, the US successfully countered the attack, damaging, sinking, or otherwise crippling two-thirds of Japan's carriers. Japan was crippled. Japanese industries did not have the regenerative might anywhere close to US industries. The remainder of the Pacific War was horrific by every measure of life, limb, and treasure. But the IJN couldn't mount meaningful offensives and conducted a costly and ultimately point-less delay of the inevitable.

How was the IJN defeated despite its advantages? *Shattered Sword* authors Jonathan Parshall and Anthony Tully show that their fate was sealed no later than 1929—more than a decade before the Battle of Mid-way.[26] This is because of the IJN's unwavering beliefs about how to man, train, and equip its surface ships and aviation units, beliefs that were put in place long before the decisive battle had even been imagined.

The IJN's operating doctrine of naval aviation was based on a weak analogy: their experience defeating an exhausted Russian battleship fleet (not freshly supplied and crewed American carriers and airplanes) that had dragged itself from the Baltic Sea around Europe in 1905 for a fight in the Tsushima Strait (not on the open ocean). Moreover, the IJN committed to this operating doctrine amid the technological innovations of the early twentieth-century, including ships, planes, armaments, radio, radar, cryp-tography, and so forth.

One can imagine such commitment so early was comforting. With "clarity" about whom to fight and how to fight, it meant that the IJN could man, train, and equip according to that established doctrine. The problem was that the manning, training, and equipping according to that doctrine actually helped script the IJN's defeat at Midway.

Parshall and Tully describe war games the IJN conducted before Mid-way. Admirals would be on one side of a table sprinkled with model ships. Junior officers acted as proxies for the US Navy leadership on the table's other side. They would begin enacting their battle plan, but the referee would quickly interrupt. The proxies were not following the plan.

Why not? The junior officers imagined that an outnumbered opponent might fight differently than the IJN leadership thought. The junior officers had identified a possible flaw in leadership thinking. However, instead of debriefing the proxies to learn from them, leadership kept replacing one proxy with another, looking for validation. It was ultimately their demise.

Case Study: The US Navy and Learning Leadership

During the same period, the US Navy leadership took a different approach. In effect, they admitted that they had no good idea how to face the enormous challenge of being a transoceanic navy. To correct this, they conducted a plethora of experiments to discover how to become successful[27] (see Table 5.1). Starting in 1923 and continuing every year for nearly two decades, the Navy ran a series of "Fleet Problems." For instance, if the Panama Canal is key for moving ships and supplies, how do we defend it from attack? "We don't know" was the basic answer, so ships and sailors were sent to sea to test ideas, seeing what worked and what didn't.

This was just one of the many problems for which they needed answers: How do we replenish at sea? How do we best fight submarines? How do we conduct amphibious attacks on island strongholds? To answer these, experiments were run onshore at the Naval War College and at sea, from which lessons were drawn and added to an increasingly rich playbook. These Fleet Problems weren't rehearsals for subordinates to act out what their superiors had scripted. Rather, these events were deliberately designed to reveal flaws in thinking long before they became consequential flaws in doing.

TABLE 5.1: US Navy Fleet Problems during the 1920s and 1930s

YEAR	PROBLEM	EXERCISE
1923	Defend Panama Canal from surprise attack.	I
1924	Advance to the western Pacific, seize an advanced base, and conduct an offensive from it.	II–IV
1925	Explore how best to attack and defend advanced bases.	V
1926	Move across the Pacific to relieve the Philippine garrison before it surrenders.	VI

1927	Simulate an advance across the Pacific and seize an advanced base.	VII
1928	Practice evading the enemy while transiting the Pacific.	VIII
1929	Execute delaying operations against a superior Anglo-Japanese coalition.	IX
1930	Test new tactical fleet dispositions and battle plans.	X
1930	Concentrate a widely dispersed fleet in the face of enemy opposition.	XI
1931	Test an aircraft-heavy force against a more conventional fleet.	XII
1932	Recapture Hawaii from an aggressive Asian power.	XIII
1933	Defend the West Coast from carrier raids.	XIV
1934	Make an opposed advance and explore advanced base operations (attack/defense).	XV
1935	Simulate an offensive Pacific campaign.	XVI
1936	Investigate operational problems associated with an extended Pacific campaign.	XVII
1937	Capture a series of advanced bases in sequence—island hopping.	XVIII
1938	Simulate a protracted Pacific campaign, including advanced base capture.	XIX
1939	Defend the Western Hemisphere from a major European fascist power.	XX
1940	Defend against Japanese attacks while much of the fleet is in the Atlantic.	XXI

Lessons and Guidance

The IJN's leadership had thought of planning as an opportunity for leadership to get its best ideas "on paper" and then use those plans as the basis for training others to follow the plan. That proved fatal. During those war games, IJN leadership ignored feedback alerting them to flaws in their plans. These flaws were evident to the junior officers playing American commanders. Those sailors were new to the plan and were not as hardened in its belief. Thus, they were less affected by biases like overconfidence, anchoring, and so forth.

By not accepting the feedback, IJN leadership didn't slow their thinking and consider alternatives. This is an example of compliance leadership, where leaders expect that instructions be followed without question.

In contrast, the US Navy conducted debriefs and reflections on what happened at sea during Fleet Problems. One can imagine the scene, as if filmed in the style of *The Longest Day* or *The Sands of Iwo Jima*. There'd be the loudmouth from New York, the stoic Scandinavian from Minnesota, and their Hispanic shipmate from LA. When senior leaders were topside reviewing the day's experience, the enlisted sailor from New York would be mouthing off, "Yo, Admiral! What was youse thinking?"

That "Yo, Admiral" attitude* is characteristic of a learning leadership style. In this situation, plans are treated as best guesses, not hardened truths. As such, they are subject to forceful backup.

This is the aggressive feedback the US Navy built into its planning. Ideas were developed and tested on tabletops at the War College and elsewhere, and every year, these best guesses were stress-tested at sea by the sailors and pilots who someday would have to perform them.

As a leader, this should make you ask the following questions: When you create plans, do you treat them as "finished," something ready for performance, for execution in operation? Do you expect a "Yes, Admiral" reply? Or, do you treat plans as your first, best guess of what to do, why to do it, and how to get it done? Do you invite challenges to all aspects of your thinking? Is your intent upon first showing your plans to get a "Yo, Admiral" push back?

Planning and Practice behind Airline Emergencies

We've presented how leaders can pause in production to create a powerful learning dynamic. And we've presented how leaders can aggressively practice to create options in performance. And the consequences when neither of these are done.

In the following case studies of two airline emergencies, we see how leaders can use slowification to enable group efforts. In this way, they are

---

* Dubbed "forceful backup" in the Navy.

more likely to succeed, particularly if performance is in a fast-moving and unforgiving environment.

Case Study: United Airlines Flight 232 Crash Landing

At 3:16 p.m. on July 19, 1989, a little over an hour after taking off, the fan disk of the tail-mounted engine of United Airlines Flight 232 disintegrated explosively, disabling all the hydraulic systems. Captain Al Haynes discovered that neither the autopilot nor manual flight controls had any effect—they couldn't control the flaps, the rudder, etc.[28]

Haynes described their predicament:

> We had no ailerons to bank the airplane, we had no rudder to turn it, no elevators to control the pitch, we had no leading-edge flaps or slats to slow the airplane down, no trailing-edge flaps for landing, we had no spoilers on the wing, to help us get down, or help us slow down. Once we were on the ground...we had no steering, nose wheel or tail, and no brakes.[29]

Their only means of controlling the airplane was by adjusting the throttles for the left and right engines under the wings.[30] This was a scenario for which no pilot had ever been trained. A complete loss of hydraulics was never supposed to happen. Despite this, the captain and crew steered toward Sioux City, Iowa, in a "series of barely controlled right spirals,"[31] with the help of Captain Dennis Fitch, a passenger who also happened to be a training instructor on that particular type of plane.* They were eventually able to line up on a closed runway and execute a (somewhat) controlled crash landing.[32]

Despite their heroics, the aircraft had descended too steeply and too fast. In the landing, a wing was ripped off, the tail section and cockpit broke off, and the fuselage rolled before coming to a stop. Of the 296 passengers

---

* His help was needed to steer using the throttles because Captain Al Haynes and First Officer William Records were focused on maintaining control of the aircraft, and neither could manipulate the throttles individually because the number two engine throttle was stuck.

and crew on the flight, 184 survived, an incredible achievement given the seeming impossibility of landing the plane with no conventional means of controlling it.[33]

Haynes credited their survival to Crew Resource Management (CRM), a set of training procedures created by the National Transportation Safety Board (NTSB) after a series of air disasters (including the one described in the next case study). Through the CRM, pilots were trained on a how to solve problems during emergencies.

CRM includes training on speaking up directly, fostering psychologically safe conditions for others to speak up, and training in simulations. This training ensures everyone's experience and input gets integrated, not solely the captain's. This prepracticed technique helps crews under great distress escape the limiting controls of "fast thinking," allowing them to use slow thinking to figure their way to a solution. In other words, CRM provided a set of Layer 3 (social circuitry) routines to aid in problem-solving under duress, preventing Layer 1 and Layer 2 habits from taking too much hold.

As Haynes later explained,

> On that day, we had 103 years of flying experience there in the cockpit, trying to get that airplane on the ground. Not one minute of which we had practiced a complete hydraulic failure, not one of us.... Why would I know more about getting that airplane on the ground under those conditions than any of the other three? If we had not let everybody put their input in, it's a cinch we wouldn't have made it.[34]

The cockpit voice recordings showed how much experimentation was going on. As Haynes described it, the conversation went like this:

> "When are we going to put the gear down?"
> "I don't know."
> "How are we going to get the landing gear?"
> "Maybe one of two ways, let's try it..."[35]

Haynes also explained how important CRM was:

Up until 1980, [flight crews] worked on the concept that the captain was the authority on the aircraft and what he or she said, goes. We lost airplanes because of that. Sometimes the captain is not as smart as we thought they were. And we would listen to him or her, do what they said, and maybe they didn't know what they were talking about.[36]

United Airlines Flight 232's flight crew pulled off a remarkable outcome given the severity of their situation. It was created as a solution to past catastrophes caused by, at least in part, crews' inability to solve problems creatively, collaboratively, and deliberately precisely when they most needed to, as we see next.

Case Study: United Airlines Flight 173 Crash

On December 28, 1978, United Airlines Flight 173, with 181 passengers and eight crew members, crashed as it neared the final approach for landing at Portland, Oregon.[37]

Captain Malburn McBroom was one of the airline's most experienced pilots, with over 27,000 flying hours.[38] The aircraft had been circling the airport for an hour because they felt a vibration and an indicator light turned on when they had lowered the landing gear. They contacted Portland Air Traffic Control (ATC), asking permission to circle the airport while they attempted to diagnose the problem.

Because the flaps had been lowered to circle the airport, fuel consumption was higher than usual. When the flight crew noticed their low fuel, they notified ATC that they needed to make an emergency landing. However, it was too late. During their landing, two engines flamed out and they lost power to the remaining engines. They crashed into a wooded area about six miles from the runway. Eight passengers and two crew members died.

The final NTSB report stated:

The Safety Board believes that this accident exemplifies a recurring problem—a breakdown in cockpit management and teamwork during a situation involving malfunctions of aircraft systems in flight....The flight crew failed to relate the fuel remaining and the rate of fuel flow to the time and distance from the airport because their attention was directed almost entirely toward diagnosing the landing gear problem.[39]

Cockpit recorder transcripts confirm that "the fuel situation was known to be on the minds of the pilot and crew to some degree."[40] The NTSB report recommended the need for more "participative management for captains and assertiveness training for other cockpit crew members."[41]

The NTSB observed that during emergencies it was not unusual for members of the flight crew to fall into the behaviors associated with duress: fight, flight, freeze, or appease.

NTSB investigator and aviation psychologist Dr. Alan Diehl studied UA173, as well as the 1977 Tenerife airport disaster, where KLM Flight 4805 collided with Pan Am Flight 1736 during takeoff, resulting in 583 fatalities, the deadliest accident in aviation history.[42]

Accident investigators noted communication misunderstandings within the KLM cockpit. Very similar to UA173, the KLM pilot, Captain Jacob Louis Veldhuyzen van Zanten, was one of the airline's most experienced pilots. In fact, Captain van Zanten was KLM's chief flight instructor, having 11,700 flight hours. Experts note that there was hesitation from the flight engineer and first officer to consistently challenge van Zanten, which could have resulted in aborting the takeoff.* Because of this series of experiences—where flight crews' thinking got locked into hierarchy, habits, and routines—CRM techniques were developed and deployed.

Lessons and Guidance

The experience of Captain Haynes and his fellow crew on UA232 offers an inspiring example of slowification in practice. When the engine malfunction destroyed the aircraft's hydraulics, the crew was no longer able to control the aircraft. A natural response in this *danger zone* situation is to fight, flight, freeze, or appease. These are the conditions that are not typically conducive to being deliberative, creative, and collaborative.

---

* Dr. Amy Edmondson describes this as the absence of "psychological safety," where social norms prevent the flow of important information.

In an emergency situation, you cannot slow down the performance environment. You cannot reduce the consequences of the situation. And you have only one shot to find the right solution.

Due to the Crew Resource Management, the UA232 crew had practiced and habituated slowing their thinking in what would otherwise be a fast-thinking situation. This gave them a priceless advantage: the tools to find a novel solution to an unprecedented problem. Because of that, 184 people lived.

In the case of UA173 and KLM 4805, the flight crews did not have dependable ways to slow down their deliberations. They had not been trained to forcefully call out the captain's possible oversights or prevent their own habits from considering new, available, and essential information.

This difference in outcomes was not due to a lack of technical skills of the flight crews (Layer 1 or 2 problem). Instead, it was due almost solely to how the social circuitry of the UA232 flight crew was wired (Layer 3). This wiring enabled effective decision-making and problem-solving, even under the most trying circumstances.

As a leader, reflect on these studies and ask yourself: When the pressure's greatest and the stakes are the highest, does that trigger you and your team into fight, flight, freeze, or appease responses? These are the behaviors that trap us in the *danger zone*. Or have you practiced recognizing these situations, with a trigger to slow things down? If yes, you're better equipped. If not, then you still have some work to do.

Practice Makes Perfect in Technology

Case Study: Google and Amazon Disaster Readiness Drills (2004 and 2001)

In the early 2000s, internet companies such as Amazon, Google, and Netflix needed to deliver reliable services in order to survive. This was especially true at Google. Founded in 1998, by 2004 Google was the second-most visited website on the internet, with ten billion visitors per day.[43] Senior leaders worried how catastrophic events, such as an earthquake in Northern California, could potentially disable critical Google services, such as Search, Gmail, and YouTube.

Kripa Krishnan ran the Google Disaster Recovery Testing (DiRT) program at the time [44] and was responsible for finding and fixing the "monsters in the tails"—those potentially catastrophic but often overlooked, dismissed, or unconsidered problems that might attack in production.

At "Google scale," there are many monsters. When services rely on potentially hundreds of thousands or even millions of servers, "even if there's only a fraction of a one-percent chance of a failure occurring, that means it's a failure likely to occur multiple times. Our plan is to preemptively trigger the failure, observe it, fix it, and then repeat until that issue ceases to be one."[45]

These controlled, simulated disaster exercises were engaged during the planning, practice, and, eventually, performance environments. For instance, Google conducted the following exercises:

- Planning: Develop a plan for responding to an earthquake in Northern California that destroys all the datacenters in that region.
- Practice: Perform an exercise to recover from all datacenters in Northern California being destroyed.
- Production: Turn off datacenters in Northern California.

These simulations revealed many issues, some that had nothing to do with technology. Some of the Layer 3 (social circuitry) issues included only one engineer knowing the recovery plan, engineers not knowing whom to call when something went wrong, and people who needed to approve certain requests not being available.

To address these Layer 3 problems, DiRT created scenarios where certain geographic areas could no longer work and help with a disaster. They purposely broke the social circuitry to see how it could be fixed. When certain engineers were marked as either "abducted by aliens" or "killed by zombies," Google teams had to execute the scenario without any help from those engineers. Instead, they had to rely on the documentation or tooling they had written.

Krishnan explained,

> An often-overlooked area of testing is business process and com-
> munications. Systems and processes are highly intertwined, and
> separating testing of systems from testing of business processes
> isn't realistic: a failure of a business system will affect the business
> process, and conversely, a working system is not very useful without
> the right personnel.[46]

Purportedly, some of the Layer 3 "monsters in the tails" that were
revealed during these mock disasters included:

- Software engineers didn't know how to access a conference call bridge,
  or the bridge had capacity for only fifty people, or they needed a new
  conference call provider who would allow them to kick off engineers
  who had subjected the entire conference to hold music.
- When the datacenters ran out of diesel for the backup generators, no
  one knew the procedures for making emergency purchases through
  the supplier, resulting in someone using a personal credit card to pur-
  chase $50,000 worth of diesel fuel.

Conducting these exercises and stress tests on the sociotechnical systems on which Google depended revealed some technical (Layers 1 and 2)
vulnerabilities. But more often, they discovered weak points in the Layer 3
social circuitry of their operations.

Krishnan stated that they designed the exercises to "require engineers
from several groups who might not normally work together to interact with
each other. That way, should a real large-scale disaster ever strike, these
people will already have strong working relationships established."[47]

By conducting these simulations, Google engineers learned whom
they needed to talk to and created relationships with those people in other
departments so they could work together during an incident, turning con-
scious actions into unconscious actions that are able to become routine.

Krishnan described the results from slowifying: "[by 2012], we retested some things that caused serious failures two to three years ago and were pleased to find they can now be resolved effortlessly."[48] She also stated, "Over the years, we've also become much braver in how much we're willing to disrupt in order to make sure everything works."[49]

E-commerce giant Amazon also had to learn these same lessons. Founded in 1994, Amazon grew exponentially, quickly becoming the largest e-commerce retailer, from 1.5 million customers in 1997 to over 35 million customers in 2002.[50] As an e-commerce retailer, Amazon needed its website to be up all the time so customers could browse, search, and order products. If the site crashed or became unresponsive, customers would get frustrated and revenue would come to a standstill. Just such an event occurred during the high-traffic Thanksgiving shopping day in 2001, when shoppers couldn't order for thirty minutes.

Jesse Robbins was hired in 2001 as the availability program manager, responsible for creating programs to ensure overall site reliability. Although a technologist, his background as a firefighter led him to conclude that "complex failures are inevitable and unpredictable...and that a service is not really tested until we break it in production."[51]

Robbins created disaster recovery exercises called "Game Days." Just like Krishnan at Google, Robbins and Amazon engineers concluded it was not enough to practice in a test environment. Instead, they would deliberately schedule bringing down critical production components that powered Amazon.com and then practice recovering.

His team would schedule a disaster, such as the simulated destruction of a datacenter, giving teams time to prepare and practice on their own. And some time on the scheduled day, as Robbins described, "we would literally power off a facility—without notice—and then let the systems fail naturally and [allow] the people to follow their processes wherever they led."[52]

By doing this, just like Krishnan had done at Google, they exposed the "monsters in the tails" (i.e., latent defects) in their system, which normally would have been discovered only during an actual outage. These exercises were then conducted in an increasingly intense and complex way, with the goal of making them feel like just another part of a typical day.

Case Study: **Netflix (2011)**

An even more extreme example of disaster readiness was revealed on April 21, 2011, when a large Amazon Web Services (AWS) cloud region (US-EAST) failed. This failure took down services running on an estimated half a million servers. Some of these services included those of some of their largest customers.

Yet Netflix, the world's largest streaming site with twenty-four million customers at the time, and which ran entirely in the AWS cloud, some-how managed to stay running. This was a feat that perplexed experts. Netflix Engineering revealed how they did it several weeks afterward. They explained that their resilience was due to decisions they had made three years earlier, describing their massive investment in planning and preparation.[53]

Prior to 2009, Netflix's internet services ran entirely in an applica-tion on their datacenters. As they began designing their systems to run in the cloud, they also designed their system to be "cloud native," able to run entirely in the Amazon public cloud and resilient enough to survive signif-icant failures.

One of their specific design objectives was to ensure Netflix services kept running even if an entire AWS availability zone went down, such as what happened with US-EAST. To do this, their system needed to be loosely coupled, with each component able to "gracefully degrade." This would ensure that a failing software component didn't bring the entire system down, because components that depended on it were designed to continue operating without it. For instance, if the personalization service failed, Net-flix showed non-personalized results.

To ensure operational resilience, they revealed that they built and had been running a surprising and audacious service called Chaos Monkey, which simulated AWS failures by constantly and randomly killing produc-tion systems.[54] They did so because they wanted all "engineering teams to be used to a constant level of failure in the cloud" so services could "automatically recover without any manual intervention."[55]

Sometimes critical services crashed in the middle of the night, but the crisis manager did not know which engineer to wake up to resolve the issue. In response, they designed Compliance Monkey, which would find all applications in the catalog of services that did not have an engineer's email address associated with them and randomly turn them off during office hours. This would keep happening until the engineer responsible for the app put their email address in the service catalog. After all, such a (hopefully) minor disruption in the middle of the working day was better than the far more disruptive event of having to wake up every engineering manager in the middle of the night to find the responsible engineer.

To gain assurance that they had achieved their operational resilience objectives, the Netflix team ran Chaos Monkey to constantly inject failures into their preproduction and production environments. This allowed Netflix engineers to constantly find and fix issues quickly and iteratively, creating a more resilient service while simultaneously creating organizational learnings.*

Lessons and Guidance

Google, Amazon, and Netflix offer examples of how to manage complex sociotechnical systems, even though they present an apparent contradiction. On the one hand, their internet services are complex, often stressed, and unforgiving when they fail in production. Yet in performance, they are somehow agile (i.e., able to be changed quickly) and resilient, performing well even when subject to severe disruptions.

Part of this contradiction is resolved when software engineers use planning and practice environments to reveal vulnerabilities, fragilities, and risks (e.g., latent defects), just as the *Apollo 11* teams did. This both informs and triggers efforts to make the system better—both the Layer 1 and 2 (technical) aspects and the Layer 3 (social circuitry) aspect of the

---

* Simplification of software through modularization is discussed in more detail in Part III: Simplification.

system—methodically running drills in planning and in practice that are offline and slow-moving. Then, drills are run in practice, offline but at the tempo of the performance environment. And finally, drills are run inside the performance environment to stress-test those situations too.

As a leader, these examples of slowification should make you ask: Are you regularly looking at situations? And before you must begin performing, are you regularly conducting some version of dress rehearsal? If not, you may be missing chances to identify flaws in your thinking and to see gaps in what you can do. If you miss those chances, they will express themselves in the unforgiving performance environment.

Conclusion

We began this book with the assertion that the enormous, observable differences in performance among those who compete in any field are explainable and are replicable. The difference between great and everyone else is not due to chance, nor is it due to esoteric, idiosyncratic factors that give one group an advantage. Quite the contrary. Superior performance (and inferior performance) is a direct reflection of management systems' capabilities—that is, the social circuitry of organizations.

Leaders must wire their organizations to create conditions where people can solve problems well and systematize new solutions. Such conditions foster individual and collaborative creativity. By creating and sustaining good social circuitry, individual contributions can combine into collective effort toward a common purpose. It is the leader's responsibility to ensure people are able to use their energy and time in ways that are productive, appreciated, and value-adding. Doing this requires resisting the pressures of maintaining operating tempo.

We saw the effect of leaders acting on this potential (or not) across the various phases of planning, practice, and performance. The best consistently slowified conditions, so people could receive feedback; update their understanding and their abilities about what to do, why to do it, and how to get it done; and bring those better approaches into practice. We summarize these below and in Table 5.2.

Planning Phase: The IJN's admiralty deliberately suppressed feedback, even as they were planning a battle critical to their fortunes.* They reverted to compliance leadership with disastrous results. In contrast, during the 1920s and 1930s, the US Navy engaged in a culture of learning leadership, the characteristics of which were expressed during Fleet Problems, run from 1923 through 1940. Ships and sailors went to sea, informed by the best thinking that could be generated through thought experiments and tabletop experiments at the Naval War College and elsewhere. By doing so, they found flaws in thinking before those flaws ever got reflected in actual battle conditions.

Practice Phase: NASA's *Apollo* lunar landing experiences highlighted the advantages of having an aggressive, feedback-rich learning dynamic during preparation. Simulations and exercises gave crews and Mission Control chances to test-drive their policies and procedures. In contrast, NASA wasn't nearly as energetic in planning and practicing for outlier events, with catastrophic consequences for *Columbia*'s twenty-eighth flight.

Performance Phase: Google, Amazon, and Netflix operate complex, high-tech, always-under-stress technical systems with high-end performance, agility, and resilience. They not only used planning and practice to stress test and improve their technology systems and their social circuitry with slow offline simulations, fast offline simulations, and regular online crisis drills, but also built capacity to deal with power outages, datacenter failures, and the like.

Similarly, the MIT Sloan sailing team created feedback-rich learning dynamics, hitting the "pause button" mid-race, so they could (re)plan and practice anew their sailing techniques. From a dead-last finish in their first race, they advanced to the fastest in the fleet. They maintained

---

* We'll revisit this contrast when we focus on amplification as a mechanism of well-wired organizations in Part IV.

that position year to year, despite the regular need to replace graduating captains and crews, by capturing lessons learned. Each season, the new crew was building on the learning accomplishments of previous crews. Their success was a direct consequence of crafting social circuitry more conducive to steady progress than their competitors. In contrast, the terrible experiences detailed in the Mrs. Morris/Ms. Morrison series were a direct consequence of not pausing during performance.

And we examined the outcomes of aircrews in distress, comparing those equipped and not equipped with sound training in Crew Resource Management techniques. In each case, there was no luxury of "hitting the pause button" to slow down the performance environment. Despite that, UA Flight 232's crew had learned to extract themselves from instinctive, fast-thinking behavior. Instead, they were able slow their thinking and engage all their collective brain power to methodically figure out what to do and how to do it. However, their counterparts, not yet equipped with CRM, met a far worse outcome.

TABLE 5.2 Opportunities Taken or Missed for Feedback-Informed Progress during Planning, Practice, and Performance

CASE STUDY	PHASES	
Imperial Japanese Navy vs. US Navy	Planning 🖊	Plans issued and compliance expected vs. plans created to generate feedback.
Apollo 11 vs. Space Shuttle Columbia	Practice ⚙️	Practice phase for finding flaws in technology (Layer 1 and Layer 2 problems) and flaws in coordination (Layer 3 problem). Forceful, aggressive simulations.
Google, Amazon, Netflix	Practice ⚙️	DiRT, Game Days: rich feedback offline slow; rich feedback offline fast.
	Performance ▯▷	Netflix Chaos Monkey: rich feedback, drills in performance.

CASE STUDY	PHASES	
MIT Sailing vs. Mrs. Morris/Ms. Morrison	Performance 🔲▷	Pause during performance.
United Airlines Flight 232 vs. United Airlines Flight 173	Performance 🔲▷	CRM: Slow down thinking even if you can't pause performance.

Across the feedback-rich experiences of planning, practice, and performance, there were deliberate, rigorous, and energetic capture of lessons learned so they could be systematized for repeated use. This is perhaps the most important benefit of slowification. As such, we'll address this in more detail in the exemplar case study in the next chapter.

QUESTIONS FOR THE READER

1. *Planning:* Identify something you are in the midst of planning or designing. Are you aggressively injecting feedback to find flaws in your thinking before they become flaws in your doing? Identify opportunities to stress test your plans. The goal is to generate feedback, constructive criticism, hard critique, and probing questions.

2. *Practice:* Identify something you have planned and are getting ready to perform. Have you set time, space, and resources aside to stress-test performance in an offline, feedback-rich fashion to find and address the "monsters in the tails"?

3. *Performance:* Identify some work you are actually doing. What have you put in place to make clear someone is having difficulty or something is going wrong? When those problems emerge, how do you call attention to them? How do you pause performance (locally or systemically) to recover and create solutions so the problem doesn't recur? As a leader, do you make it a habit to schedule routine pauses or take breaks in performance when it feels like the gracefulness of execution

is slipping? This allows you and your colleagues to use planning and practice to study what you've been doing and formulate an improved approach.

4. *Performance:* Identify some work you are actually doing that cannot be paused (e.g., a medical procedure). What have you done to teach your colleagues to recognize their situation is getting increasingly abnormal? How do you help them deliberately enter a slow-thinking routine?

CHAPTER 6

Slowification: Exemplar Case Study and Further Examination

April 15, 2013, Patriots' Day, a regional holiday marking the start of the American Revolutionary War. But instead of the typical celebrations, two brothers placed pressure-cooker time bombs at the Boston Marathon finish line, transforming the holiday into multiple days of terror and trauma for the city and its surrounding communities.

Thanks to emergency responders—EMS, fire, police, and area hospitals—a day of tragedy eventually became one of community triumph. In this chapter, we will examine what those first responders and medical care providers did and how they did it. Their exemplary performance sets a high bar for us all. It is through this final case study that we can see the full importance of slowification as a mechanism to build great advantages for ourselves and the enterprises we lead.

Exemplar Case Study:
Preparing for a Mass Casualty Event

In years past, the Boston Marathon had been marked by wet and cold or hot and humid weather. But 2013 was a nearly perfect race day.[1] Half a million spectators were yelling encouragement. Wellesley College students flanked Commonwealth Avenue, forming a "scream tunnel" of support at the half-way mark. Twelve miles later, the marathon's winners were crossing the finish line, followed by thousands of other runners, with thousands more still on their way.

But at 2:49 p.m., all that changed. There was an explosion and then a second at the marathon finish line. Three people—a local restaurant manager, a foreign graduate student, and an eight-year-old boy—were killed by the blast. Some 281 other people were injured, 127 of whom needed immediate care at Level I trauma centers.[2]

Despite the devastation of the blasts, any trauma patient who made it to a Boston-area emergency department survived.[3] The local medical community had been rigorous in preparing for a mass casualty event. Through the use of slowification during planning, practice and performance, they were ready.

Amid the shock, confusion, and chaos that immediately followed the two blasts, victims received immediate, life-saving aid from first responders at the blast site. Within forty-five minutes, the injured were cleared from the scene.[4] Lessons learned from improvised explosive devices in Iraq and Afghanistan had been institutionalized in Boston's EMS practices, meaning life-saving treatments were used immediately.[5]

This astounding feat was possible partly because of the number of medical workers on hand. Given the tens of thousands of runners and the hundreds of thousands of spectators, Boston and neighboring communities were already set up to deal with a large number of medical emergencies.[6]

At Brigham and Women's Hospital (BWH), the emergency operations center had been opened at 8:00 a.m., as the marathon is typically considered a potential mass casualty event.[7] This is because during a typical marathon, there are usually hundreds of medical encounters.

When nearly thirty thousand people are running more than twenty-six miles, one expects issues such as low sodium levels from dehydration, hypothermia, and cardiac events spread over several hours. However, one does not typically expect the trauma injuries from street-level bomb blasts all needing care at once.[8] This was a crisis greater in scale and severity than typical, and hospitals had been going about their routine business that day.

When the hotline at Brigham rang and told them there'd been explosions and that patients were on the way, the emergency response contingency plans kicked in. The lead emergency medicine doctor, an incident commander in previous practice drills, had the emergency department cleared of the fifty-five patients who had been filling its beds. Eight medical psychiatry patients were moved to a different facility, and claims were made on operating suites that weren't in use (thirty of forty-two were already active).[9] And a good thing too, for of the thirty-one trauma patients who were transported to BWH, twenty-three arrived within thirty minutes of the blast.[10]

Likewise, at Beth Israel Deaconess Medical Center, where twenty-four bombing victims were treated,* alerts of the disaster triggered the hospital's emergency activation plan. Patients who'd come to the emergency department earlier in the day were discharged or admitted to beds elsewhere in the facility. A hazardous-materials tent was set up and incoming patients were scanned on the chance that the bombing was chemical or radiological. Entrances were manned to control who had access to the hospital, and a gathering space was created for people who were searching for friends and family.[11]

At Massachusetts General Hospital, operating room schedules were booked and the emergency department was full. Yet, of the five critically injured patients who arrived at Mass Gen, all were in the operating room within eight minutes.[12]

All this preparation and coordination contributed to the remarkable survival rates of those injured in the bombing. This was not by chance. Instead, it was the result of nearly a decade of preparation.

What Happened in the Years Before

Planning for each Boston Marathon starts months in advance. And that planning draws on the experience gained from previous large public events in the Boston area. First responders and hospitals have used those opportunities "to train, anticipating and preparing for mass casualties in case something goes wrong."[13] Additionally, they had ample training that was not opportunistic; it was deliberate.

For example, eleven years earlier, in November 2002, the City of Boston, Boston EMS, and fourteen Boston-area teaching hospitals ran a

---

* To give some sense of the severity of the injuries caused by the explosions, of the twenty-four patients treated at Beth Israel, sixteen required amputations.

disaster drill called Operation Prometheus, simulating the explosion of a dirty bomb on an inbound airliner. In that drill, BWH received seventy-two patients (almost as many as were distributed across the network the day of the marathon bombing). From 2006 to 2012, BWH ran seventy-three other disaster activities and in total ran 623 separate exercises, including some that tested communication and power systems and technical parts of the sociotechnical system.[14]

The community also took lessons from the 2012 Aurora, Colorado, shooting, in particular the realization of how quickly casualties would be arriving at hospitals. That proved a valuable insight, since, as mentioned, of the thirty-one patients transported to BWH, twenty-three arrived within thirty minutes of the blasts.[15]

In 2008 and 2009, Boston also hosted symposia on planning for and responding to bombing incidents, drawing on lessons learned from London, Madrid, and Israel.[16]

These lessons were captured and rolled into practice. The BIDMC plan, for instance, incorporated lessons learned from previous marathons and other emergencies, and considered areas and departments throughout the facility that might be affected. The 2013 plan had been updated to include social workers to help reunify runners with their families.[17]

Lessons Learned for Next Time

Given the investment made to build up capabilities in the decade preceding the Boston Marathon bombing, it is no surprise that the community has continued to capture lessons learned and make them available. For instance, the citations on which this case study is based are a tiny sampling of what's been written as after-action reviews by those who were involved. Moreover, with the particular emphasis on medical casualties we have here, we're not even referring to lessons learned by law enforcement and others.[18] What's noteworthy is that the lessons learned are not solely "pats on the back of how great we were." Instead, they are self-critical after-action assessments of what went wrong and how it could go better.

For instance, there are reflections on things as mundane as the emergency departments not accounting for unidentified patient naming conventions. Unlike emergency department admissions from car crashes and other tragedies, where patients would, by and large, arrive with IDs, runners often arrived with only their number. Keeping track of patients' physical locations also proved challenging when many arrived in one group.[19]

Dealing with a surge in well-intentioned volunteers proved another challenge (e.g., people trying to insert themselves into the social circuitry without having been wired in deliberately).[20]

The community also discovered other opportunities to improve; after all, knowledge capture and the potential for continued progress are nev-er-ending. For instance, "mass casualty triage tags" were used by first responders, but only 50% of patients arrived at the hospitals with them. Also, tourniquets as a first-aid tactic were widely employed, but they weren't always properly applied.*[21] Because the bombing occurred so close to several Level I trauma centers, equipment and instruments were gen-erally available, but the after-action review did see some difficulties when sharing across institutions was needed.[22]

How Well Do We Capture Knowledge?

Knowledge across performance, practice, and planning phases was used by all the organizations in the successful case studies of Chapter 5. The MIT Sloan sailing team deliberately created a book of lessons learned from the repeated pauses in performance, so those lessons could be reused, not only race to race but season to season and crew to crew. Tech leaders used feedback-rich practices to manage infrastructure failure and build reusable knowledge as the basis of surviving bona fide infrastructure failures.

Likewise, NASA's Apollo program succeeded, in part, because of the steady accumulation of lessons learned during a variety of simulations, exercises, and so forth. The US Navy, with its Naval War College war games

---

* In years past, there was an accepted notion that using tourniquets was counter-productive, raising the risk of losing the limb. However, lessons learned within the trauma community and informed by the military's experience in Iraq and Afghanistan reversed that belief. Using tourniquets had become more widely publicized. That said, of the tourniquets used on patients, two-thirds were used by bystanders and were not properly applied. The community learned there was a need for more education of the general public, not only to use tourniquets but how to do so properly.

and Fleet Problems, gradually evolved an operating doctrine that was the basis of victory over the Imperial Japanese Navy at Midway and later. And knowledge capture provided particular importance and great value to enabling first responders and medical care providers to deal with the marathon bombing so capably.

These examples set us up with some questions to consider: Regardless of which phase we find ourselves in—planning, practice, or performance—how often and well do we capture lessons learned in a way that is easy to access? And how well do we create opportunities for those lessons to be learned so they can be incorporated into future planning and used in future practice?

As we think through opportunities in our own work, consider that knowledge capture has been a key mechanism leading to betterment through human history, taking full advantage of writing, imaging, modeling, and so forth.

Capturing knowledge in books and making them available in libraries has allowed experts to share wisdom with practitioners, even when they were separated by years or decades. Newton discovered the laws of mechanics and motion, but it wouldn't have mattered if he did not also write down what he learned, print it, and have it curated and distributed to scientists through the Royal Society.

Knowledge can be captured in physical objects as well (e.g., fixtures to hold materials in place, jigs to guide work, and gauges to ensure thing are fabricated correctly).[23] These tools mean experts' wisdom are expressible through the hands of many, even those of amateurs, leading to radical gains in productivity.[24] This can even enable new organizational architectures and forms[25] (which will be discussed further in Part III: Simplification).

Knowledge can also be captured in code. For instance, numerical control of machines means knowledge can be created and captured for repeated use.[26] Twenty-first-century machine learning and other data science techniques to achieve pattern recognition continue this trend (e.g., diagnosing a medical condition from a large number of medical charts).

Of course, knowledge capture can be conveyed in routines. "Standard work" is not peculiar to repetitive manufacturing. For instance, an engineer responsible for firmware debugging realized he kept re-creating solutions to problems he'd already solved. Worse, colleagues spent time solving problems when their teammates already had solutions. So, his team began cataloging existing problems and solutions, generated "standard work" on how to put known debugs in place, and increased throughput eighteen-fold.[27]

And, of course, thanks to lessons learned and knowledge captured, *Joy of Cooking* fan Julia Child could teach many more people to master the art of French cooking.

How to Capture and Use Knowledge

Figure 6.1 is an example of visualizing knowledge capture. It was generated out of the review of a situation that had gone wildly out of control. It provides a way to visualize a postmortem on what had happened and prevent it from happening again.

FIGURE 6.1 Turning Planning, Practice, and Performance into Feedback-Rich Opportunities to Make Progress

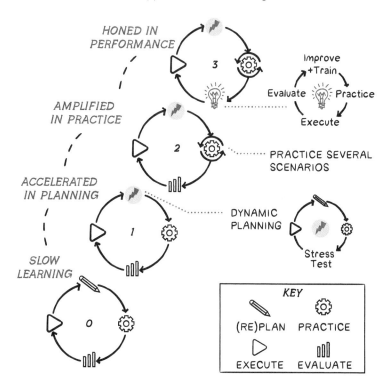

#0 Feedback-Free, Non-Learning Dynamic: In this situation, the norm had unfortunately become for leaders to develop plans and brief or explain those plans to their subordinates, with the expectation that they would execute (perform) the plan as it was written and conveyed. That's the (non-learning) loop in the bottom left of Figure 6.1. Evaluation would occur, but it would largely be an evaluation of the subordinates and how well they'd adhered to the plan, not if the plan was reasonable or not. This was the feedback-free dynamic that characterized the Imperial Japanese Navy's leadership.

#1 Incorporating Feedback into Planning: There was recognition by US Navy leadership that, at the very least, feedback should be built into planning, with leaders offering what they designed, not as a complete and flawless solution but as a best guess. Whatever was designed, planned, or otherwise suggested was framed by the figurative or literal statements: "This is my imperfect best." Or "What can be made better?" Or, even more certainly, "I just don't know." This is captured in the second loop in the diagram, showing feedback during planning. This led to energetic feedback during war games at the Naval War College, during the Fleet Problems, and at other times.

#2 Incorporating Feedback into Practice: Often "practice" can be framed, like planning, as something that "the peons" do to master what they've been told to do. Indications that people are having trouble performing the play as written are not accepted as a sign that something is wrong with the play. Rather, it's (wrongly) interpreted as indicating there's something wrong with the people (performers): "If only they'd try harder or paid more attention." Imagine that if each time the Apollo crews in the simulator had splattered themselves across the landing zone, Gene Kranz had said, "Well, if Neil Armstrong and Buzz Aldrin had more commitment to the mission...."

#3 Incorporating Feedback into Performance: Listen and look for problems so we see them, early and often. This creates the chance for us to solve them more quickly and more easily while suffering fewer consequences from delays. We saw the downside of not being attuned to problems in performance when reviewing the Mrs. Morris/Ms. Morrision medical incident.

The Learning Leader

Another key aspect in the slowification *winning zone* case studies was the presence of learning leaders, like those in the US Navy leading up to the Battle of Midway. A learning leader (also known as developmental leadership) creates a culture where people can say what they really think. This is a psychologically safe culture that encourages people to share ideas, resulting in the flow of important information.

Let's look at an example. A colleague of Steve's, who works in an exceptionally high-performing organization, concluded a meeting and was sitting down to debrief. The majority of those in the meeting felt it had gone quite well, even surprisingly so. But Steve's colleague's first words were, "Hold on. Give me a second to think about what went wrong."

A learning leader is comfortable with not knowing the answer. They are more concerned with asking the question and listening to their team. A learning leader makes training a priority and trusts their team to fulfill that training. Finally, a learning leader actively engages in slow thinking; this is the learning leader's superpower. (We detail even more on the learning leader, aka developmental leadership, in Appendix B of this book.)

Wrapping Up Slowification

The very best performers succeed because they create the conditions in which people can be the most effective. To accomplish this, leaders must focus on the social circuitry (Layer 3) of their organizations. If this is done correctly, people exert less time and energy to navigate Layer 3 problems, and focus on Layer 1 and 2 problems. The solutions to these problems are what help an organization fulfill their mission. Slowification makes it easier to manage Layer 3 problems. It shifts problem-solving from the *danger zone*'s demands for fast thinking into the *winning zone*'s allowance for and encouragement of slow thinking.

In Part III, we will focus on the mechanism of *simplification*, which changes the nature of the problems themselves, making them easier to solve. We'll explore how the techniques of incrementalization, modularization, and linearization help simplify products and processes. These techniques make managing those products and processes easier, moving them away from the *danger zone* and into the *winning zone*.

PART III

Simplification

CHAPTER 7

Simplification:
A Theory Overview

On September 26, 2022, NASA's Double Asteroid Redirection Test (DART) spacecraft was on track to collide with the 5-million-ton (4.8 billion-kilogram) asteroid Dimorphos. This was the first-ever attempt to collide a spacecraft with an asteroid with the intention of changing its trajectory. If successful, this technique could be used in the future to deflect asteroids that pose a threat to Earth.

The 1,345-pound (610-kilogram) DART spacecraft was traveling 14,000 miles per hour (22,500 kph) when it slammed into its target, which had a cross-section about that of a football field. That collision occurred 6 million miles (11 million kilometers) from Earth and happened after DART had pursued the asteroid pair of Didymos and Dimorphos for ten months, traveling 7 million miles to do so.

DART was a David-versus-Goliath experiment for NASA. It was a step toward seeing if near-Earth objects, or NEOs (of which there are an estimated 25,000), could be intercepted in such a way that could prevent a catastrophic collision with Earth.

The DART mission was a success. Dimorphos's orbit was altered around Didymos, the 500-million-ton (523 billion-kilogram) asteroid that Dimorphos is gravitationally tethered to.[1]

The mission was a technological marvel. Tremendous Layer 1 technical competency was reflected in the design of the DART spacecraft, the propulsion systems that got the spacecraft to where it could greet Dimorphos so kinetically, and the LICIACube (created by the Italian Space Agency) that traveled with DART to the intercept spot so it could record the collision and its aftermath and report those events back to Earth.

Terrific Layer 2 technical competency enabled the fabrication and assembly of these designs—conducting tests, validating plans, and otherwise giving form to the many great ideas that came together to make the mission a success.

However, the fact that so much individual creativity could be integrated into such a massive undertaking is a testament to outstanding social circuitry (Layer 3). Without this social circuitry, the myriad talents of engineers, technicians, scientists, and mechanics would not have been integrated for mission success, and deflecting a potentially destructive NEO would have remained the stuff of Hollywood fantasy.

How Do We Simplify?

DART's success shows us techniques we can use to achieve aspirations that might otherwise have seemed impossible due to their ambition, complexity, or scope. These *simplification* techniques (see Figure 7.1) help move us from the *danger zone* to the *winning zone* in a different way than slowification.

Remember, slowification makes it easier to solve problems by changing the *conditions* in which the problem-solving is occurring. Simplification makes the problems *themselves* easier to solve. It achieves this through three techniques—*incrementalization*, *modularization*, and *linearization*. In short, simplification breaks up situations that are big, complex, convoluted, integrated, or highly intertwined and makes them more manageable because they are smaller, contain fewer departures from what is already known, and are easier to understand in their construction.

Moreover, simplification offers another advantage: breaking large, complex problems into smaller, easier pieces means more problem-solving can occur simultaneously (in parallel) with less coordination required. The net result is making problems easier to solve and solving more of them at once. This ability to solve more problems independently and in parallel is a consequence of all three simplification techniques partitioning large systems into smaller, coherent pieces.

In Chapter 2, we defined coherence as a component within a system that has all the elements internal to it that interact frequently and intensely, so their interactions can be easily managed. A component is coherent when all

FIGURE 7.1 Shifting from the *Danger Zone* to the
Winning Zone by Simplification

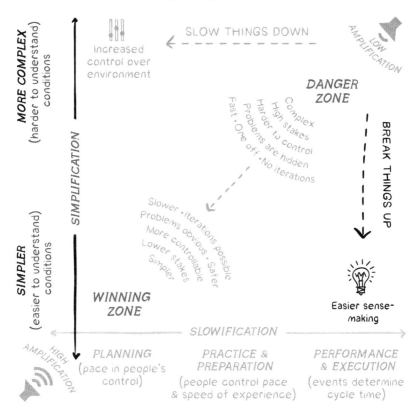

the elements that are necessary to generate an output are included. In this way, the component is a self-contained, unified whole that can behave in a logical, consistent, and independent fashion, which often requires teams to be "cross-functional."

We saw this in the moving-and-painting vignette when Gene and Steve created room teams and then phases within room teams. This allowed work in one room to be managed independently of work in other rooms. And later, the movers and painters were even able to work independently of each other within each room.

In contrast, as Gene and Steve discovered initially, their silos of movers and painters were not coherent. Neither movers nor painters were able to refurbished rooms independently, even with Gene and Steve's best attempt to assign them to rooms through scheduling and expediting.

When a coherent unit is decoupled (i.e., partitioned, separated) from others, disruptions in one don't spill over. In the moving-and-painting vignette, this was accomplished by being sure people and resources weren't shared across rooms to avoid a higher-than-normal pull of one room's workers and depleting what was available to workers in other rooms.

To achieve this, simplification uses three techniques:

Incrementalization: Partitions what is novel (which needs to be tested) from what is known (which is already validated) into their own self-contained, coherent units and adds to the novelty in many smaller increments rather than in a few large attempts. The benefit is that we iterate and test changes on fewer factors and on a smaller portion of our system more quickly and safely.

Modularization: Partitions a large, integrated system that is unwieldy in size, complexity, or intertwined relationships into smaller, simpler, more numerous coherent pieces. These coherent modules are less coupled to each other because they are connected through only a few well-defined and stable interfaces. The benefit is that small teams gain independence of action, enabling them to work and experiment on more manageable parts of the problem in parallel and more quickly and safely, with lower costs of coordination, .

Linearization: Partitions operations that are complex and share resources to accomplish multiple objectives into independent (decoupled) and coherent workflows. Each is focused on one or a few objectives that can happen in parallel. Coherence is achieved by committing all resources needed to generate outputs to workflows and sequencing them in the order that work needs to be performed. Partitioning across workflows is achieved by preventing the sharing of resources between them. Similarly, partitioning within workflows is achieved by defining handoffs between steps. The benefit of both types of partitioning is creating independence of action (decoupling), which contains disruptions during performance and makes improvements during planning and practice easier to do.

FIGURE 7.2 The Three Techniques of Simplification

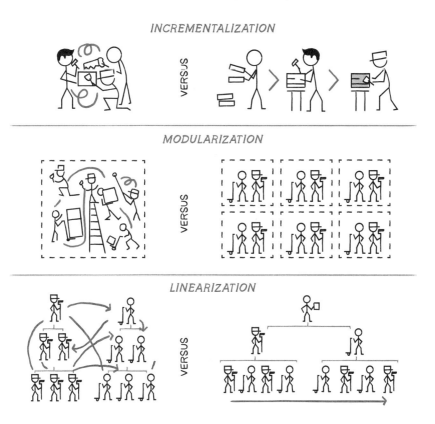

We can see these three techniques at work in the moving-and-painting vignette in Chapter 2.

- Within the painting teams, Gene and Steve used *incrementalization*. It was easier to paint newer plasterboard walls as it did not require any experimentation to prep or paint (in other words, this was known work). Time for this routine work was blocked out from time to figure out how to treat older plaster walls and wood that needed staining (the novel work).

- The work of refurbishing the hotel was *modularized* into room teams, each with their own dedicated painters and movers. This partitioned each room team from others, enabling them to work independently.
- Within each room team, movers and painters *linearized* their work across and within phases, creating clear boundaries and specifications of how movers handed off the room for the painters and how the painters handed the room back to the movers. This created independence of action for the movers and painters to perform and change their work within phases (e.g., moving the largest furniture first, rearranging the steps of paint prepping and coating).

In each case, coordination costs—the time and effort needed to get the right people doing the right thing at the right time in the right place— went down while freedom of action went up. Furthermore, people working within the system had significantly lower cognitive load and were better able to focus on the necessary Layer 1 and Layer 2 problems versus the incidental problems of Layer 3.

Dr. John Sweller, a cognitive psychologist, explained why it's so important to worry about cognitive load: to protect cognitive capacity for useful purposes. He characterized cognitive load as "the total amount of mental effort being used in the working memory."[2] He observed that if the cognitive load of a task is too high, it can hinder learning and burden our cognitive capacity.

Multitasking is another source of cognitive load. Studies have shown that multitasking degrades the performance of completing even simple tasks, such as sorting geometric shapes.[3] The serious impact of this phenomenon was shown by Harvard researchers Dr. Steven Wheelwright and Dr. Kim Clark. They wrote about the problem of spreading engineers' attention over too many projects simultaneously. As the number of projects went up, the time spent on productive tasks (e.g., problem-solving, interpreting data) went down by more than half, from 70% or more of their time to about 30%. The increased nonproductive activities included status meetings (communicating and coordinating across teams), switching costs (time required to reestablish context from one project to another), and so forth.[4] Wheelwright concluded, "If an engineer was on one major project and one smaller project, they not only were working on productive tasks 70%–75% of the time, but they felt much better about their work and their role in the company."[5]

In other words, when leaders create great Layer 3 wiring (social circuitry) through simplification, people can do their work easily and well. This is because they can focus on a small number of novel items in a small number of projects and interact with the smallest number of people necessary to achieve their goals. Next, we'll examine how the three techniques of simplification helped set up the NASA DART mission for success.

Incrementalization

Incrementalization made it easier for NASA to achieve success with the DART mission because only part of its requirements were novel. Rendezvousing with an NEO and landing on one (if not deliberately colliding with it) wasn't entirely new for the US space agency (see Table 7.1).

TABLE 7.1 Previous NEO NASA Missions

YEAR	MISSION	DETAIL
1996	Near Earth Asteroid Rendezvous (NEAR)	*Shoemaker* spacecraft landed on asteroid 433 Eros after traveling for four years and then orbiting around it for an additional year.[6]
1998	Deep Space 1	Mission visited the 9969 Braille asteroid.[7]
2003	*Hayabusa* spacecraft	A NASA partnership with Japan's space agency, collected sample material off the Itokawa asteroid.[8]
2004	Rosetta mission	Flew by the asteroids Steins and Lutetia.[9]
2007	Dawn mission	Visited the asteroids Ceres and Vesta.[10]
2000–2020	Multiple missions	Many other missions to study asteroids were conducted..

NASA and its partners *simplified* the collision problem by building upon a sound foundation of already-validated science and technology. Therefore, the creative energy necessary to accomplish the DART mission didn't have to be diffused over everything; it could be focused on the particulars of a rendezvous and intercept that had a specific new purpose, not of study but of deflection. The DART mission team partitioned its work so novelty was added only on the margins, not across the entire undertaking.

Incrementalization is likely already familiar to you, as it is the basis of many management systems used in industries. For instance, agile software development practices are a response to waterfall approaches. In waterfall approaches, characteristic of the 1960s and 1970s,[11] the entirety of the system is considered at each step in its creation:

- Analysts first gather all the necessary requirements, comprehensively documenting every aspect of the system to be developed.
- System designers create the architecture and design.
- When the design is approved, software developers begin writing the code for the system.
- After the software is written, quality assurance tests it against the original requirements to identify any defects or inconsistencies.
- Once the system is tested, the software is installed and configured in the production environment.
- Users can finally use the software, often to their vast disappointment.

The result is that all the system's novelty has to be tackled at once. This is difficult, if not impossible, to manage. Too many factors have to be considered by development, design, building, and testing. Thus, coordinating among these functions can be overwhelming. Furthermore, user feedback comes only at the very end,* potentially meaning the restart of the whole process on the whole system.[12] This contributes to massive rework, driving projects over deadline and over budget. It creates dismal outcomes not only in software, but in industrial products too.[13]

Instead, agile software development takes a different approach. Rather than "everything all at once through design, development, testing, and

---

* This is poor "amplification," the third mechanism used by organizations wired to win, as we describe in Part IV.

delivery," the idea is to iteratively design, develop, test, and deliver to the user in small increments, ensuring the amount of newly added novelty remains small. This informs the next iteration of design, development, testing, and delivery, as well as adds to the ever-growing base of validated understanding.[14]

FIGURE 7.3 Contrasting Waterfall Approaches with Incremental (Agile) Ones

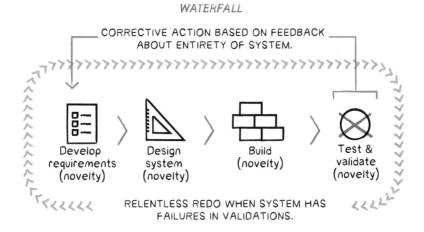

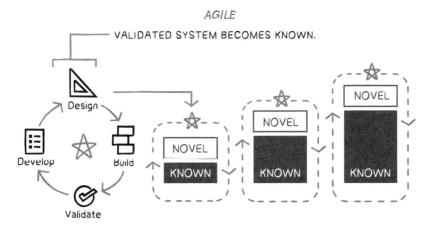

Lean startup methodologies, as defined by Steve Blank and Eric Ries, are also an alternative to waterfall-like approaches to business planning. There are simply too many untested assumptions in product development and customer discovery to have a reasonable prediction of features, including customer ability and willingness to pay, readiness of suppliers to provide technology, and so forth. Concocting an elaborate plan based on these and countless other assumptions is fragile. It is better to generate a few hypotheses, test them out, capture the ones that have been validated, and build on those, as Blank emphasizes.[15]

In other words, agile software development, DevOps, and Lean startup methodologies are examples of incrementalization for specific applications. Incrementalization is a general approach to make it easier to solve difficult problems more reliably, quickly, and safely in any application or industry.

Modularization

Modularization is the act of partitioning large, highly integrated situations into smaller, simpler, more manageable pieces. It helped with the successful refurbishment of the hotel in the moving-and-painting vignette by modularizing the entire project into independent room teams.

Modularization helped NASA's DART mission succeed by enabling a vast team across a diverse range of specialties to contribute. Modularization partitioned a very difficult problem into many smaller and simpler ones. Numerous organizations contributed to the DART mission, including the Falcon 9 launch system from SpaceX (which carried DART) and the LICIACube from the Italian Space Agency. Other technology firms, universities, and laboratories also contributed a part to the much larger whole.[16] By doing so, the large, complex whole was broken into discrete, coherent pieces so that specific groups responsible for each particular module had freedom of action to develop, design, build, and test independently.

Modularization freed each of these organizations from having to synchronize every design decision in one component of the mission with every other. The looser coupling allowed the DART teams to solve more problems directly related to the mission simultaneously rather than one at a time.

Each of these organizations further modularized their systems to enable even smaller teams to work in parallel. For instance, on the DART probe, the solar-powered ion propulsion systems were developed by

NASA's Glenn Research Center and Aerojet Rocketdyne, the navigation systems were developed by the Johns Hopkins Applied Physics Laboratory, and the roll-out solar arrays were developed by Redwire's Deployable Space Systems, just to name a few.[17] Each, in turn, further partitioned their components to enable smaller teams to work on their portions of the system.

Modularization, like incrementalization, makes the problems themselves easier to solve. Partitioning a large system into smaller and coherent components means each component is simpler, making it easier to manage, understand, and experiment with.

Modularization also makes problem-solving easier. By reducing the roster of each team required to solve problems related to each component/module, modularization reduces the costs of coordinating across teams as a whole. And in Layer 3 (the social circuitry), because teams that are responsible for different modules are more loosely coupled, they can experiment in parallel. The combination of Layer 1 and Layer 3 changes creates a higher yield of creative output with substantially reduced costs of coordination.

Modularization is likely familiar to you. It is everywhere around us. Consider the electrical outlets in your home. In this case, the modules are your home and the power company providing electrical power to you, and the interfaces are all of the electrical outlets. The Layer 3 implication is that you have independence of action (i.e., the ability to plug and unplug appliances without needing to coordinate with your power provider). Conversely, the power provider also has independence of action. They could switch from fossil fuels to renewable energy without having to coordinate with you. Similarly, effects are isolated within modules—electrical problems in one house do not affect its neighbors, so you do not need to coordinate with them either.

Applications on mobile phones are another example of modularization. In this case, the modules are the phone operating system (which is the responsibility of the mobile phone vendor) and the applications that run on it (which are the responsibility of the developers who create them). If done well, the operating system hides details of the underlying phone model (e.g., screen size, cellular radio) so that the phone hardware can be changed independently and the applications don't also need to be changed. Conversely, applications can be changed or new applications can be added without having to change the operating system. This creates Layer 3 benefits. Developers for an application can innovate independently. They don't have to coordinate with developers working on another application or the operating system.

In their book *Design Rules*, Drs. Carliss Baldwin and Kim Clark show how system modularity creates option value. They build on the work of Drs. Robert Merton, Fischer Black, and Myron Scholes, who showed how to quantify the monetary value created by options on financial instruments. Merton, Black, and Scholes showed how one can decouple (temporally) decisions tomorrow from conditions today, giving latitude of action to decision-makers that they otherwise wouldn't have. Baldwin and Clark showed how one can decouple actions (spatially) in one location from those in another, providing independence of action that otherwise wouldn't have existed.

To illustrate this point, consider a system made up of ten gears that are all coupled together and therefore composed of only one module. To perform an experiment in this system, you must spin all ten gears at the same time because no gear is independent of the others. This means that for someone responsible for a gear to make a change, they must coordinate with the owners of the other nine gears, even if what is being changed doesn't affect the other gears (e.g., changing only its material composition).

On the other hand, if each gear were its own module, each of the ten gears could be changed independently (that's the spatial dimension), potentially more frequently (because of independence of action), and decisions could be delayed until after the result of the experiment is known (temporal dimension). The result is that the more modules there are in a system, the space that can be explored is greatly increased, often by orders of magnitude.

While modularization enables independence of action, it creates the potential downside of incompatibility: A team may make a decision based on their unique situation but inadvertently create issues they did not foresee elsewhere in the system. For instance, if every team chooses to use a different set of software or tools, other teams may not be able to use what they create (e.g., files that cannot be read without purchasing that software), or people will have difficulty switching to a different team because they use entirely different tools for similar tasks.[*]

Other examples include misspecification at the interfaces (e.g., one uses metric units while the other uses imperial units) or inability to change the interface when it proves to be inadequate (e.g., the architecture is created too early, before the problem space is sufficiently understood).[†]

Modularity continues to influence modern software architectural practices, such as service-oriented architectures (e.g., the Amazon e-commerce example in Chapter 8), microservices, software containers, and technologies such as Kubernetes. Similarly, in manufacturing and elsewhere, modularity enables rapid changeovers from one product to the other within a production cell and the ability to rapidly reconfigure lines from one workflow to another.[‡]

It is important to note here that the leader has the Layer 3 responsibility to balance independence of action with ensuring enough compatibility that all the components integrate into a cohesive whole.

Linearization

The last technique of simplification is linearization, which partitions problem-solving within sequential workflows. This makes the problem easier to solve by reducing the number of interacting factors that have to be

---

[*] In Chapter 9, we describe how modularity in the Apollo space program resulted in the incompatible air scrubbers in the lunar module and command module, leading to the problem of "how do we fit a square peg into a round hole."

[†] These challenges will be explored in the following chapters, including principles and practices to overcome them.

[‡] *The High-Velocity Edge* provides the examples of the factory for a supplier to Toyota that burned down in 1997. It was the sole supplier for a production-critical part. Predictions were of weeks to months before production could be restarted. However, because other suppliers were so adroit at reconfiguring their systems, replacement parts were flowing within days and routine production was quickly reestablished. In 2002, North American production was at risk because labor disputes in West Coast ports threatened the importation of certain critical parts and subsystems. Also, in short order, alternative routes were created. Because supply chains had already been modularized into coherent portions, the entirety didn't have to be re-created, only key portions.

considered simultaneously. It also reduces the number of people whose creative collaboration has to be coordinated. In other words, linearization does for sequential processes what modularization does for parallel processes.

Linearization has four elements:

- Sequentialization: All system outputs are generated along the single, dedicated, non-looping pathway of connected activities.* This is how system outputs take form (e.g., products, services, or information), from the start through the finish of their generation to their delivery.†

- Standardization: This is comprised of (1) the explicit and prespecified definition of what a subsystem is meant to deliver in terms of the *output* it is meant to generate, (2) the sequence of steps to be performed to generate that output (the *pathway*), (3) the nature of the exchanges or handoffs over the *connections* linking one step to the next, and (4) the methods by which work is done at each individual *activity*.‡

- Stabilization:§ Triggers are built into outputs, pathways, connections, and activities so when a surprise inevitably arises (because of delays, defects, difficulties, etc.), the surprise (i.e., problem) is seen and resources (especially people's time and attention) are swarmed onto the problem. This is to contain the problem, so its duration is curtailed and its ability to escape and have systemic effects is diminished.¶

---

* This is called the outputs, pathways, connections, activities (or OPCA) framework in *The High-Velocity Edge*.

† The physical substantiation of this is the assembly line, on which work is completed step by step. However, assembly lines are not the only application. Linearization has great effect in medical care, engineering design (as we'll see in the Pratt & Whitney case below), drug development, and many other situations.

‡ In *The High-Velocity Edge*, this is called "prespecification."

§ In *The High-Velocity Edge*, this is referred to as "built-in tests" that trigger problems being solved once problems are seen.

¶ Standardization and stabilization are explained in *The High-Velocity Edge* as all processes level with the OPCA levels of design being "prespecified" before operation with "tests built in" to indicate where problems need immediate attention during operation.

- Self-synchronization: The production system can automatically self-pace without elaborate scheduling systems.

Sequentialization creates clarity about what activities are upstream and downstream of each other. Standardization makes clear what is exchanged one step to the next and makes signaling possible when intermediate inputs are needed and outputs are done. Stabilization ensures that surprises, one step to the next, are minimized. So, changes at one step are communicated directly to supporting and supported steps.* In short, a workflow is fully linearized when the four elements of sequentialization, standardization, stabilization, and self-synchronization (the "4 S's") have been employed.

Linearization solves a common problem in the design of Layer 3 (social circuitry), such as the examples in Chapter 2 of Steve's daughter and Gene's father becoming "stuck" in a hospital system, the valve in the oil refinery, or the checkbox in the mobile phone service provider. What could be sequential work is instead assigned and scheduled across different functions or departments.

In the production of automobiles, work is divided into styling, design, and production (and subdepartments like body, trim, interiors, power train, etc.), even though a single car has elements of all of those.

In healthcare, work is divided into medical specialties, such as cardiology, pulmonology, infectious diseases, and psychiatry, and the work of doctors is separated from nurses and technicians, even though patients may have multiple maladies and need the attention from all those specialists to occur in an integrated fashion.

Ideally, regardless of context or industry, there should be coordinated collaboration among those whose work depends on or is depended on by other specialists. However, too often, coordination is done only "at the top of the silo," as shown in Figure 7.4. This makes collaborative problem-solving less effective due to the loss of frequency, speed, and detail with which collaboration can occur.

---

* This is an attribute of "pull systems," just in time, etc., which is the antithesis of using schedules and expediting. Likewise, the concept of value streams from Lean captures many of these concepts.

FIGURE 7.4 The Coordination Required in Layer 3
across the Top of the Silo

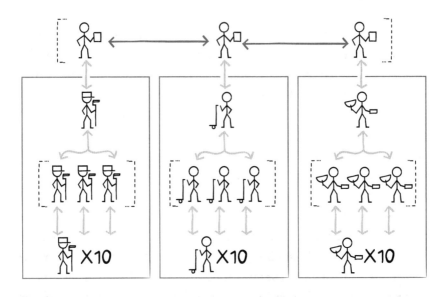

How the 4 S's of linearization played out in the DART mission's success is less obvious. While we can see the architecture of the system used to accomplish the mission, we have less insight into the processes by which the mission was planned and the technical systems were designed and built. It's in those processes that linearization has application.

Despite this, you'll likely find much of linearization to be familiar. This is because linearization draws upon and incorporates many of the key concepts from the study of management going back hundreds of years. In this section, we will present some of the most prominent examples of linearization.

Some readers might recognize linearization as the thesis behind high performance in Dr. Wickham Skinner's "The Focused Factory."[18] There, he explained the difference in performance between the many manufacturing plants that had the common experience of adding significant production volume and product variety but only a few having superior performance across many metrics: quality, productivity, etc.

Skinner explained that the superior plants had leaders who had chosen to create "factories within factories." There were separate production lines dedicated to some subset of the facility's overall production. Coherence was achieved because individual functions committed resources to each line's pathway of connected activities.*

Once coherence was achieved, each line was decoupled from the other lines. This enabled sequentialization, dedicating resources to specific activity steps, so alignment or arrangement of resources didn't have to be repeatedly reconfigured. Decoupling and sequentialization made it easier to create alignment around objectives, create more opportunities to build competency around relevant tasks, and so forth. That made standardization around specialization easier too.

In contrast, leaders of the poorer-performing plants had chosen a more job-shop approach. Subgroups of people and capital equipment were not committed to producing a subset of the production mix. Therefore, "jobs" bounced between different departments (creating a scheduling problem) or left one set of processes queued for the first available machine at the next process.

As a result, moving work required either complicated and sophisticated scheduling systems or queues to hold intermediate products as they waited for machines and machinists to become available. Machine operators were often surprised by what work was coming next and by where it was going. In short, without sequentialization of workflows, creating standards was difficult. There was more need to invent on the fly or improvise.

The impact of nonlinear systems affects the performance of people within the system and the performance of the system as a whole. For instance, Don Reinertsen has written about how scheduling and queues in both manufacturing and software development led to "increased cycle time, delayed feedback, constantly shifting priorities, and status reporting...[which] hurt economic performance."[19] This happens, at least in part, because nonlinearized flows need considerably more Layer 3 coordination.

In contrast, according to Reinertsen, "[Linearized] factories do far less status reporting than traditional factories....A traditional factory with a

---

* This is an example of functions providing resources to the lines rather than the lines sending work to the functions. In software, there is a similar philosophy: send work to the teams instead of sending teams to the work.

16-week lead time may use 60 move transactions....A [linearized] factory making the same product might do two transactions, one to start the work order and the other to close it out."[20]

Skinner and Reinertsen are not alone in celebrating linearization. There's a long history of linearization being used as a technique for making social circuitry easier to design, operate, and improve. This allows people's cognitive capacity to be directed toward Layer 1 and Layer 2 problems, without being cognitively overloaded by trying to figure out where and how they fit into Layer 3.

Adam Smith, in his 1776 *Wealth of Nations*, wrote about the enormous advantages of 1700s factory production over craft production. His quintessential pin factory allowed specialization of production equipment, skills, and focus (i.e., lowered cognitive load). Per capita productivity was hundreds of times greater than that of individual craftspeople, who had to do every step in the production from start to finish. The factory allowed knowledge about production to be generated and concentrated in the minds and hands of experts and reused through collective action.

In the 1800s, factory production was further improved by the introduction of fixtures, jigs, and gauges. Fixtures held a workpiece in place so it wouldn't slip and require repeated realignment. Jigs guided workers, meaning that non-experts could shape material because the experts' wisdom was incorporated into the tool itself. Gauges could be used after the fact to ensure each part was made to its standard.[21]

However, as Skinner would later observe, a new problem that emerged with factories was managing the flow of work (and the corresponding flow of information) across different departments. Machines of similar types were clustered together because it brought together the equipment with those who know how to set up, run, and maintain it effectively. But this created its own problems: as production variety and volume went up (a direct consequence of the factory system—specialization and fixtures, jigs, and gauges), it became more difficult to track what jobs were where, in what stage of completion, and in need of which next steps to advance.

This inadvertently shifted the factory from a Layer 1 engineering problem to a Layer 3 information-processing problem. In other words, factory managers found themselves facing the same problems Gene and Steve first faced when scheduling the movers and painters. The problem of getting parts and materials where they needed to go became overwhelming.

This is what pioneers in assembly line techniques addressed. Ransom Olds and then Henry Ford made breakthroughs by linearizing Layer 2, which, in turn, linearized Layer 3. They arranged equipment so it was placed when and where it was needed in the workflow. If something had to be drilled twice, then better to have two drill presses—one farther upstream in the workflow and one farther downstream—than having to carry the part back and forth between the drilling area and other parts of the factory.

This meant no longer having to track what was where, at what degree of completion, and where it had to go next. Instead, jobs could be queued at just one end of the pipeline, where cognitive capacity could be shifted from the information management issues of running a factory, with its specialized production centers, to the engineering issues of solving technical problems that impacted safety, quality, yield, and cycle time. For Olds, linearizing production contributed to a five-fold production increase; for Ford, making the assembly line move contributed to a six-fold reduction in assembly time, from twelve hours to fewer than two.[22]

To put Skinner's 1974 article in context, what he saw was that as production volume and product variety were increasing amid post–World War II economic growth and technological advances, leaders were regressing in terms of how they managed complex operations. Those lesser-performing plants, where work advanced only through sophisticated scheduling or by waiting in interminable queues, had backed off of the lessons realized by Olds and Ford and were backtracking to job-shop approaches.

Skinner was hardly the only or the last researcher who had a keen interest in practice to chide leaders for periodically backtracking from simplified, linearized, easier-to-manage workflows to far harder to operate job shops. For example, Dr. Eliyahu Goldratt and Jeff Cox's book *The Goal* depends on linearized processes to find and remove bottlenecks that inhibit process flow to increase productivity, as well as reduce the information process requirements.[23] A key insight was that managing how work was performed at the bottleneck was much simpler and more effective than scheduling the entire factory.

In another example, *Dynamic Manufacturing*, by Dr. Bob Hayes, Dr. Steve Wheelwright, and Dr. Kim Clark contrasted two companies. The first was a lower-performing factory organized around silos with senior leaders having to literally helicopter into situations to get problems solved and efforts aligned. In effect, that company had backtracked to a siloed job-shop approach that required relentless expediting (much like with Gene and Steve's first attempts to manage the movers and painters). The second, higher-performing one had much simpler (linear) systems, which made cross-boundary collaboration easier and more productive. It was the authors' exemplar of "the learning organization."[24]

Similarly, Dr. Michael Hammer and James Champy's "manifesto for business revolution" also insisted re-engineering enterprise-wide business processes that were stovepiped or siloed in a more linear fashion.[25]

Lastly, Toyota's much-storied management system depends on linearization for reliability and stability in the short term because it is easier to see and swarm problems immediately, when and where they occur, to contain them. Linearization is also essential in high-speed, sustained improvement. This becomes evident with a close read of Taichi Ohno's book about the development of the Toyota Production System. It shows how the linearization of systems created conditions far more conducive for people to use their ingenuity effectively.[26]

Toyota's approach is perhaps the most consistently comprehensive application of each of the 4 *S*'s. As Spear documented in his book *The High-Velocity Edge*, there's simplification of (in the extreme) all workflows: assembly lines, supporting lines, employee training and onboarding, product design, supply chains, new product launches, establishment of new production lines, and even creation of new production systems under duress. Across all those, there are standards about outputs being generated, sequences of tasks on pathways and assignments of responsibility for those tasks, handoffs between tasks, and methods for each individual task. Consistent with the theme of designing all systems with prespecified standards with tests built in to reveal problems in operation, there's persistent stabilization so local problems are transitory blips, not the start of an avalanche of trouble.[27] (We'll pick up on stabilization in Part IV: Amplification.)

Conclusion

With DART, we saw NASA and its partners successfully change the conditions in which people solved the problem of deflecting a potentially threatening near Earth object. They used at least two of the three simplification techniques—incrementalization and modularization—to change the nature of the problems being solved so they could be easier, simpler, quicker, etc.

For DART, incrementalizing the solution meant building on past successes to develop, design, test, validate, and deploy the incremental novelty. Even with incrementalization, the novelty was still gigantic, so the DART program modularized the mission into discrete, coherent components around which teams could orient, acting somewhat independently because their work was more loosely coupled to the system as a whole.*

In this regard, there is a "model line" element to the DART mission too. We've talked about having model lines as platforms in which new ideas can be tested and generated, new capabilities can be developed, and the appropriate new social circuitry can be wired. This allows us to generate more, less costly, less disruptive learning loops than if we tried to transform a system in its entirety all at once.

It's consequential that DART aimed at Dimorphos and not Didymos. First off, Dimorphos was small, relative to the asteroid it orbits, so DART could be smaller, easier to build, lighter to lift into space, easier to propel, and so forth. Though a major project by most standards, it was still smaller than might be necessary to deflect a larger and more threatening NEO.

There's more to the story. The objective in testing the possibility of "kinetic deflection" was to alter the smaller asteroid's orbit around the larger one. If calculations were off and the orbit was altered in unforeseen ways, Dimorphos would continue to orbit Didymos, and both would continue their travels around the sun without posing a threat to Earth. However, if NASA did its test on Didymos or tried to alter how some other

---

* NASA also applied some slowification techniques. DART wasn't chasing an actual NEO threat across those seven million miles. It was chasing a "test dummy," bringing problem-solving back into a planning and practice environment.

asteroid orbited around the sun, there was always the chance—maybe small, but still some—that the orbit could become more perilous than less.

In the next chapter, we will explore a series of case studies that further illustrate the three techniques of simplification. The case studies are broken into three sections: linearization, modularization, and incrementalization. In Chapter 9, we present an exemplar study that shows all three techniques working together in one case.

QUESTIONS FOR THE READER

1. As someone responsible for creating, maintaining, and improving the social circuitry of an organization, take a look at the situations for which you are responsible. Have you mapped which aspects are truly novel and need to be treated as such and what portions are known, in that you can take advantage of preexisting, validated solutions to fulfill some critical functionality? If your answer is yes, that's good. If not, then you may be making your problem harder than it needs to be.

2. Have you adequately partitioned (modularized) the big problems on which you are working into smaller, more tractable pieces? Here's a test: every time you want to develop or try something new, can it be done quickly, or do you spend so much time trying to schedule discussions and solicit cooperation and approvals, that nothing ever actually gets done? If you answered the latter, you have something that needs to be broken into smaller pieces so you're not crushed by the burden of coordination costs.

3. Take a look at some sample flows of work in your organization, diagramming where ideas, information, materials, and the like travel as they get from where they are generated to where they are next needed. Do those flows look like spaghetti on a plate? Or do those flows require permissions going up one function before being passed over to the top of another before they flow back down to the place

of work? If you answered the latter, you've created opportunities for impedance, congestion, misdirection, turbulence, and the like, and linearizing those flows with more direct connections is likely to help.

Simplification: Case Studies in Incrementalization, Modularization, and Linearization

Where slowification changes the nature of the problem-solving experience, simplification changes the nature of the problems being solved. By utilizing simplification, teams can avoid addressing complex, integrated systems where coherence exists only for the system as a whole (e.g., everyone has to have their hands on the couch all at once). Instead, simplification partitions systems so smaller problems are decoupled from each other.

As a result, problems can be solved quicker since they are easier, and more problem-solving can occur simultaneously since teams have the freedom to act independently of each other. To illustrate this, case studies are drawn from diverse situations or are illustrated with counterexamples to show how simplification provides value across multiple industries. We'll focus on each of the three techniques in turn: incrementalization, modularization, and then linearization.

If you're a fan of details and examples, then this chapter is a treasure trove. If you'd rather skip the detailed examples, head over to Chapter 9, where we provide a single exemplar case study of simplification.

Simplification by Incrementalization

Incrementalization simplifies problems by partitioning what's novel (new) from what is already known. Then fast, small bites are tackled one after the other, rather than trying to swallow one large bite. By holding the base of what is known as constant, modifications can be focused on a smaller portion of the larger system.

Incrementalization allows fewer factors to be considered simultaneously. So, action and outcome (cause and effect) are easier to determine. Testing changes is quicker and easier because only part of the whole system has to be modeled. Feedback is faster because of the smaller scale of experiments. And, because only the novel part of the system is being tested, the number of people involved is fewer and less coordination is required.

Incrementalization has been used in Layer 3 by the Wright brothers in pioneering heavier-than-air flight, in software development to support the launch of new products like the iPhone, and even in creating great art. In all of these case studies, incrementalization helped people move from the *danger zone*, where solving problems is difficult if not impossible, to the *winning zone*, where success is quite achievable.

We now look at two aspects of incrementalization: (1) isolating what is novel and in need of intense study from what is already known (i.e., designed, tested, and validated), and (2) adding novelty gradually but quickly rather than attempting to perform full-scale deployment and validation of the entire system all at once.

Case Study: Incrementalization in Achieving the Wright Brothers' First Flight

The Wright brothers are famous for pioneering powered flight of a heavier-than-air aircraft in 1903.* What's remarkable is that their entire effort cost about $1,000† (approximately $35,000 today[2]); in contrast, the Smithsonian's Samuel Langley spent $50,000 ($625,000 today)[3] but was

---

* Shockingly it took many years after the first flight at Kitty Hawk for the Wright brothers' seminal achievement to be recognized. Their achievement didn't get "media attention" until 1905, two years after Kitty Hawk. And that was from Amos Root, editor of *Gleanings in Bee Culture*. Five years after Kitty Hawk, the brothers finally became celebrities, with Wilbur setting world records for flight duration in France and Orville making similar demonstrations at Fort Myer in Virginia.[1]

† If you factor in the labor costs, it gets to be more than $1,000. However, it was still much less than Langley's effort.

unsuccessful in getting his Aerodrome to fly. Numerous French aeronautical dilettantes, though well funded, also couldn't approach the capabilities the Wrights demonstrated.

Each of these failed attempts had something in common: they did not incrementalize. Instead, they designed, built, and tested their "aircraft" all at once. Without feedback along the way, there were flaws in what they thought and in what they built, and they ended up running out of resources before they could try a second or third time.

FIGURE 8.1 Comparison of 1903 Flight Trials of the Wright Brothers vs. the Langley Aerodrome

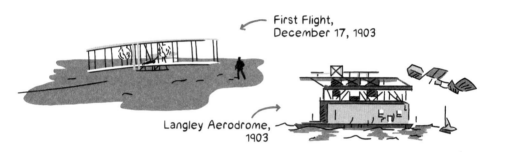

The Wrights used incrementalization to break the big problem of heavier-than-air flight into smaller component pieces. Then, they quickly advanced their understanding bit by bit. Each step supported each subsequent step of inquiry. They believed they couldn't think their way to the right answer; instead, they experimented relentlessly with great frequency and at low cost.

The Wright brothers were unabating experimenters. Their experiments included model gliders flown like kites, months spent with gliders at Kitty Hawk modifying structures and flight controls while gaining flying experience, a self-fabricated wind tunnel in which they could test scale models of airfoils to better understand how to generate lift, etc.

Kitty Hawk was even deliberately chosen as a relatively simple place to test their ideas: wide open spaces and consistent wind speeds and directions. In 1900, they first tested with gliders and a tethered kite before having a person on board. This was to isolate and test ideas for controlling roll and pitch. They went back to Kitty Hawk in 1901 to work on lift, with disappointing results. So, they ran experiments, first rigged up on a bicycle and then in a wind tunnel.

They continued this cadence of first testing and then modifying before putting all the lessons they'd learned about flight controls, lift, propulsion, etc, into their first plane. Even then, the addition of the engine to the aircraft increased its weight. The aircraft needed a new way to launch, which required iterative improvement too.[4]

Their Layer 3 social circuitry enabled every experiment to provide fast feedback. And the experiments themselves were easier to create and understand because each was a small increment relative to the whole (see Figure 8.2). That gave the Wrights more opportunities to gain useful feedback and build know-how quickly. Furthermore, the results of each successful experiment could be added to the validated base and could be built upon further.

FIGURE 8.2 Comparing Langley's "All at Once" Experiment (left) with the Wright Brothers' Incremental Experimentation (right)

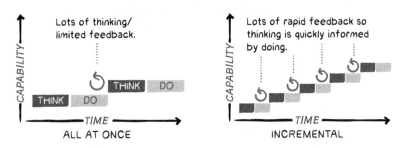

Samuel Langley, on the other hand, had a considerable head start on the Wrights but wired his organization differently. He had built and successfully flown a powered, *unmanned* aircraft in 1896. It was so impressive that he received $50,000 in grants to continue his work. In 1903, he attempted to launch a manned aircraft from a catapult over the Potomac River (his aircraft needed to land on water because he hadn't figured out landing gear). It crashed, and though the pilot survived, his resources had run out.[5]

The degree of complexity he attempted to incorporate in his first, large bite is not inconsequential in its degree of complexity: the complexity of his aircraft, the complexity of his catapult, the complexity of trying to fly over a river with whatever turbulence the wind and current introduced, etc. Langley had tried to do too much all at once and didn't succeed.[6]

As we'll see in the two cases that follow, incrementalization is not limited to early-stage innovation of new technology. The strategy of incrementalization is common across disciplines. Breaking large problems into smaller pieces, around which it is easier to experiment and learn, is a common feature of some great achievements.

Case Study: Incrementalization in the Arts

In 1997, the Brooklyn Museum staged an exhibition, *Monet and the Mediterranean*, which included seventy-one paintings Claude Monet created during trips to the French and Italian Rivieras (in 1884 and 1888) and to Venice (in 1908).[7] Instead of single, signature works, the exhibition showcased how Monet experimented, changing one variable at a time.

For instance, for his Grand Canal series, Monet painted the same church from the same location but at different times of day to study changes in lighting. He also painted the Doge's Palace for another series, showing the same building from different perspectives. Monet used this method of painting the same subject with small variations to perfect his technique.[8]

This illustrates the aspect of incrementalization in Layer 1, isolating and iterating the novel parts of the problem from what is considered already developed, tested, and validated.

Monet was not alone. Pablo Picasso also used this incremental technique, as seen in the painting *Science and Charity*.[9] The massive painting, over six feet tall and eight feet wide, shows a bedridden patient. On one side of the bed, a doctor is checking the patient's pulse. On the other side, a nurse stands with a child, presumably the patient's.

But, this painting didn't simply spring from the young Picasso's imagination in a eureka moment. Rather, as displayed at the Museu Picasso in Barcelona, he first generated many small studies. In the series, you can see his single-variable experiments, where he changes each of the major figures in the painting, converging into its final form. Through incrementalization, Picasso was able to iteratively experiment his way to a master painting.

Next, we return to incrementalization in Layer 3 (social circuitry), where step-by-step introduction of novelty to an otherwise validated system helped a leading technology organization gain significant competitive advantage over the established market leader.

Case Study: Incrementalization in Software Development: Apple iPhone vs. Nokia

Apple

On June 29, 2007, Steve Jobs, cofounder and then CEO of Apple, announced the groundbreaking iPhone to a crowd of three thousand people at Moscone Center. It was heralded as three devices in one: a music player, a phone, and an internet communicator. It looked very different from other mobile phones of the time. Compared with phones with a physical keyboard, the iPhone was dominated by an enormous screen with the keyboard displayed upon it. It was an instant hit, with $118 million in sales in its first quarter.[10]

The iPhone's development ultimately required the work of more than a thousand engineers over three years.[11] But success wasn't a function of brute force. Rather, it depended on Layer 3 wiring that enabled them to use incremental approaches. This allowed engineers to experiment and iterate rapidly, figuring out how to introduce a groundbreaking product that revolutionized mobile computing.

Two years before the iPhone launched, there were only fifteen software engineers working on the iPhone user applications and the user interface libraries, part of a project code-named Purple.* One of the important decisions they made was that the iPhone operating system would be based on OS X, the operating system that had been powering their Macintosh desktops and laptops for over a decade, which itself was an evolution of another operating system going back to the 1980s.†

---

* The name "iPhone" would not be known to the team until Steve Jobs announced it onstage three years after initial development had begun.

† OS X (later renamed to macOS) was based on NeXTSTEP, which was created in the late 1980s at NeXT, a company that Apple acquired in 1997. And, in turn, NeXTSTEP was based on the prior work of the Mach kernel research project and the BSD (Berkeley Software Distribution) operating system.

These fifteen engineers were responsible for a small, coherent unit. For example the iPhone applications would support only one phone model, and there would be only sixteen software applications (e.g., Safari web browser, calendar, contacts, etc.). This freed up those engineers' cognitive capacity to focus on problems unique (novel) to creating the iPhone.

Because the team chose to focus on a very small subset of functionality, the first iPhone was missing many features that were typically found on smartphones at the time, such as copying and pasting, sending photos in text messages, and recording video.

The team was able to change nearly every aspect of the iPhone application software and the user interface. While most of the iPhone applications initially had fewer than one full-time engineer assigned to them, collectively all the iPhone applications were owned by every software engineer on the team. Each member of the team routinely interacted with every other team member.

In September 2005, the team encountered a potential problem that could have led to the project's cancellation. Ken Kocienda, a software engineer on the team, wrote,

> I remember Scott Forstall [SVP of Software and in charge of the secret project] sitting in an office chair, leaning forward, cupping the Wallaby screen [the name of the iPhone prototype that was tethered to a Mac computer] in his hands as he attempted to use the keyboard demo....Try as he might, Scott repeatedly failed to thumb-type anything intelligible...Scott kept trying, deleting backward and then typing again...Holding it closer, he focused intently on the screen and slowly moved his right index finger toward the S key, intending to type the first letter of his name. He couldn't. The keys were too small, and the software was hopelessly confused. No matter what he tried, Scott couldn't type 'Scott.'[12]

Two days later, Forstall instructed everyone to stop what they were doing and work on solving the keyboard problem. No one had ever tried to make a usable keyboard on a screen with a width less than the height of a credit card. As Forstall discovered, people couldn't aim their fingers accurately enough when the keyboard letters were shrunk that small. In the following month, everyone on the team worked to individually create prototypes of potential ways to allow people to type using a non-hardware keyboard.

The designers understood the stakes of not solving this problem. Kocienda wrote, "Would Purple be cancelled? [Forstall] didn't come out and say it that way, but he didn't have to. In all my years at Apple, we'd never halted a fifteen-person project to focus everyone on a single problem."[13]*

At the end of the month, Forstall tried each of the prototypes the engineers had prepared in a "keyboard derby." Kocienda had created five different prototypes and submitted the one he thought was most promising. After evaluating all the proposals, Forstall chose Kocienda's. It was the only one that seemed to impress Forstall, generating the reaction "This is amazing!" It was novel because it used a dictionary to present candidate words to the users.

Kocienda was given the responsibility of continuing the research and creating the final keyboard design. He continued to iterate and experiment, able to make changes to the keyboard code and test them within minutes or hours. Each day, his teammates would load the updated keyboard software onto their Wallaby prototype devices to try it out. However, for months, despite his attempts at improvements, "the feedback came back to me loud and clear. It was too hard to build up typing speed. The keys were too small, key-by-key accuracy was too low, and entering text involved too much looking in the suggestion bar. Those suggestion bar bubbles were like speed bumps."[14]

After months of iteration, Kocienda had a colleague try a prototype that autocorrected when the space bar was hit. He was astounded at the results: "He thumb-typed as fast as he could. He typed, typed, typed. He never paused or stopped to look up. He trusted the software. When he was done typing his long sentence, he typed a period. Then he looked up at the text to see how he did. [It was] just as he intended."[15]

"We couldn't believe how well the dictionary figured out everything. Richard just typed far more quickly than anybody had ever typed anything

---

* Inability to type accurately on the iPhone would have likely led to its cancellation. The inability to input text on Apple's previous handheld device, the Newton, led to widespread industry ridicule.

on a Wallaby," Kocienda wrote.[16] Suspicious that somehow the results weren't real, Kocienda checked the log file on his Mac, and "it showed that Richard's actual typing was horribly imprecise, a complete mess, like a person hilariously failing a spelling sobriety test: Tge quixk brpwm foz jimprd ivrr rhe kazy..."[17]

Even after this success, Kocienda continued to refine the keyboard code, nearly until the phone started shipping six months after Jobs's announcement in June 2007. The iPhone became a massive success, partially enabled by how quickly people, even young children, could immediately pick it up and use it.

FIGURE 8.3 Incremental Prototypes of the Apple iPhone Keyboard

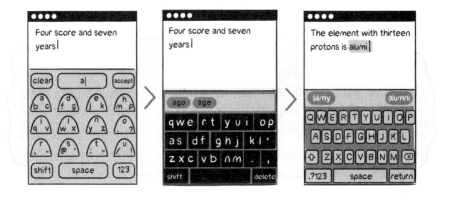

The leftmost picture shows Kacienda's original prototype; the rightmost, the finished product that shipped with the iPhone.

Adapted from: Ken Kocienda, *Creative Selection: Inside Apple's Design Process During the Golden Age of Steve Jobs* (New York: St. Martin's Press, 2018).

The success of the iPhone software (and its on-screen keyboard) was made possible because the iPhone software team used an incremental approach. Among other things, they used the already-validated OS X operating system and concentrated their attention on novel problems instead, such as the keyboard. The small team, working in this new model line, was able to rapidly iterate and explore a huge number of possibilities and create a mobile phone that looked nothing like what had come before.

Nokia

Nokia, the leader for mobile phones when the first iPhone came out, struggled to get a competitive smartphone product to market in 2008, despite a workforce of 123,000 employees and €51 billion (~$79 billion) in revenue. In their smartphone operating system, Nokia did not create the Layer 3 wiring to adequately separate the novel from the known. Instead, they were forced to use an "everything all at once" pattern that slowed down the development and deployment of new ideas.

The problem was evident as early as 2006. Nokia was introducing dozens of phones each year. But the most sophisticated phones, which might compete against the iPhone and soon-to-be released Android phones, were suffering from software delays.

In 2009, Risto Siilasmaa, a Nokia board member, learned it took engineers over forty-eight hours to compile the Symbian operating system.[18] Worse, Siilasmaa discovered that it took two weeks for engineers to get a software build that they could run on a prototype because software needed to be integrated from teams spread out around the world.

Part of Nokia's troubling situation was that they couldn't partition the novel from the known and add novelty in small bits. Unlike Apple, which had their own operating system that they could modify for the iPhone, Nokia's phone ran on an operating system licensed from Symbian. Symbian was also licensed to and supported 150 other models from Nokia rivals, such as Sony, Ericsson, and Panasonic.

In the past, Symbian customers were able to get to market faster, but when it came time to transition from cell phones to smartphones, Nokia (and presumably the other Symbian customers) didn't have enough control over the core technology: they couldn't add or remove functionality quickly enough to incrementally build the needed novelty. In other words, they couldn't break the big problem of developing a competitive smartphone into smaller, more manageable pieces.

This was further exacerbated by customizations created by the multiple Nokia phone teams that were never added to a common stable base, meaning Nokia phone software teams couldn't build upon the work of other teams. Nokia's Layer 3 decisions and resulting situation serve as a striking contrast to the minimalist, focused approach that Apple adopted.

To turn the situation around, in May 2010, Nokia's board replaced its CEO,[*][19] hiring Stephen Elop from Microsoft. He abandoned Symbian, instead adopting Windows Mobile OS.[†] But it was too late. By 2013, Nokia's market share had fallen from 39% to 3%.[20] Microsoft bought what remained for $7.2 billion, just 3% of their peak valuation of $250 billion in 2000.[21]

Lessons and Guidance

There are two aspects of incrementalization: (1) partitioning what is known from what is novel and (2) adding novelty in many small bites rather than a few large bites. The Apple iPhone team did just this. They were a small team in the larger enterprise (i.e., a model line). In other words, they created a Layer 3 partitioning of processes and procedures.

In terms of Layer 1 technical problems, the iPhone team based their operating system on the tried-and-true (known) OS X, which was already validated on other Apple products. The iPhone team also reduced their design reach for the first iPhone's software, restricting it to a small number of applications and only one phone model.

This partitioning of Layer 1 technology and Layer 3 processes meant the iPhone team could quickly iterate and experiment, adding novelty bit by bit, as with the iPhone keyboard. The resulting product redefined what consumers expect from mobile devices.

In contrast, Nokia's reliance on the Symbian OS made it difficult to incrementally develop novelty to compete with the iPhone. Having more engineers didn't prove to be an advantage, as teams enjoyed no independence of action and couldn't test novel ideas quickly and nondisruptively. Their changes were snarled in the complex whole of the Symbian OS. Compared with the iPhone software team, they iterated far more slowly and could try out only a much smaller number of options, limiting their ability to experiment and iterate in a fast-moving market. By the interplay of Layer 1 and Layer 3 architecture, they weren't wired to beat Apple.

---

* In Part IV: Amplification, we will discuss further how the discovery of the two-day compile times led to Siilasmaa and the board of directors searching for a new CEO.

† This bet did not work well either but was arguably the best bet to achieve Nokia's strategic goal, which was to either create or participate in a winning software ecosystem.

In other words, Apple had created a small couch, which a few people could move, while Nokia had a large couch that was also attached to all the other furniture in the room, which all had to be moved at once.

There are Layer 3 generalizations we can pull from the Wright brothers, Apple, and Nokia case studies of how groups of people must work together to achieve a goal. And, as much as the final products of groups doing science and art differ, it's perhaps not surprising that the creative processes underpinning both depend on incrementalization to achieve great outcomes. For both, people are trying to generate something that doesn't yet exist. They start with only a limited and certainly insufficient understanding. They develop their understanding of what to do and how to do it by putting their intellect to good use and in ways that harness its strengths and also respect its limitations.

For instance, strengths might include its generative ability, the possibility of drawing on multiple inspirations, and synthesizing them into a unique and novel conclusion. Limitations include being unable to make sense of highly complex situations, those in which many factors are at play simultaneously and being changed by large measures along many dimensions.

This same logic underpins creating model lines (an example of Layer 3, incrementalization) or building minimally viable products (an example of fast-feedback experimentation using Layer 1 incrementalization). The result is to test and refine ideas at a small scale, with reduced complexity and subject to fast and frequent feedback before injecting ideas into actual performance.

QUESTIONS FOR THE READER

1. As a leader, take a moment to conduct a self-diagnostic challenge. Examine some initiative for which you are responsible. If you sketched it out, is it obvious what's novel? Has it been partitioned from what is known? If not, you are making the work more difficult than it otherwise might be.

2. When you consider the increments with which you are testing and introducing novelty, are there many small steps or giant leaps? For instance, is the new idea being cycled back and forth among sketches or their equivalents (e.g., scale models, mock-ups, simulations, simplified prototypes)? If not, you might think you're saving yourself time and money by skipping these incremental bits, but taking fewer, larger bites may well set you up to fail.

Simplification by Modularization

The second technique of simplification is modularization, which simplifies problems by partitioning large, complex systems (which have highly intertwined interdependencies) into systems that are more modular. Within this structure, each module has clearly defined boundaries and established conventions for interactions with other modules.

In the following selection of case studies, we'll see this technique used across a variety of circumstances, from a school district navigating the COVID-19 crisis to software design at Amazon. In each case we see how modularization helps organizations move from the *danger zone* into the *winning zone.*

Case Study: School District Modularization and Safe School Reopenings

In March 2020, the approximately fifty million children who attended US public schools[22] were told to stay home. The COVID-19 pandemic had spread quickly, many people had already been killed or made seriously ill, and societal quarantine seemed to be the best way to slow its spread and keep healthcare systems from being overwhelmed. However, there were reasonable and well-founded fears that closing public schools would cause dramatic and lasting socioeconomic consequences on students and families.

So, while closing was necessary, many realized the urgency of getting schools safely reopened. How well that was accomplished across the country differed considerably depending on how senior leaders managed the process. Some took top-down approaches, with "headquarters" developing policies and procedures to be followed throughout their systems. Others delegated authority from the center out to districts, schools, and even individual classes to develop methods for safely reopening that fit their own circumstances. The latter approach, which enabled distributed experimentation and learning, worked much better, as we'll see.

But first, let's break down the differences between top-down and center-out leadership (as illustrated in Figure 8.4). In a top-down approach, leaders keep data and decision-making to themselves. They try to develop solutions for the system as a whole and then push those out to everyone. As we'll see, this is what many school administrators did around the country.

However, this approach immediately impairs people's ability to solve problems iteratively and therefore more quickly. By trying to develop solutions that fit the entirety of their systems, leaders curtail the number of people who can be involved in problem-solving efforts, tethering them in the *danger zone*. This is reminiscent of Gene and Steve in the earliest part of the moving-and-painting vignette but on a much larger scale and with much graver consequences.

FIGURE 8.4 Top-Down vs. Center-Out vs. Hands-Off Approaches
for Leading Distributed Operations

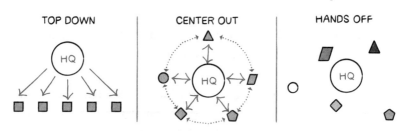

Now consider the advantages that center-out leaders create. They collect as much information as they can get and push it out to those running local operations. Then they delegate authority to local leaders to generate solutions that work for their unique situation. Then the center gathers local lessons learned and synthesizes them into shareable, collective wisdom.

In other words, center-out leaders move themselves and their systems into the *winning zone*. By partitioning the problem (e.g., reopen the entire system) into smaller pieces (i.e., districts, schools, and even classes), center-out leaders increase the number but decrease the complexity of the problem that needs to be solved. Moreover, each partition creates more, smaller coherent units, which means many more minds can be engaged simultaneously rather than sidelined and idled, as in the top-down approach.

Not only that, the center-out approach solves another problem that top-down leaders can't resolve. Because the center-out leaders delegate responsibility, the individual modules have independence of action to create local solutions that fit local conditions. In addition, by maintaining regular communication with and among the localities (e.g., the districts, schools, and classes), leaders at the center can identify and create targeted solutions that align with system issues.

By doing so, they avoid the problems of prescribing a one-size-fits-all solution. They also avoid the perils of leaving everyone to their own devices, as in a hands-off approach. Let us look at the experiences of one exemplar school district, Menomonee Falls in Waukesha County, Wisconsin, to illustrate these points.

On Friday the 13th, March 2020, Wisconsin governor Tony Evers ordered that all K-12 schools be closed.[23] This was consistent with what was happening nationwide. Across the country, school systems struggled to switch to remote learning, some taking weeks to do so. The school district in Menomonee Falls was an exception to the rule. They were running remote lessons by the first week after schools were initially shut down,

Nine months later, at the start of the spring semester, most students around the country still weren't back to in-person learning. Many had to wait until that fall (2021) to finally return (only after vaccinations had finally started to be widely available). By that time, these students had been without in-person learning for more than a year. The terrible consequences of such prolonged absences are still being tabulated.[24]

Menomonee Falls, however, was able to bring students back into classrooms by the fall of 2020, merely months after they had initially closed. They focused on bringing in-person learning to the youngest students first because learning on digital platforms made the least sense for them. They then quickly brought back the rest of the elementary age students, then middle schoolers, and finally high schoolers.

Their leaders made it an imperative to open as quickly as possible. After all, they knew the consequences of prolonged school closures. For instance, at both the county and district levels, they knew that on ordinary snow days staffing at hospitals was difficult because parents had to stay home with their children. School closures also caused businesses to suffer and meant many people weren't drawing a paycheck.

Amid a public health crisis, hospitals had to be fully staffed. People needed to work, and employers needed to operate. And not going to school, particularly for long periods, is disastrous for children. Not only is there steady atrophy of academic lessons previously learned, there's the drop of learned social skills through lack of socialization.

Additionally, schools offer much-needed safety nets for vulnerable children, with school lunches helping to alleviate food insecurity,[25] school nurses giving access to basic healthcare, and the school system providing access to other social services needed for children. Schools, particularly public schools, are linchpins for communities.

Key to Menomonee Falls' success was that at no level of the organization did anyone assume they could generate all the answers for everybody. For example, Dale Shaver, a senior county administrator who was one of the county's resident internal process improvement experts, and other county leaders connected with superintendents of local districts, including Menomonee Falls' Corey Golla. The county executives offered to share what they were learning about COVID-19 transmission, testing, treatment, and the like. The county would also facilitate connections with public health and medical care resources. With these resources in hand, they left it to the superintendents to develop safe reopening plans that fit their districts.

At the district level, Golla took an identical approach. He offered what information and resources he had to the district's school principals. They were given the latitude to develop plans that worked for their parents, teachers, staff, and students.

In return, the district asked to be kept abreast of what was going on so that lessons learned locally could be shared systemically. For instance, early in the pandemic, when schools had been forced to close, a high school librarian and that school's technology director had developed and tested a virtual learning platform. They invited teachers to test the application and rolled out the feedback-driven solutions widely. This system had immediate bene-fit. It was also used during the transition to hybrid learning later that year.

This same center-out approach was used for developing reopening plans—learning occurred locally and informed what happened systemically. Teachers performed experiments that informed principals, and schools performed experiments that informed the district as a whole.

Consider this remarkable learning dynamic: literally the week after the governor closed schools, Menomonee Falls started working toward reopen-ing. Teachers, parents, and students started testing ideas daily. Teachers had meetings each week to compare and contrast ideas they were piloting. Principals learned from those lessons and also met with each other weekly to gather ideas and share what had been discovered. Each Friday, there was a community debrief with parents, staff, and administrators.

Additionally, hospitals in the area were developing safety protocols, and they had relevant data on disease spread. County and district officials didn't try and develop their own approaches, nor did they try to copy and paste hospital approaches onto schools. Instead, officials provided resources and guidance and then delegated decision rights to the schools. School nurses, faculty, and staff were able to take protocols tested in the healthcare sector and apply them in the classroom. Not surprisingly, the nurses had their own collaborative exchanges going on too. Likewise, the chamber of com-merce worked to educate parents about what was being done to keep their kids healthy and what they could do at home to help.*

The result of this modularization across the school district was that, unlike most of the country, Menomonee Falls reopened in-person learn-ing for their youngest students on September 1 of 2020. By October, all of K-12 was doing some form of hybrid learning, with all children having some in-person experience.

---

* Contrast that with another system where "HQ" surveyed parents to find their preferences and capabilities about at-home or in-person learning. However, HQ never shared the detailed data by school, by grade, etc. with principals. Instead, they shared only the aggregated data for the school system as a whole. You can see the obvious problem. Getting policies to work would have required dealing with the local idiosyncrasies in the system, those factors that accounted for the variability between some of the wealthiest neighborhoods in the country and some of the poorest. The average actually had little descriptive or normative value.

To be clear, this wasn't a reckless reopening, putting staff and students at risk to achieve some other objective. Of the approximately seventy-five thousand K-12 students in Waukesha County, about 1% tested positive, and only 1% of those were attributed to in-school transmission. The health department confirmed that cases of transmission from student to staff was three, in total. No in-school transmission between separate classroom cohorts was reported.[26]

In contrast, the districts that took the top-down, non-partitioned, non-modularized approach kept children remote through the spring of 2021, with everyone left waiting for the top-down dissemination of plans, policies, and procedures. In effect, all that ingenuity in local operating units (classes, schools, etc.) was asked to sit idle.

FIGURE 8.5 US Schools vs. Menomonee Falls During COVID-19 Crisis

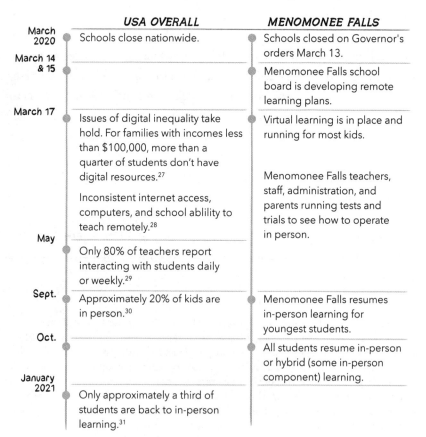

	USA OVERALL	MENOMONEE FALLS
March 2020	Schools close nationwide.	Schools closed on Governor's orders March 13.
March 14 & 15		Menomonee Falls school board is developing remote learning plans.
March 17	Issues of digital inequality take hold. For families with incomes less than $100,000, more than a quarter of students don't have digital resources.[27]	Virtual learning is in place and running for most kids.
	Inconsistent internet access, computers, and school ability to teach remotely.[28]	Menomonee Falls teachers, staff, administration, and parents running tests and trials to see how to operate in person.
May	Only 80% of teachers report interacting with students daily or weekly.[29]	
Sept.	Approximately 20% of kids are in person.[30]	Menomonee Falls resumes in-person learning for youngest students.
Oct.		All students resume in-person or hybrid (some in-person component) learning.
January 2021	Only approximately a third of students are back to in-person learning.[31]	

As you saw in this case study, organizations that are good at creating the conditions in which people can solve difficult problems typically use several mechanisms and techniques at once. For the purposes of reopening, Menomonee Falls and Waukesha County used modularization heavily. To start up online learning quickly after schools were ordered closed, they depended on incrementalization as a useful technique. Menomonee Falls had lots of practice building reliable systems for remote learning for snow days. This was Wisconsin, after all. So, when schools were shut in March 2020, they weren't starting from scratch. They built on what they already knew and added the novelty of snow day education, but for an extended period.

Next, we look at an example of the rapid learning that a center-out modular approach enables in a totally different context: the US Navy.

Case Study: **Modularization in Mastering New Naval Technology**[32]

The US Navy landed on a center-out instead of a top-down approach to leadership in the early 1900s. At the time, ship technology was going through a massive change. For centuries, warships had been configured with side-mounted guns. Previous ship advances—shifts from sails to steam and from wooden hulls to steel—hadn't affected tactics. Line up your ship within some hundreds of yards of your foe and trust that you can blast them away more furiously than they can blast you. For centuries, naval warfare was very personal, conducted over small distances.

Turreted guns, which could be elevated vertically and rotated horizontally, changed the equation. Individual guns could be aimed and targeted, not the whole ship, somewhat independently. And they could fire upon targets much farther away. The war-fighting problem went from maneuvering the entire ship to aiming each weapon at a target that might be out of sight. That wasn't easy. For instance, at Manila Bay and Santiago during the Spanish American War (1898), hit rates were between just 1% and 2%.

The Royal Navy had introduced "continuous aim and fire." Rather than fix the guns' pitch and wait for the deck to roll onto target, crews would continually adjust to stay on target. Doing so offered the chance of firing at any moment, not just during a roll down or up. As Lieutenant Commander Benjamin F. Armstrong wrote, "The British had improved their accuracy by an order of magnitude while nearly quadrupling their rate of fire."[33]

FIGURE 8.6 Changes in Naval War Ships Pre- and Post-1900

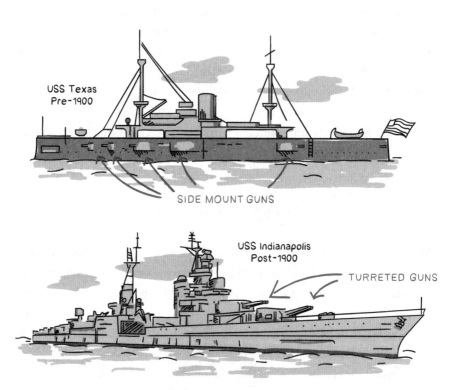

When the US Navy lacked such an approach, one might have expected top officers to take a top-down approach, assigning the problem to some dedicated team of "experts," having the experts determine solutions, and then having those solutions assigned to ships to be followed compliantly. Instead, leadership partitioned the larger system into many smaller, coherent, modular units; supported each unit in running experiments; and gathered the lessons learned for shared benefit.

William Sims, a junior officer, established target ranges where ships and their crews could test their approaches for targeting and firing accurately. The range gave them an opportunity to experiment, and it became a forum for disseminating lessons learned—from failures and successes—and advancing the collective understanding.

The problems revealed and solved were plenty. Giving liberty to turrets to aim and fire revealed inadequacies in ship-wide communication. This prompted more experimentation and the creation of "fire control systems." Someone aloft would spot targets and call for corrections.* Further experimentation revealed the need for range finders and range projectors, substituting for visual judgment and manual calculation.

As experiments were carried out, each problem that was resolved led to the realization of a new problem. Many were ship-level problems, like just described. Others, like coordinating battleships versus coordinating those with side-mounted weapons, rose to the fleet level for command, control, coordination, etc. Lt. Commander Armstrong wrote, "The system they introduced increased the speed with which American gunners hit their targets by 100 percent and the effectiveness of American batteries by 500 percent."[34]

Lessons and Guidance

The experience of Waukesha County and Menomonee Falls illustrates the power of modularization in the form of center-out versus top-down leadership. Top-down leadership tries to promote uniformity through the commonality of policies, procedures, routines, and regulations. When everyone adheres to the same standards,† and those standards are imposed and monitored by a central authority, there's limited discretion to act locally.

---

* This problem of range finding was, in fact, the origin of naval aviation. Coming out of World War I, navies experimented with having float planes assigned to battleships set aflight for a long-range view of targets and feedback on accuracy.

† There's a risk of interpreting "standards" as meaning something that, once written or otherwise established, is unchanging and immutable. That may be true, sometimes. But in the MIT Sloan sailing case study and in other organizations that are wired to win, especially when linearization is employed, standards are used quite differently. For them, standards are an articulation of the best-known approach, in the moment, of how to accomplish something. They adhere to this standard because it increases their chances of being successful. However, relentlessly declaring a standard and using it rigorously also makes it much easier to see when something is going wrong; that is, when the standard is being refuted in practice. In this situation, organizations that are wired to win swarm and solve the problems, making the organization more agile and quicker to improve.

In certain situations, this is done in order to minimize variance in how work is performed, such as when preparing accurate financial reports, training retail staff to ensure a consistent customer experience, or ensuring uniform operations across fast food franchisees, at the expense of accommodating local idiosyncrasies and allowing local problem-solving or improvement.

In contrast, partitioning of authority within Waukesha County allowed more people's ingenuity to be fully engaged. At the local level, individual schools and even individual classrooms were able to address issues for which they had contextual understanding. At the same time, at the core, they could focus on issues that were systemic. Partitioning at the county level gave latitude to districts. Partitioning at the district level gave latitude to schools. And partitioning within schools gave latitude to individual teachers to work with parents to arrive at useful solutions.

The top-down school districts got the worst of all worlds, not the best. They didn't taking advantage of operating-edge understanding of contextual issues, and they allowed only a few to make creative contributions, without the benefit of that contextual understanding. No wonder Menomonee Falls opened by summer 2020's end, whereas places that took the centralized approaches remained closed well past a year.

The same benefits occurred to the US Navy, more than a hundred years earlier, when it partitioned its fleet to individual ships, gave those coherent "modules" latitude to experiment, kept lessons local, gathered general insights to be shared systematically, and converted itself from one of the worst to one of the best navies in terms of gunnery expertise.

In a top-down approach, like that used by many systems, a few people are "allowed to think" while the many—who might have great insights from experience and great minds to interpret and put their findings into action—are sidelined. The center-out approach flips that, making sure that those on the operating edge can contribute.

Certain types of operations are conducive to center-out partitioning. For instance, when operational responsibility is distributed. Or where work happens in coherent local units that do not affect each other, such as schools or ships at sea. In other words, the operating units at the edge are decoupled from each other.

Other examples include different production cells in a factory or different factories in a company; hospitals that have different units in each facility and often several hospitals in a network; drug development that occurs in different labs or different kinds of labs doing work of different types in different parts of the world; or retailing that happens in different stores across a wide geography and markets. There are distributed efforts in hardware and software engineering, education, social services, and just about all other aspects of our commercial and civic enterprises.*

Case Study: Modularization in Computer Software Design: Amazon (Pre-2002)

When an organization is wired to win, teams can do what they need to do because they form a complete, coherent unit and have independence of action. However, teams often find themselves in the opposite situation: they don't form a coherent unit and they are unable to create their desired output independently due to dependencies with many other teams.

This is the situation in which Amazon software engineers found themselves in 2004. In 1997, Amazon had 1.5 million customers and $150 million in revenue. By 2002, they had 35 million customers and $4 billion in revenue.[36] Amazon's growth was propelled by selling an increasingly vast number of products. In 1997, Amazon sold books and music. In 1998, they started selling electronics and toys. By 2002, they were selling products in thirty-five different categories, such as clothing and apparel.

This growth put enormous pressure on the business systems. User and sales growth put pressure on capacity, which put the site in danger of outages, as described in the case study presented in Part II. Also, like most e-commerce sites, Amazon had separate development teams for the home-

---

* Center-out in book retailing has been credited for the surprising rebound of Barnes & Noble's book sales in 2023, where CEO James Daunt gave autonomy of book buying to the local store managers instead of it being dictated by corporate. This enables stores to stock their shelves with the books that are particularly relevant or of interest to their local clientele. On the other hand, corporate alleviates store managers from having to make decisions on non-book (non-idiosyncratic) merchandise (e.g., LEGO®s, stationary, etc.), reducing the store manager's cognitive load. Center-out explains what enables decentralization done well.[35]

page, product pages, shopping cart, checkout, and search. Those teams needed to interact with the teams from product categories, such as books, music, digital, and apparel. Each of those types of products needed to be correctly displayed, added to the shopping cart, shipped to customers, etc. This required a combinatorial increase in the communication and coordination between those teams from small (initially) to insurmountable (eventually). (See also Figure 8.7.)

FIGURE 8.7 Communication between Product Category Teams and E-Commerce Teams at Amazon

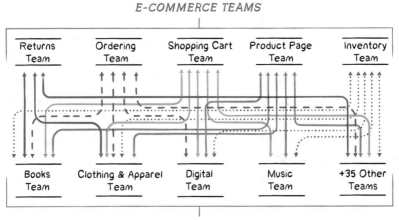

E-COMMERCE TEAMS

PRODUCT CATEGORY TEAMS

During this period, high coordination costs caused certain teams to become "stuck." For instance, with the introduction of digital products, Dr. Werner Vogels, Amazon CTO, described that when those teams "wanted to add something to the order pipeline, a physical delivery address was required....[To change the ordering process, the digital teams] would walk to the 80 different ordering teams and say, 'We need to change this.' The ordering teams would respond that they hadn't budgeted for it."[37*]

Even adding new physical product categories was surprisingly difficult, such as supporting apparel and clothing because of SKUs (stock keeping

---

* This is known as *design-time coupling*, which is the degree to which one service is forced to change because of a change to another service.

unit numbers). Every retailer has SKUs, which are the product numbers used to keep track of inventory and stock internally. However, clothing SKUs are much more complex. They contain varieties, such as category (sweater, T-shirt), size (small, medium, large), style (regular, oversized, slim), color, and so forth.

Because of this, the apparels team not only had to coordinate and work with all the e-commerce teams (e.g., product page, ordering), but their changes to how SKUs were defined potentially affected all the other product category teams as well. Jesse Robbins, availability manager in operations, described the impact: "Changing product SKUs required database schema changes, which were very disruptive. They caused many global outages at Amazon, sometimes even corrupting the database, sometimes causing multi-hour outages. Before apparels, we never had any SKU variants, let alone fifty."[38]

Each year, it took longer and longer to ship features to customers, and the risk of even small changes causing major problems kept growing. In 1998, developers could make changes and deploy them immediately. By 2004, pushing code changes into production required hours, even days, to be deployed.[39]

Teams were no longer able to solve Layer 1 problems because they were too mired in Layer 3 problems—communicating and coordinating to get even small things done. This is because the smallest coherent unit at Amazon became all the software engineers at Amazon, whether in development or operations. Every engineer had to talk to every other engineer because everything was coupled together, depriving everyone of the ability to act independently of each other.

The tightly coupled architecture also made it more difficult to do Layer 1 work. Ruth Malan, an expert in software architecture notes, "As the complexity of the system increases, so, generally, do the cognitive demands on the organization building and evolving it. Managing cognitive load through teams with clear responsibilities and boundaries is a distinguishing focus of [effective] team design."[40]

One more notable problem contributed to the difficulties at Amazon. There were two silos: developers and operations. Developers, who were either in the e-commerce platform teams or in the product category teams, would write the code. The code would then be given to operations, who would test, deploy, and run the code in production, often without ever having the ability to test it in a safer, preproduction environment.

Robbins said of those deployments, "The constant issues and outages that developers caused sometimes ruined lives of operations people, whose job it was to keep Amazon running. Someone would want to launch a product on a Friday, which meant that my team needed to work all weekend to recover from all those problems."[41] This was due to runtime coupling between components in the system.*

Like many other organizations in this situation, their response had been to hire more project managers to help coordinate the work and to put in more approval processes in an attempt to reduce outages. However, this was very different from what Jeff Bezos, founder and then CEO, had hoped for. In the early days of Amazon, Bezos described how he wanted all new hires to be "doers—engineers, developers, perhaps merchandise buyers, but not managers."[42] In other words, he wanted people to be able to spend their time working in Layers 1 and 2 as opposed to coordinating in Layer 3.

His response in 2002 was that the entire company would be restructured around what he called "two-pizza teams"—teams with fewer than ten people (the most that could be reasonably fed by two pizzas). These teams "could be independently set loose on Amazon's biggest problems."[43] Bezos wanted teams to "figure out a way...to communicate less with each other, not more."[44] In effect, he realized that for Layer 3 processes to enable people to use their ingenuity well, Layer 1 and Layer 2 systems had to be designed in such a way that working in small, coherent teams was possible.

To do this, they needed to partition the software that powered Amazon from a large, unwieldy, monolithic whole into many smaller, modular, coherent pieces. Bezos issued a series of mandates, which were described by Steve Yegge, a senior engineer at Amazon, that included the following:[45]

- All teams will henceforth expose their data and functionality through service interfaces.
- Teams must communicate with each other through these interfaces.

---

* *Runtime coupling* is defined as the degree to which the availability of one service is impacted by the availability of another service.

- There will be no other form of interprocess communication allowed.
- Anyone who doesn't do this will be fired.

As a result, for years, engineers had to figure out how to partition their code from everyone else's. They created hard modular boundaries between the different parts of the systems that supported Amazon, with strict interfaces between them (APIs, or application programming interfaces). The only way to access the module was through those APIs. As Bezos said, modules were not allowed to have back doors or direct access to their databases because this would allow components to become tangled again.*

In Figure 8.8 (see page 180), you can see the product page, product categories, and shopping cart are all part of one module and that they share the same database (left-hand side). Changes to any of those components could negatively affect all the other components.

However, after that one module was split into several modules, each gained independence of action (right-hand side). Furthermore, each module had its own database that other modules could not read or modify. This simpler system, made up of more modules but with fewer connections, made the system as a whole easier understand and to change safely.

Now teams could make internal changes to their module without any need to communicate or coordinate with other teams, lowering their coordination cost.† Teams supporting a module could develop, test, and deploy to production independently of each other. No longer could a single database schema change take down all of Amazon.com.

Teams were also reorganized from the functional silos of development and operations into service teams, which had combined development and operational responsibilities. As Vogels described,

---

* The software engineering term for this is *service-oriented architectures*, and this type of effort is often called "monolith to microservice."

† In software engineering, this property of being able to invisibly make internal changes to the internal details and implementation of a module without affecting components that rely on this module is called "information hiding." This property is what enables changes to the module to be made without having to communicate or coordinate with other teams. This decoupling is what allows changes to be made on only one side of the interface.

The traditional model is that you take your software to the wall that separates development and operations, and throw it over and then forget about it. Not at Amazon. *You build it, you run it* [emphasis added]. This brings developers into contact with the day-to-day operation of their software. It also brings them into day-to-day contact with the customer. This customer feedback loop is essential for improving the quality of the service.[46]

FIGURE 8.8 Amazon.com's Evolution from a Highly Integrated Monolith (on the top) to Modular Architecture (on the bottom)

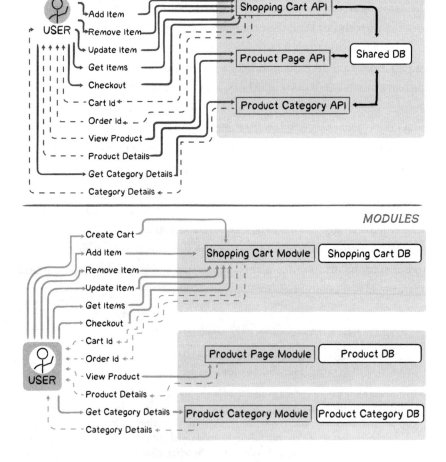

Amazon went from having one module in 1998 to tens of modules in 2004. By 2011, they had hundreds of modules, each able to work independently of each other. The impact on teams' ability to deploy to production is breathtaking.[47]

- 1998: Hundreds of deployments per year (est.)
- 2002: Twenty deployments per year (est.)
- 2011: 5.4 million deployments per year (15,000 deployments per day)
- 2015: 49 million deployments per year (136,000 deployments per day)

This re-architecture reportedly cost $1 billion over about five years[48] but had significant benefits. Amazon engineers could easily scale capacity to keep up with customer growth. They could ship more features that would attract more customers, increase average order size, and create new offerings (e.g., Amazon Prime, Amazon Music, Amazon Video, Alexa). This architecture helped propel Amazon revenue from $2.8 billion in 2000 to $34 billion in 2010 and $386 billion in 2020.[49]*

Case Study: Modularization in Computer Hardware and Software (1960s)

Amazon's engineers were not the first to modularize a large technical system (Layer 1) to reduce the cognitive overload of people in Layer 3 (social circuitry). IBM adopted such an approach for similar reasons some fifty years earlier. In 1960, IBM was the leading mainframe computer company, with a revenue of $3.3 billion,[51] but its market position was at risk. Competitors were entering the market, and IBM needed to figure out how to deliver faster computers (and the software that ran on them) to market more quickly.† Their time-to-market problem was due, at least in part,

---

* Notably, some of the internal services that Amazon.com created to enable scalability and reliability became the basis of Amazon Web Services (AWS), a technology any company can now use for their own purposes. AWS is now the largest profit generator for Amazon, generating $80 billion in revenue in 2022 and 75% of overall profits.[50]

† This rate of CPU performance increase is called Moore's Law, which held true for nearly sixty years.

to coordination costs. Design teams had to be highly integrated, which meant they had limited independence of action (Layer 3), because the systems they designed were tightly coupled (Layer 1). A CPU change might require a memory change and maybe even software changes. This coupling compounded to make any change difficult, requiring communication, coordination, or approvals across thousands of engineers.

And worse, because software design was so tightly coupled to the underlying hardware design, software was incompatible from one hardware system to the next, requiring customers to rewrite their software every time they changed computer systems. And if customers had to rewrite their software anyway, it became easier for them to consider another vendor.*

In response, IBM developed the System/360 family of computers. They varied by processing power, depending on customer needs, but they all ran the same software, solving for the compatibility and upgrade problem. This project was the first to decouple software from the hardware it ran on, giving software and hardware engineers the independence of action they lacked.

But the hardware designs were still highly coupled. This created the same struggle with coordination costs. This impacted development and delivery speed, as well as compatibility issues that affected customer migration from one system to the next. To address this, IBM made the revolutionary decision in 1961 to modularize hardware components (such as CPUs, memory, tape and disk drives, terminals, and keyboards), making them "plug compatible" and interchangeable, available to be used across the entire System/360 family of computers.[52]

By partitioning the system into modular components that connected through stable interfaces, IBM made it possible for groups to work, experiment, and make improvements in parallel, without the constant communication, coordination, and joint approvals previously required.

In *Design Rules*, Dr. Carliss Baldwin and Dr. Kim Clark wrote, "For the first time in history, a computer system did not have to be created by a close-knit team of designers."[53] Like at Amazon fifty years later, chang-

---

* This was in an era when almost all software was custom built, so replacing the software from a commercially supported package or competitor was rarely an option.

ing the technical system's architecture (Layer 1) created opportunities for designers to work independently (Layer 3) and for customers to have a range of options they previously lacked.

The System/360 program would be the largest hardware and software effort ever undertaken up to that point,* with a cost estimated over $5 billion,† two times higher than IBM's annual revenue at the time,[54] and involving thousands of engineers.[55] When the System/360 computers were introduced four years later in 1964, they launched five compatible computers, with 150 interchangeable peripherals and software products.[56]

It was an enormous commercial success, giving IBM market dominance that lasted thirty years. Revenue grew from $3.3 billion in 1960 to $7.5 billion in 1970 and $26.2 billion in 1980, with descendants of the System/360 increasing IBM's cash flow by twenty times during that same period.[57]

Lessons and Guidance

Both Amazon and IBM were able to create huge advantages for themselves by modularizing their systems. They partitioned the whole into smaller, more coherent, and less tightly coupled pieces so that they could be designed and delivered independently.

They solved for *design-time coupling*, which had forced engineering changes to be coordinated across a vast surface area. This led to high coordination costs, such as Amazon engineers having to talk to sixty other teams.

They also solved for *runtime coupling*, where failures in one area of the system had caused other areas of the system to fail. For instance, with Amazon Obidos, if searching the product database became overloaded and slow, it likely meant that all other areas of the site became slow as well.

This is similar to the moving-and-painting vignette. During Gene and Steve's first attempt, there was no modularization. Gene and Steve approached the entirety of the project as a coherent unit, trying to schedule all the people across all the work, all at once. This was an impossible coordination problem, just as it was for Amazon and IBM. Changing the

---

* This would remain unsurpassed until the 2010s, with the emergence of cloud vendors (e.g., Amazon, Google, Microsoft), which each built scores of datacenters, operating hundreds of thousands, sometimes millions, of servers for their customers.

† $50 billion in 2022 dollars.

architecture of technical systems (Layer 1) liberated people from having to navigate and solve coordination problems (Layer 3), enabling them to better focus on the work at hand.

By creating modules, they significantly reduced the design-time coupling, if not eliminated it. Reducing design-time and runtime coupling contributes to agility in software development and resilience in operations. In software development, architecture dictates how organizations are wired and has been shown to be a top predictor of performance. The research for the State of DevOps Reports from 2013 to 2019 was a cross-population study that spanned over thirty-six thousand respondents over six years. It showed that architecture determined if it was possible for teams to:[58]

- make large-scale changes to the design of the system without the permission of someone outside the team or depending on other teams;
- complete their work without fine-grained communication and coordination with people outside the team;
- deploy and release their product or service on demand, independent of other services the product or service depends upon; and
- do most of their testing on demand, without requiring an integrated test environment.

But beware. It is possible to over partition systems. In software engineering, teams have sometimes overly modularized their system to the point where modules are no longer coherent units. As a result, to get something meaningful done requires coordinating across many teams. It is as if Gene and Steve sawed their couch in half for the purpose of gaining independence of action but ended up with neither a couch nor a chair.*

QUESTIONS FOR THE READER

1. Once again, let's take a moment as a leader to conduct a self-diagnostic. As we asked at the end of the section on incrementaliza-

---

* This happens when a "microservice" strategy is taken too far.

tion, examine some initiative for which you are responsible. Particularly for what is novel and also for what is not, have you found ways to partition the large integrated whole of the system into distinct, coherent pieces? Do those pieces contain some small subset of the system's total functionality?

Simplification by Linearization

The final technique within simplification is linearization, which simplifies processes by directly connecting people who need to collaborate, so they don't have to communicate up and down through siloed functions, thereby losing frequency, speed, and detail in their communications and collaborations. This frees people's time and energy from having to figure out *how* to get things done (a Layer 3 problem), so they can actually do their Layer 1 and 2 work. When linearization is wired into our work, the key elements of standardization, stabilization, and self-synchronization become the norm.

Linearization is used across a variety of circumstances, from developing new medications to designing new jet engines to planning and conducting military operations. In each case, we see how linearization helps organizations move from the *danger zone* into the *winning zone*.

Case Study: Using Linearization to Accelerate Drug Development

When medications are successfully brought to market, society benefits greatly. We all shared this experience, globally, in 2021 when COVID-19 vaccines became available, allowing society to return to some normalcy. Unfortunately, in general, developing safe and effective medications has low odds, high and rising costs, and lengthening lead times.[59] This means greater cost to society, even for successful therapies, with painful consequences to people for whom relief does not arrive.

Many factors make developing medications challenging, including the biochemistry and technology involved (issues in Layers 1 and 2). In addition, the social circuitry of drug development can be hampered by siloed processes that limit creative collaboration. People can have different priorities, so they aren't working toward a common purpose. Also, they can suffer delays because people whose work is interconnected are not in direct communication with one another.

One top pharmaceutical company recognized this problem and used a model-line team to linearize their siloed processes. In doing so, they cut the time required for an early phase of discovery by half. They delivered better output into the next steps of drug development, and spread what they learned to two dozen other areas in their firm. Here's how that happened.

Discovering promising medications starts with identifying proteins that are causing symptoms (targets). Next comes identifying potential therapies in "high-throughput screening" (HTS). HTS generates "hits," chemicals that indicate some promise. Next comes "hit to lead." Informed by what hit, chemists, biologists, and their colleagues design, synthesize, and test molecules that might have promising properties. The best of those become leads, where the most promising are developed further.

At this pharmaceutical company, the area of hit-to-lead was picked as the perfect place for a pilot model line to test ways to linearize their siloed work. Hit-to-lead had active interest from leaders, and it contained sufficient complexity and novelty for it to be a microcosm of the broader drug development undertaking.

The linearization of the workflows in hit-to-lead established unifying priorities across different functions. This helped people to start linking their individual efforts into a collective purpose. It also created an opportunity for rich, collaborative discussion between people whose work was interdependent.

In the past, chemists and biologists communicated mainly through physical material (e.g., molecule samples to be tested and test results sent back with rudimentary explanations). In contrast, linearization created the opportunity for cross-functional problem-solving.

Let's break down the details of what this model line did. Each specialist has a unique role to play. Chemists envision molecules that will "modulate" the target and develop designs for them. Then, they have to figure out the steps, the series of chemical reactions by which the molecules can be constructed (i.e., made, synthesized).

Biologists develop and conduct tests to assess how those molecules might bind to the target, to what degree the binding might affect their behavior, and otherwise give early indication to how they might behave as a valuable medication.* Together, their work forms the design-make-test cycle (Figure 8.9), the learning engine by which the possibility of good ideas (i.e., hits on targets) are turned into promising leads.

FIGURE 8.9 Design-Make-Test Cycle Connecting Chemistry and Biology Labs with Supporting Services Indicated

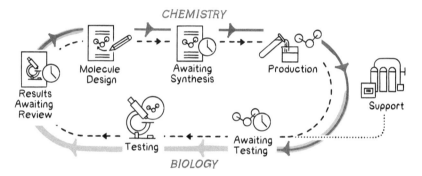

More has to occur in support. There are elaborate purification steps so what was synthesized can be tested. Oftentimes, materials that are needed to run experiments, both in chemistry and biology labs, are esoteric and have to be acquired or created, hence the criticality of "chem supplies" as part of the team.

During the pilot model line, the team first assessed how long it took molecules to be developed. Records showed that for whatever the indicated total time spent on the direct work of designing, making, or testing molecules was, the elapsed time was two or three times longer. Clearly, the parts weren't coming together. Part of the problem was silos. Coordination and prioritization occurred episodically. Typically, problems had to be escalated to lab directors or even higher to get things reprioritized and coordinated.

Integrating work wasn't a problem just across functions but also within each lab. For instance, one chemist was curious about a particular feature

---

* Their relationship is similar to design/development and QA/information security in software design and delivery, design/engineering, and those who create the functional and stress tests for new engineered systems in aerospace, and so forth.

of a certain molecule, so he synthesized it and sent it for testing. Unbeknownst to him, creating and running tests consumed three work weeks in the biology lab and yielded results that did little to inform the program that had been prioritized.*

To align individual efforts, the chemistry lab leader worked with her colleagues to prioritize the questions they asked and the top problems they would study and resolve first, second, and so forth.† Establishing near-term goals helped them decide what tasks needed to be performed, in what order, and by whom to meet those objectives. In other words, they created a temporary standardized workflow and near-term plan.‡

This standardized workflow within chemistry also established the workflow downstream, for purification and biology. Knowing the sequence, those departments could set a sequence by which they could purify which materials or run which tests. In other words, they could align with their own colleagues on a committed workflow. Chem supplies also had better orientation about what they needed to accomplish when.

When things were siloed and connections haphazard, there was little opportunity for chemists to clarify what they hoped to learn from the tests in biology. Nor could biologists explain important insights provided by the data they were generating.

When they created linear flows, it became more obvious who was doing what and from whom and to whom work was being passed; there then

---

* Another chemist, when he moved on to another assignment, left behind some two hundred molecules that he had synthesized because he was curious about them and how he might actually construct them. They sat in his locker and weren't even sent forward to the biology lab.

† She well understood that with science so cutting edge, there would be no consensus as to what these priorities would be, nor was she trying to impose her will on her colleagues, regardless of their points of view. Rather, they all agreed to establish a flow of work, so it would be more obvious what their collective hypotheses were and what they were actively trying to learn.

‡ This alludes to a framework introduced in *The High-Velocity Edge* that all systems can be specified in terms of: (1) what will be generated as output, (2) the sequence of tasks that will generate that output and who is responsible for doing what, (3) how exchanges will be made between adjacent tasks, and (4) how individual tasks will be performed. For each of these prespecifications, there can be tests built in to indicate early and often that there are problems that, once seen, can be swarmed to prevent their spread and to begin their solution.

could be conversations between particular chemists, biologists, and people working in purification and supplies to establish what was needed from one another.

With those handoff conditions better established, the chemists and biologists formed a coherent unit. They could now could do their work of designing and making molecules or creating and conducting tests without anyone constantly reprioritizing their efforts. These direct connections meant quicker turnaround on results and a richer discussion about what the results meant.

As the pilot model-line's leaders linearized the system from loosely connected silos to more direct connections along the flow of work, they had another realization; they couldn't fully load everyone's time with work. Otherwise, when one person had delays or difficulties, those would spread, impacting other people in the workflow.

Before, in pursuit of high output, they had assigned work to avoid wasted time. Even leaders assigned themselves a full load of hands-on research work. However, once they linearized, that proved counterproductive. If someone had a particularly hard problem, they had a dilemma. They could push their work forward before they were really done to pick up the next piece in the flow. Or, they could continue working on the problem but create delays for those waiting on them.

The leaders recognized this conundrum and put in a stabilization mechanism: they assigned only enough work to account for 85% of their colleagues' time. This gave everyone some slack to deal with unexpected challenges. In addition, leaders stopped assigning themselves hands-on (bench top) work, so they could lend their own minds and hands to resolving especially hard problems. By creating simple flows, establishing standards, and having stabilizing mechanisms, they had no more need for elaborate schedules or crazed expediting. With everything simpler and more self-evident, work became more naturally self-synchronizing.*

---

* Don Reinertsen has written extensively on the need for people in a system to have "slack time" in software development. The wait time for a service (such as a functional expert working on a job) increases exponentially as their utilization goes up. For instance, the wait time is nine times longer when that resource is 90% utilized versus 50% utilized. (For the curious reader, this is a property of queues such as those at supermarket checkouts and customer service calls, known formally as M/M/∞ queues.)

It is important to note here that linearized processes can be fragile. By lining work in sequence and having a minimum buffer between steps, an aberration at one location can, if not contained, rapidly cause cascading effects. Delays get imposed by those downstream who are starved for inputs or those upstream who are blocked from delivering their outputs. Defects become required rework on those accepting them, and ambiguity requires someone else reestablishing clarity. Without various stabilization mechanisms, workflows can quickly devolve into "job shops," with all the characteristic reporting, monitoring, scheduling, expediting, firefighting, and other harried behavior.

Bear in mind, everything done on this model-line pilot was focused on rewiring the social circuitry (Layer 3). No people or other resources were added (Layer 1), nor was there new equipment (Layer 2). Nevertheless, the results achieved on this pilot were significant.

The pilot program benchmarked itself against projects that had been considered successful. A previous benchmark project had needed more than a year to complete hit-to-lead. The model-line pilot completed this in only six months. The benchmarked programs had required up to sixty design-make-test cycles. The model-line pilot team needed only nineteen. Moreover, the model-line pilot team was able to deliver more leads of higher quality and greater promise then the previous successful benchmark programs.

TABLE 8.1 Results of the Model-Line Experiment

	BENCHMARK PROGRAM	PILOT PROGRAM	IMPROVEMENT
Total time	13 months	6 months	2x faster
Design-make-test cycles	55	19	3x more efficient
Results transmitted to "lead development"	72 qualified hits (< 10 clusters) ~14 internal chemists 5 lead series delivered	340+ qualified hits (100+ clusters) ~16 internal chemists 5+ lead series projected	5x more hits (All achieved with approximately the same size of staff.)

There's one last point. Earlier, we made the case that model lines create opportunities to test ideas and build capabilities on a small scale. The opportunity to learn through fast, frequent feedback from experiences that are nondisruptive to the larger enterprise creates that latitude. Once built, there's a chance for those who've created competency to fan it out.

That's exactly what happened. Not only did the pilot's leaders get a significant reduction in effort required to get better results, but their example also became an example of how to linearize other aspects of drug development, including ten other R&D efforts, thirteen enabling technologies that could be used in other programs, and even three other non-R&D efforts, affecting hundreds of scientists within the firm.

Case Study: Using Linearization to Accelerate Jet Engine Design[60]

Using linearization to improve development and design processes is certainly not limited to early-stage drug development. Improving social circuitry through linearization and standardization, with mechanisms to keep workflows stable and self-synchronized, paid huge dividends to Pratt & Whitney's jet engine efforts.

In the 1990s, Pratt & Whitney had been suffering a series of expensive losses in contests to get their engines on new aircraft, both military and commercial. They were organized in functional silos, like the pharmaceutical company, and suffered the same attendant downside. People worked with a limited sense of the overall program. And, coordination and integration didn't occur within the flow of work but was done by senior leaders at the top of the silos. This made Pratt & Whitney uncompetitive in timeliness, cost, and quality of its designs.

The company remedied this by creating processes that followed how work had to flow across functional silos (the social circuitry of Layer 3). They also created standards to provide clarity around design objectives, a linearized workflow to cut across functions, and standards for handoffs between one step and the next. Such clarity made it easier for engineers to understand how to conduct their own work. And such clarity not only equipped people to succeed on their first passes, but to succeed every time a standard was used, because there was feedback about how it could be improved.

For Pratt, the benefits were enormous. The pilot program completed development in three years versus an expected four. And it had half the engineering change orders than typical (an indicator of quality and cost). With this new workflow, Pratt & Whitney won the contest for the F-35 Joint Strike Fighter. With expected production for the US and allies of 3,500 jets at $10 million per engine, it was a $35 billion revenue win, and that's before maintenance contracts and replacement parts.

Case Study: Linearization: Team of Teams as Another Process-Building, Silo-Bridging Case[61]

There is a common theme that organizations siloed around functions and technical specialties have trouble integrating individual effort into collective action toward a common purpose. Because of that inability to integrate easily, performance suffers. This is true not only in the private sector but for high-stakes military operations as well.

The book *Team of Teams* by Stanley McChrystal, Tantum Collins, David Silverman, and Chris Fussell introduced a paradox. On the one hand, the US military's Joint Special Operations Command (JSOC) had highly trained, well-equipped, motivated soldiers, sailors, airmen, marines, and civilians in its ranks. They were assigned the important mission of defeating Al Qaeda in Iraq. Al Qaeda, on the other hand, was operating seemingly unchecked, using nihilistic terrorist tactics (roadside explosives, suicide bombers, etc.).

The problem was, JSOC depended on the contributions of numerous military, intelligence, and diplomatic organizations whose efforts weren't well integrated. For instance, information might be gathered on a raid, but it took too long to get to the analysts. By the time that data was analyzed, it was stale and could not be used to direct other operators to capture or kill the enemy.

To solve this problem, leaders linearized the process from when information was first gathered, through when it was analyzed, to when it was acted on. This created the social circuitry (Layer 3) that matched how one action fed the next, increased processing speed, and lowered the need for senior leaders of each silo to coordinate.

Lieutenant Commander David Silverman, a former US Navy SEAL and one of the coauthors of *Team of Teams*, described how "these communication mechanisms gave leaders the ability to...empower them to operate at the local level....[We knew] the person closest to the problem is best situated to solve the problem."[62] Leaders were then able to redirect their attention to supporting those in the field and otherwise putting their minds and hands directly on JSOC's work. With no extra people, money, or other resources, JSOC's operational tempo increased from five raids per month to three hundred.[63] Silverman described the result as a "shared consciousness" that enabled over fifteen thousand people across twenty-seven countries to achieve their goals of dismantling Al Qaeda in Iraq.[64]

Lessons and Guidance

The drug development model-line pilot team was wired across several silos (chem lab, bio lab, purification, and chem supplies) and myriad disciplines. This challenged the notion that cutting-edge, novel work has to be processed in an unstructured, serendipitous fashion. Rather, they realized that the experimental discipline they used on their bench tops to build knowledge rigorously and well around Layer 1 problems could be applied to Layer 3 problems as well.

The *Team of Teams* and Pratt & Whitney case studies show that as different as organizations are in Layer 1 and Layer 2, when it comes to Layer 3, issues of designing effective systems for coordination and collaboration, the same principles apply.

- Define objectives for the group as a whole.
- Create a simple workflow that cuts across functions (by assigning resources from particular functions into the workflow).
- Create partitions within the flow so how people interact across specialties is clear. This allows independence of action to be enjoyed behind the partition.
- Build slack and stabilization mechanisms into the work, behind partitions, to keep problems isolated.

QUESTIONS FOR THE READER

1. Once again, as a leader, take a self-diagnostic challenge. Examine some initiative for which you are responsible. For the flow of work required, have you identified where people in different functions, departments, etc. have to have ideas bubbled to the top of their operating unit for integration by those in charge of each of those?
2. Are direct connections made between people who create and deliver output from one step to be used as inputs at the next (and where creative collaboration has to occur across the boundaries)?
3. Do people receive inputs of the same type from many sources (versus one or a few) and deliver output (of the same type) to many users (versus one or a few)?
4. Can you create parallel simpler flows (rather than the intertwined ones) so it's obvious to people on whom they are dependent, who depend on them, and with whom they should be in creative collaboration?

Conclusion

The enormous, observable differences in performance among competitors are explainable by differences in the overlay of social circuitry—the processes, procedures, routines, and norms that exist at Layer 3. These determine the conditions in which people solve technical problems individually and collaboratively at Layer 1 and Layer 2.

Simplification highlights how leaders can manage the conditions in which people are operating, so solving problems—particularly complex ones—is quicker, easier, and more productive. Simplification moves people in the direction of the *winning zone* via the following:

- Easier experiments: Simplification creates opportunities to solve smaller problems; experimentation is quicker, easier, and cheaper.
- Easier learning from experience and experiments: Through simplification, sense-making becomes easier (e.g., action-and-out-

come, cause-and-effect, action-reaction) because the situations are simpler, with fewer factors in play that have less intertwined relationships.

- More experiments: Simplification enables more frequent iterations, happening either in parallel (through modularization) or within sequential processes (through linearization), which require teams performing the experiment to be a coherent whole (through incrementalization).

- Distributed learning across the enterprise: Simplification allows problem-solving to occur in parallel because of partitioning, multiple experiments occurring in parallel, or partitioning of linear workflows by creating standards and stabilization.

How the three techniques of simplification play out in the cases we've reviewed is summarized in Table 8.2.

TABLE 8.2 Simplification Techniques in Each of the Case Studies

KEY I: Incrementalization, M: Modularization, L: Linearization

NASA DART	I: Make kinetic collision the novelty on top of validated launch, flight, rendezvous, landing communication, and other technologies and techniques of previous missions.
	M: Separate responsibility for launcher, the probe that collided, the probe that did the surveillance and data capture, etc., among different entities.
ARTISTS AND WRIGHT BROTHERS	L: Generate multiple prototypes to test ideas around single problems quickly (like Monet did by using several easels to focus just on lighting in Venice; Wright brothers did this with their high-volume experimentation at Kitty Hawk and elsewhere) or build micro prototypes first, before incrementally building to full-scale model (like Picasso did by having several smaller, rougher test canvases before committing to the masterpiece).
APPLE VS. NOKIA	I: Base the iPhone operating system on the Mac operating system, and focus innovation on the novel problems presented with the applications and their user interfaces of keyboard and screen.

KEY I: Incrementalization, *M:* Modularization, *L:* Linearization

----

SCHOOL REOPENINGS AND NAVY	*M:* Drive data, already-known facts, resources, and authority to act ("independence of action") out to the local operating units; allow experimentation in localized operating units.
	Have "the center" (headquarters) provide resources and do synthesis of local lessons learned into common, shareable knowledge.
AMAZON AND IBM	*M:* Decompose large, highly integrated systems into coherent pieces, each focused on a small portion of the overall functionality. That way, problem-solving happens within the module without needing to coordinate everything at the system level.
	This gives independence of action to the teams, reducing the need to coordinate across boundaries with those responsible for other component subsystems.
DRUG DEVELOPMENT, PRATT & WHITNEY, TEAM OF TEAMS	*L:* Link all contributors to a sequential flow of work that progresses from start to finish. That way, what tasks have to be done, by whom, in what sequence, with what exchanges at the boundaries is made obvious. This allows work to flow more easily and for collaboration to occur more easily from one function to the next, as opposed to when integration occurs only at the tops of the functional silos.

CHAPTER 9

Simplification: Exemplar Case Study and Further Examination

The *Apollo 11* slowification case study in Chapter 5 focused specifically on the crew's successful moon landing, made possible by feedback-rich planning and practice. However, there's more to the story. The vast undertaking that culminated in *Apollo 11* was made possible because NASA also exploited simplification through the techniques of incrementalization, modularization, and linearization.

Exemplar Case Study: NASA Space Program: Mercury, Gemini, and Apollo

In the following sections, we describe how the US space program in the 1960s benefited from simplification by making it easier to solve difficult problems, both individually and collaboratively. First, NASA identified the novel parts of the problem. Then they partitioned those larger problems into smaller, coherent parts (incrementalization). This meant problems could be tackled in parallel because of the independence of action afforded by modularization. After that, problem-solving was made more linear to reduce the cost of coordination and to make collaboration easier.

Incrementalization

Armstrong's declaration that he was taking a small step for man, a giant leap for mankind was certainly poetic. It was also (almost) literally accurate. His step was the culmination of the many previous accomplishments, so many that they might be described as "inchstones" rather than milestones.

This was in contrast to what might have been a "start from scratch and develop a giant leap solution" moment. Rather, each step was added to an already-established foundation. This simplified the problem being solved from "everything all at once" to "new added on top of old."

FIGURE 9.1 Incrementalization of the Space Race

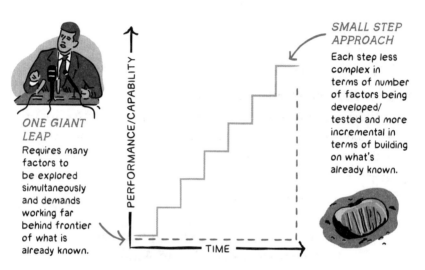

ONE GIANT LEAP
Requires many factors to be explored simultaneously and demands working far behind frontier of what is already known.

SMALL STEP APPROACH
Each step less complex in terms of number of factors being developed/ tested and more incremental in terms of building on what's already known.

The myriad problems that had to be solved for the massive challenge of going to the moon, landing on it, and returning safely to the Earth were partitioned across three distinct programs: Mercury, Gemini, and Apollo, each with their own incremental approach.

The space race started in the 1950s during the Eisenhower administration with the Mercury program, years before Kennedy's 1961 challenge. But it didn't start from scratch. Rather, the first objective wasn't to go to the moon; it was to get astronauts safely launched into orbit and then recovered safely on Earth.

For this, NASA took what was already known and (somewhat) validated. The first class of astronauts was recruited—the Mercury Seven—from experienced pilots from the military. NASA likewise built their missions around rockets that had already been designed, built, and validated. The first flights were suborbital (requiring less boost) and used the Redstone rocket that was taken from an Army missile program. For later orbital flights (needing greater boost), NASA took Atlas D rockets from the Air Force's intercontinental ballistic missile program.

By using booster technology that already had been tested and validated, NASA and its contractors partitioned the known and turned their attention to the novel: developing and deploying technology necessary for human flight in space (communication; navigation; combinations of ground-based, automatic, and manual piloting; life support; reentry; and recovery).

Having partitioned the problems associated with rockets and launch from issues of human flight (the space capsule), NASA and its collaborators further incrementalized their approach. For instance, Alan Shepard was the first American astronaut, conducting a flight of about fifteen minutes and at about 115 miles in altitude.

At first glance, the next flight, by Gus Grissom, seemed repetitive: it was also atop a Redstone rocket, also lasted for about fifteen minutes, and also flew to an altitude of about 115 miles. However, Grissom's flight had been outfitted with different windows, the test-drive of a modification necessary for more complex orbital flights. The controls were also modified to make it easier for the astronaut to control the capsule, which more complex missions would require.

FIGURE 9.2 Incremental Modifications in Mercury Program Flights

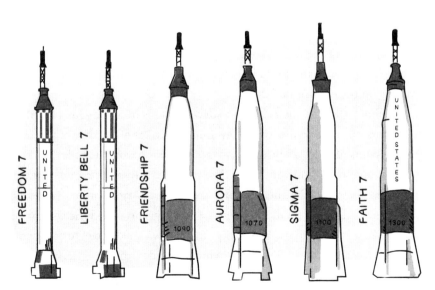

Those first two flights established some stability of the space capsule design—a foundation for the next novelty. John Glenn was launched aloft an Atlas D rocket so he could reach Earth orbit. Modifications of his spacecraft (informed by previous flights) were focused on navigation and communication while orbiting and maneuvering to ensure reentry. The key was navigating into the correct reentry angle (too acute and he'd burn up, too little and he'd be deflected into perpetual orbit).

Scott Carpenter (the Mercury's fourth pilot) repeated Glenn's experience but with the added complexity of various science experiments. The fifth Mercury flight nearly doubled the duration achieved on the previous flights to nine hours. The last Mercury flight lasted thirty-four hours, nearly four times longer than the previous flight. With these accomplishments under their belt, NASA could use astronaut Gordon Cooper's experience to test both the equipment and the pilot more severely. All told, each flight added additional novelty to what had already been validated rather than trying to accomplish everything all at once.

While NASA was experimenting and validating ideas with Mercury, it was also readying the Gemini program for more sophisticated missions and developing its capabilities even further. Gemini crews had two astronauts instead of one, meaning missions could be longer and of greater complexity.

Here, too, NASA maintained a similar incrementalist approach. Gemini missions continued to push the envelope, as it were, adding proficiency in tasks like rendezvousing and working in space suits outside the spacecraft (a capability that had to be developed, tested, and validated in Earth orbit as preparation for astronauts leaving their lunar landing craft and actually walking on the moon's surface).

In short, Gemini was a chance to develop skills necessary for a flight to the moon, but practiced within a few hundred miles of Earth, not the tens of thousands of miles away an actual moon mission would entail.

Incrementalization continued throughout the Apollo program, bringing more clarity to the (near) literal accuracy of Armstrong's statement about having taken a small step. The *Apollo 7* mission tested the command module (the vehicle in which the three-man crew would travel to the moon and back) and the service module (which provided thrust, steering, electrical power, communication, and so forth to get from Earth orbit to lunar orbit and back). These first manned tests were conducted in Earth orbit; however, *Apollo 8*'s crew then built on these accomplishments by making the first flight to the moon and back.

Apollo 9 built on the achievements of *Apollo 7* and *8*. Their mission lasted over a week, maintaining NASA's focus on the physiology and supporting technology for the astronauts' well-being and capability. And while it remained in Earth orbit, it added complexity to *Apollo 7*'s experience. Not only did it launch and orbit, it practiced rendezvousing with a lunar landing module, which had been carried aloft in a separate compartment, thereby pulling forward lessons and skills from Gemini's rendezvous and docking exercises but with equipment that was closer to what would be used for the moon mission. Again, novelty was added in small steps not giant leaps.

Apollo 10 repeated many of the exercises completed by *Apollo 8* and *Apollo 9*. But *Apollo 10*'s mission was not just a synthesis of previous lessons learned. In addition, the crew added novel complexity by descending from sixty miles above the moon's surface to within forty-seven thousand feet.

FIGURE 9.3 Size of Rockets across Mercury, Gemini, and Apollo Programs as Metaphor for Accumulated Knowledge

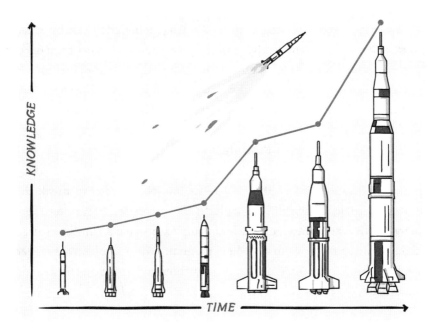

By the time Armstrong and Aldrin left command module pilot Michael Collins behind for their milestone mission with *Apollo 11*, they were drawing on the incrementalized accomplishments from all previous Mercury, Gemini, and Apollo missions. In fact, they built incrementally on their own accomplishments as well, not only from previous Apollo missions. Collin's was on *Gemini X*, which included a rendezvous and an extra-vehicular activity, Aldrin completed a record EVA on *Gemini XII*, and Armstrong docked with another vehicle on *Gemini VIII*. In truth, Armstrong and Aldrin took far more than just "a small step." That said, what was truly novel about their mission was the final forty-seven thousand feet of descent, landing, ambulation on the surface, and return.

Notably, the Soviets started the space race with a substantial head start. For instance, not only was Yuri Gagarin the first person in space, he orbited on that first flight. On the second Soviet mission, cosmonaut Gherman Titov spent a full day in space. In comparison, it wasn't until the third Mercury flight that Glenn orbited, and it wasn't until the sixth flight that Cooper was aloft for a full day. By 1962, the Soviets were flying joint missions of two spacecraft, something the US didn't do until 1965.

But then, the Soviets lost their lead. They didn't achieve a docking until 1969, years after the Gemini accomplished that in 1965. And it wasn't until 1970 that they were achieving long-duration flights in Earth orbit, by which time the Apollo program had been to the moon and back more than once. They had taken a different, non-incremental path to space. The Soviets had fewer learning cycles, each of which required more to be learned. This may be part of the reason why the Soviet's head start soon dissipated.

Modularization

Incrementalization wasn't the only technique NASA used to break the immense problem of sending people to the moon and returning them safely to the Earth into smaller, less complex problems. They also used modularization to break up the whole program, which involved over three hundred thousand people across twenty thousand industrial firms and universities.

We saw just some of that with the Mercury program. NASA picked the Redstone rocket for the first suborbital flights and the Atlas D for the later orbital ones. But it was careful to maintain a common boundary between the space capsules and the rockets, so NASA could experiment with navigation, communication, life support, and the like within the capsule without having to unduly coordinate those changes with changes to the booster rocket itself.

They partitioned further by separating Mercury's one-person missions from the two-person, longer-duration, more complex ones of Gemini. NASA gave itself and its contractors the latitude of extracting lessons from Mercury into Gemini while maintaining independence of action to develop ideas and technology.

For instance, McDonnell Douglas, which was the contractor for the one-astronaut Mercury capsule, was also responsible for Gemini's two-person capsule. But even for the capsule design, McDonnell Douglas took a more modular approach on Gemini than it had on Mercury. Whereas the first capsules had all functions integrated in them, in Gemini, everything needed for reentry was incorporated into the capsule, while propulsion, power, water, and air were contained in a separate adapter module. This gave designers the option to design and test some components simultaneously without having to coordinate those changes or interfere with work being done on other modules.[1]

As systems got greater in scale, scope (functionality), and consequent complexity, modularization continued to be a valuable strategy. *Apollo 7*'s Earth-orbit test of the command and service modules wasn't boosted by the Saturn V rocket that took astronauts to the moon. It was launched on a lesser-powered, less complex Saturn 1B. The lunar landing module was developed as a separate component from the command and service modules (albeit with concern for how it interacted for docking and maneuvering when coupled). This modularization meant the lander could be designed and built by Grumman while separate teams worked on the command and service module at North American Aviation and Rockwell.

As with Amazon and IBM in the previous chapter, modularization reduced the costs of coordination because fewer people needed to be synchronized in joint effort. This increased the creative output of the enterprise by allowing many people to solve problems simultaneously, generating and delivering more value with greater volume and speed.*

Linearization

The manned space missions were not only astounding technological accomplishments; they were also outstanding managerial accomplishments. After all, the cost of the first landing was $19 billion.† It involved the work of three hundred thousand people working for twenty thousand contractors and two hundred universities located in eighty countries.[2]

Integrating efforts from so many people, spread over so many institutions and organizations, across so many locations could not have been possible without a reliable and productive overlay of procedures, processes, and routines (Layer 3 social circuitry).

In fact, its absence contributed to the failures in NASA's earlier Ranger satellite program, whose mission was to gather data about the moon and potential landing sites before manned missions commenced. Those failures were not necessarily attributable to failures of particular components. Rather, failures occurred because of interactions between components at their interfaces (e.g., mismatched connectors, different electrical voltages).[3]

NASA's response to this failure was to implement "systems engineering," as explained by Dr. Stephen Johnson in his book *The Secret of Apollo*. Systems engineering has characteristics similar to linearization, in that it is not only a deliberate approach to managing how different component pieces interacted with each other (e.g., making clear how pieces interacted in Layer 1 and Layer 2). It is also a deliberate approach to managing how the people responsible for different components interact with each other

---

* We also saw a consequence of modularization during the *Apollo 13* emergency. After an oxygen tank inside the service module exploded as the spacecraft neared the moon, one of the many problems was trying to figure out how to use the CO_2 scrubbers from the command module in the lunar module, where the astronauts were. The famous challenge of "figure out how to fit a square peg into a round hole" was because the scrubbers were never intended to be interchangeable.

† $152 billion in 2022 dollars.

in a more predictable and productive fashion (the Layer 3 issue of social circuitry's processes, procedures, and routines).

This might not be quite the taut, stretched-out spaghetti of dedicated process flows like Ransom Olds and Henry Ford created, nor exactly the more flexible and agile dedicated process flows of Toyota's fabrication and assembly lines. However, there's marked similarity on examination.

As Johnson highlighted, systems engineering rigorously describes how different subsystems connect with each other to ensure well-functioning integration while avoiding and preventing inadvertent interferences. By having clarity around how these technical subsystems interact at Layer 1, organizations can be formed on how they should interact in Layer 3.*

To make this massive undertaking work, NASA needed a way of delineating who had to be in direct collaborative conversation with whom, about what, and across what reliable interfaces. By making interactions clear they reduced cognitive load for engineers, technicians, and scientists, and allowed them to focus more fully on their portion of the system.

This also clarified where their work fit into the larger enterprise. People explicitly knew how their work connected with the other systems on which it depended and which depended on it. In that regard, NASA created connections between component parts and the people working on them, just as leaders did for the drug development experience, in the Pratt & Whitney case, and in the JSOC experience.

For example, the early Atlas program had reliability rates of about one-in-two (the Atlas was the rocket booster on which most of the Mercury missions were launched). As these systems engineering approaches took hold, reliability was raised to about three-quarters by the 1960s and over 90% thereafter.[4]

As we've discussed, it is important to take large problems and break them into smaller, self-contained pieces. This partitioning means fewer people have to coordinate their efforts to solve problems collaboratively, and more problems can be solved in parallel. However, that does raise the

---

* Readers may notice similarities in how Layer 1 and Layer 3 interact here, just as we saw in the Amazon e-commerce case study, in which the introduction of APIs (a Layer 1 solution) made it possible to have two-pizza teams (a criterion for effective Layer 3 problem-solving).

issue: How do partitioned pieces interact productively without compromising local functionality, let alone the system as a whole?

In the space program, because of the complexity of the rockets being used and the way in which they were being used, managing the interactions between adjacent pieces was challenging.[5] Electronics systems could generate signals that inadvertently affected the performance of other systems, causing them to misperform.

Compared with airplanes, rockets depend on more electronics. Aside from all the monitoring of systems and signaling to components that are internal to the system, there has to be more signaling back and forth with ground-based controllers because there had been no pilot on board to interpret data and make adjustments. In contrast, strategic bombers of that era had crews that could consist of a pilot, copilot, flight engineer, radar operator, and navigator. More generally, mismanaging the interaction between adjacent pieces was a potential problem.

The Air Force and NASA recognized that organizational and communication problems could cause interface problems. In other words, problems in social circuitry (Layer 3) could cause problems in technical circuitry (Layer 1). Organizations had different cultures and work methods, meaning there was miscommunication across boundaries. Components and subsystems developed by one organization in parallel with those designed by another organization (a consequence of using the modularization technique) may accidentally be incompatible, discovered only when they were first connected and tested.

For example, in the Mercury program, during a 1960 Redstone unmanned test flight, the launcher lifted only four inches before settling back onto the launchpad. The launch had been automatically aborted because the capsule's escape rocket mistakenly launched. The failure was due to mistiming between the rocket's electronics and those of the launch complex, caused by differences between the weight of the *Mercury* capsule and those of payloads normally flown on Atlas. In effect, mis-wiring on Layer 3 (who was or was not talking to whom about interferences) led to technology problems in Layer 1.

This inability to integrate work effectively across boundaries pushed programs into the *danger zone*. The corrective action was to create documents and processes that determined not only how technological components interacted with each other, but also how the organizations responsible for those interacting components should interact.

As we will explain next, this was to maintain *isomorphism* between the technical architecture/wiring of Layer 1 and the social architecture/wiring of Layer 3. Given that Layer 1 (technology) was still being invented and refined, Layer 3 (social circuitry) also had to be invented and refined. It wasn't enough to just create these interface documents and assume they were set. Rather, they had to assess how the interface was experienced by both sides, and that it was documented (designed), used, and updated.[6]

One might reasonably ask the benefit of managing the social circuitry. As Johnson, author of *The Secret of Apollo*, documented, the early Atlas, Titan, and Corporal projects had reliability between 40% and 60%. Reliability improved to the 60% to 80% range during the 1950s and early 1960s, and increased to +/-90% after that.[7] In contrast, the European Space Vehicle Launcher Development Organization (ELDO) had far less systems-management discipline. None of its rockets ever launched.[8]

Isomorphism

Isomorphism is the quality of related items having similar structures. Design requires isomorphism between Layers 1 and 3* (between the technology and the social circuitry). Production requires isomorphism in all three layers.

This is a recurring theme: the social circuitry (Layer 3) must support the technical work (Layers 1 and 2). Throughout the organization, people need to support their work, whether it is information, approvals, requirements, time, attention, or expertise. And these problems will vary by severity and frequency. When the social circuitry is wired properly, everyone gets what they need quickly and easily.

---

* For sufficiently complex processes that involve things small enough in time or space, we may need Layer 2 in design as well, such as in software, quantum physics, etc. For instance, a developer very rarely manipulates the production executables directly but instead will use tools like editors, compilers, debuggers, and so forth. An example of problems when Layer 2 tooling is incongruent with Layers 1 and 3 would be having to manually copy (transport) compiled executables from a developer laptop to a production server.

This was a key insight of the widely cited article by Dr. Rebecca Henderson and Dr. Kim Clark on why firms were losing their competitive advantage.[9] Others speculated that it might be due to radical innovation versus incremental innovation. But Henderson and Clark pointed out something others had missed: problems won't be solved if there's a mismatch between the design of a product (Layer 1) and the way the organization works (Layer 3), whether the changes are radical or not.

They illustrated their point with cases of photolithography aligners. These are the devices that hold silicon wafers in place for images to be projected onto them. They also hold steady the "mask" through which light is shined, which put the pattern of electrical circuits onto the wafer.

Henderson and Clark's study looked at two technologically decoupled subsystems in these aligners. Initially, across the firms who made them, there wasn't need for interactions between the engineers of those systems. Each firm had two separate groups of engineers, each dedicated to one subsystem or the other.

However, as these aligners got more sophisticated, there was an inflection point where the interaction between the two subsystems mattered. This was when firms divided into leaders and laggards. The leaders were wired differently: they still had the two groups of engineers managing each subsystem, but they also had a third group of engineers managing the design of the interface between them. The laggards did not. Not only could they not solve the interface problem; they didn't even realize how much of a problem it was.

Henderson and Clark were not alone in seeing the need for isomorphism between technology (Layer 1) and social circuitry (Layer 3). Clark previously described that as the architecture/technology changes, the organizations responsible for designing and producing the system will also change.

In software, Dr. Melvin Conway independently observed that any organization that designs a system (defined broadly) will produce a design whose structure is a copy of the organization's communication structure. The larger an organization is, the less flexibility it has and the more pronounced the phenomenon. What Conway observed was that once an organization's social circuitry (Layer 3) is set, it will dictate the architecture of the technical systems (Layer 1).

This was also observed by Drs. Alan MacCormack, Carliss Baldwin, and John Rusnak when they extensively studied software projects. They found that regardless of whether Layer 3 evolved in response to Layer 1 (like Henderson and Clark demonstrated) or Layer 1 was shaped to match Layer 3 (Conway's Law), if there was a mismatch, organizations underperformed. Product architecture influences product performance, the possible variety, and eventually the success of the firm. As they summarized: "We find strong evidence to support the mirroring hypothesis"[10] that mismatching product architecture and design process architecture was a disadvantage in achieving good designs.

A misalignment (lack of isomorphism) between the architecture and distribution of problems at Layer 1 and the collaborative opportunities at Layer 3 can have dire consequences. It can affect the firm's ability to see and solve problems, to work collaboratively, and to deliver new and useful solutions into practice.

Gene and Steve discovered this with their first, futile attempts to manage the hotel refurbishment. They attempted to manage painting and moving as independent silos, which could not accommodate the frequency and intensity of the interactions needed between the movers and painters. The solution was to create flows that cut across functions, which matched the physicality and the information-flow needs of the work.

Gene and Steve had wired their organization in such a way that prevented movers and painters from doing their work well. In other words, Layer 3 was not isomorphic to Layer 1, forcing all the necessary flow of information and interaction between the movers and painters to go through Gene and Steve (the functional silo heads). In contrast, at the end, Gene and Steve created an isomorphic Layer 3 organization that cut across the functional specialties and better supported the Layer 1 work. (As we will explore shortly, there are similar consequences when there is no isomorphism between Layer 2, how we architect the instrumentation through which we work, the processes and procedures by which we coordinate our actions, and Layer 3.)

Both Olds and Ford created congruence between Layers 1, 2, and 3; they pioneered the assembly line, an example of achieving simplification through linearization. However, this introduces a new problem. When work requires a sequence of steps in Layer 1 (e.g., grind then polish, prime before paint), work is no longer where it needs to be. Instead, it must be lifted and carried to the next operation.

Moving materials from place to place has all the attendant costs of time and expense, risks to personal safety, damage to products and equipment, etc. It also puts more information and coordination burden onto Layer 3, which has to continuously track what work is in what location and in what degree of completion. Then, it has to determine where work should go next and onto what machine it should be placed.

Olds and Ford solved for this incongruence. They had each function commit to putting all needed resources in their workflow, with people and equipment lined up in the sequence where their contributions were needed. This created isomorphism* between the Layer 1 architecture of the product and the Layer 2 architecture.

Changing job-shop layouts to linearized workflows may align Layer 1 and 2. However, Layer 2 can still be incongruent to Layer 3, such as when functional managers (e.g., grinding and polishing) can dictate how their people do their work and determine when, how, and in what form work it is presented to those who depend on it. This can create rework and contention, and make it difficult for people to do their work easily and well.

This is similar to when Gene was trying to manage painters, and Steve was trying to manage movers. There was little opportunity for movers and painters working in the same room to collaborate directly with each other. The problem was that no one was actively managing the interfaces between adjacent segments of the system. In contrast, when movers and painters were able to coordinate, integrate, and harmonize their work within their room teams, it made Layers 1, 2, and 3 isomorphic to each other.

In effectively run organizations, the functional leader is responsible for "who" and "how"—providing trained people who are competent in their profession to be used in sequentialized flows. The flow owner (e.g., project leader, program leader, value stream leader) is responsible for the "what" and "when" of how those people are deployed to achieve the system goals.

---

* We may use the words *isomorphic* and *congruent* interchangeably, as well as *not isomorphic* and *incongruent*.

This leader establishes what outputs that system is meant to generate. They ensure that the pathway of what work is done in what order is sequenced properly. They ensure balance in terms of cycle times and work load. And, they ensure that one step to the next has established the conditions for exchanges and handoffs over connections, by which the outputs of one step gracefully become the inputs to the next.* Management that cuts across functional silos creates isomorphism, or congruence, between Layers 2 and 3.†

The need for isomorphism between Layers 2 and 3 is the key insight from such luminaries as Skinner, Hammer, Champy, Hayes, Clark, and Wheelwright. They showed the value created by isomorphism and the consequence of not having it: functional organizations that have only a loose connection to the actual flow of work.

Isomorphism is a theme in several of the case studies we have presented: For example:

- In the Amazon case study, there was realization that software development had stalled, slowing to only twenty deployments per year. This was caused by the large number of people whose contributions had to be simultaneously coordinated. This led to the edict that teams be limited to a size that could be fed by two pizzas. That was a decision to modularize Layer 3 into more, smaller coherent units (i.e., their equivalent of Gene and Steve's room teams). As a consequence of this Layer 3–decision, the software those teams worked on in Layer 1 needed to be modularized too. This created isomorphism between Layers 1 and 3. Without it, the Layer 3 architecture would have been inadequate to manage the design, operation, and improvement of the Layer 1 work.
- In the case study of NASA's management of human space flight, there was an isomorphic relationship between the partitioning of Layer 3 social circuitry and Layer 1 technical system through modulariza-

---

* For more on this framework of systems existing to generate outputs over pathways of connected activities (O-P-C-A framework), please see Chapter 6 in *The High-Velocity Edge*.

† This match is something Toyota managed to tighten even further by overlaying information flows on top of materials flows, with the creation of just-in-time "pull" systems.[11]

tion. And there was a similar partitioning of Layer 1 and 2 technical responsibilities of the many corporate and academic contributors. Systems engineering became a tactic for ensuring clarity of partitions, definitions of interfaces, and management of interferences to maintain the isomorphism of Layer 1 and Layer 3.

- In the case study of the drug development team, we also see how isomorphism affected their work. Before the pilot, Layer 3 work was organized in functional silos, with coordination often done at the top of the silos. But, scientific problems were concentrated not only within functions but at the interaction boundaries between chemists, biologists, chem supplies, etc. By linearizing the drug development process through hit-to-lead, the team directly connected those who needed to interact frequently. Doing so enabled people to solve problems, especially those that were most frequent and most severe. This was an experience repeated with both Pratt & Whitney and JSOC.

Simplification's Implications for Leadership

How you lead an organization that has been simplified—through some combination of incrementalization, modularization, and linearization—differs massively from how you lead one that has not been simplified.

Incrementalization in Leadership

In Table 9.1, we contrast the "all at once" leader versus the "incremental leader." The "all at once" leader suffers from cognitive overload and attempts to solve all their problems at once. They must hold in their heads the entire Layer 1 system for which they are responsible and must coordinate nearly everyone and everything in Layer 3.

In contrast, the incremental leader enjoys and protects their cognitive capacity to create enduring solutions. They use their technical experience to help people solve their Layer 1 and 2 problems when needed because they have redesigned processes in support of that goal. This is beneficial because their intense attention is needed only on the novel portions of the problem, and they need to create new collaborative processes only for those portions.

TABLE 9.1 Leadership Challenges with All-At-Once vs. Incremental Approaches

	ALL-AT-ONCE LEADERSHIP	INCREMENTAL LEADERSHIP
Attention	Diffused over many things, simultaneously.	Focused on what is novel but not yet functional or reliable.
Leadership priorities	Giant leap.	Many small steps.
Leadership challenges	Keeping pace with systems scale, scope, complexity, and speed.	Maintaining channels of communication and mechanisms for knowledge sharing and exchange.
Key responsibility	Determining who should be doing what, for what reason, in what fashion. This is by necessity fast-paced, complex, and highly detailed.	Partitioning novel from validated and ensuring experiments are being conducted rigorously and frequently.
Problem-solving	Forced into a few cycles of complex experience and experimentation; difficult sense-making with few learning-loop iterations.	Allowed more cycles of experimentation with easier sense-making and gradual introduction of scale, scope, and complexity.

Modularization in Leadership

When discussing school reopenings in Waukesha County and Menomonee Falls, we distinguished between top-down and center-out leadership. In top-down leadership, access to data and authority for decision rights is centralized. This means leadership has to coordinate over the entirety of the potentially sprawling operations for which it is responsible. Top-down coordination and scheduling is difficult if not outright computationally impossible to do correctly in a finite amount of time. For even simple scenarios, as Gene and Steve discovered in the moving-and-painting vignette, there are too many people and idiosyncratic conditions to keep track of. The pace at which things change overwhelms the pace at which data can be gathered and processed, decisions made, and instructions issued. The delayed feedback makes problem-solving more difficult. As a result, top-down leadership is frazzled with data-processing and decision-making tasks. Leaders can rarely use their own slow-thinking capabilities, because they are forced into fast-thinking, impulsive behavior (see Figure 9.4).

FIGURE 9.4 Top-Down vs. Center-Out Leadership

TOP-DOWN APPROACH (CENTRALIZED)

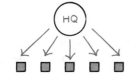

CENTER
Assume possession of data decisions, expertise, and authority.

EDGES
Either paralyzed and waiting for direction or continuously out of compliance.

CENTER-OUT APPROACH (DISTRIBUTED)

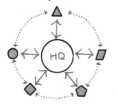

EDGES
Generating variety of approaches and outcomes.

CENTER
"Mining" across rich data, sythesizing and sharing, evolving best collective known methods.

The experience of center-out leaders is quite different. They're responsible for creating, sustaining, and improving the mechanisms by which more colleagues can contribute to the enterprise's collective problem-solving. Not only are center-out leaders addressing topics different than top-down ones, they're able to stay in a deliberative, slow-thinking mindset.

With the hotel refurbishment, Gene and Steve's minds were wildly active in the beginning of their experience, but they were not terribly productive. In contrast, when work had been partitioned, Gene and Steve were less frenetic and better able to add real value.

Table 9.2 contrasts this difference between top-down and center-out leadership. The top-down leader suffers from cognitive overload and deprives everyones else of their ability to contribute. In contrast, the center-out leader liberates the ability of everyone to contribute and help facilitate, communicate, synthesize, and share local learnings globally. They accommodate many solutions to be generated and tested in parallel. And, with the right leader, those many solutions can be parsed between those broadly applicable and those that are valuable locally but are not scalable.

TABLE 9.2 Comparing Top-Down vs. Center-Out Leadership

	TOP-DOWN LEADERSHIP	CENTER-OUT LEADERSHIP
Data	Centralized.	Distributed.
Decision rights	Centralized.	Distributed (but bounded).
Solutions	Homogeneous	Heterogeneous.
Leadership priorities	Coordination and control.	Facilitation, communication, and synthesis.
Leadership challenges	Keeping pace with systems scale, scope, complexity, and speed.	Creating and maintaining channels of communication and mechanisms for knowledge sharing.
Key responsibility	Determining who should be doing what, for what reason, in what fashion. This is by necessity fast-paced, complex, and highly detailed.	Creating mechanisms by which people can arrive at their own solutions and have local discovery synthesized into system solutions.
Mode of problem-solving	Leaders are forced into fast-thinking habits, routines, and impulses to be responsive to demands from operating units.	Leaders are able to maintain deliberative, slow-thinking approaches of designing, assessing, and improving the mechanisms they've created for data sharing and knowledge synthesis.

Linearization in Leadership

Just as modularization and incrementalization change the nature of leadership, so does linearization. As mentioned previously, the additions of fixtures, jigs, and gauges to factories were huge multipliers in productivity compared with the craft systems they replaced. This contributed to abundance, not scarcity, being characteristic of industrially and economically advanced societies.

However, the factory system had its limitations. As product volume and variety grew, it became increasingly challenging to manage materials, machines, and mechanics, tracking the conditions of each and figuring out what each should be doing next and where. Management devolved into a data-processing problem requiring expediting and exhortation to keep things from getting wildly out of line.

The linearization brought about by the assembly line solved that problem. No longer did managers have to worry about where everything was, what it was doing, and where it had to go next. Rather, they could focus on engineering "a pipeline" and queuing work of similar types to enter that pipeline. That was the extent of the data-processing demand—establishing the demand signal into the system.

After that, production issues reverted to engineering issues. If things slowed down, then they found the bottleneck and either sped it up or offloaded work from it. If a node in the system was found to be struggling, then they made sure that point was well supported by all the flows of material and information needed to support it. That too kept problem-solving as an engineering challenge, not an information-processing one.

Shifting from job-shop management to linearized workflows partitions the entire enterprise into distinct pieces. That has benefits, like shifting from top-down to center-out management. Leaders have to spend less time doing frenetic, impulsive, fast-thinking work. Instead, they can be more deliberative, first figuring out the partitioning that allows for linear flows. That's deliberative slow thinking, a more productive use of people's minds. Then, they can continue in the slow-thinking, deliberative, productive mode by solving the engineering (technical) problems that affect safety, cycle time, quality, and yield (see Figure 9.5).

FIGURE 9.5 Job Shop for Flow Production

KEY: —— Material Flow   - - - Information Flow

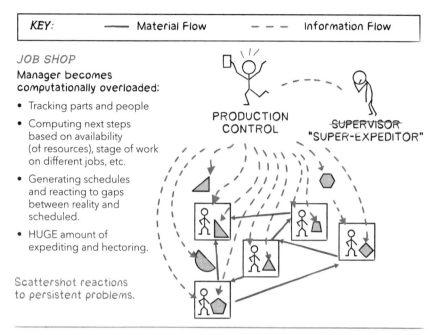

JOB SHOP
Manager becomes computationally overloaded:

- Tracking parts and people

- Computing next steps based on availability (of resources), stage of work on different jobs, etc.

- Generating schedules and reacting to gaps between reality and scheduled.

- HUGE amount of expediting and hectoring.

Scattershot reactions to persistent problems.

PRODUCTION CONTROL

SUPERVISOR "SUPER-EXPEDITOR"

FLOW PRODUCTION
Management becomes cycle-time opportunity.

- People and parts have set location.

- Work has set sequence across all the steps in the flow.

- Scheduling is just on the sequence with which work enters the pipeline.

- Management attention can be refocused on technical, scientific, and engineering challenges.

  - Cycle-time reduction.

  - Reduction in cycle-time variance.

  - Line balancing.

  - Change-over-time reduction.

Persistent solutions to real problems.

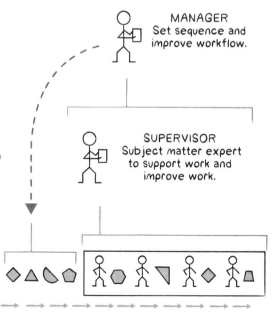

MANAGER
Set sequence and improve workflow.

SUPERVISOR
Subject matter expert to support work and improve work.

At the same time, those doing the direct work of the organization (mechanics, technicians, scientists, engineers, designers, clinicians, and so forth) can be more locked in on Layer 1 and 2 issues (see Figure 9.6).

FIGURE 9.6 Flow Production vs. Partitioned Flow Production

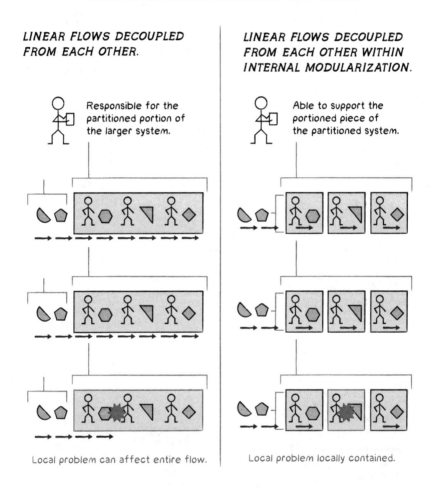

Standards and stabilization mechanisms allow for even more partitioning. This is not just decoupling one workflow from others; it is insulating one step from those before and after, allowing for even more shifts in how and on what people spend their precious creative energy.

Table 9.3 contrasts "job-shop leadership," "flow leadership," and "partitioned-flow leadership."

TABLE 9.3 Leadership Challenges with Nonlinear vs.
Linear Flows of Work

	FLOWS OF MATERIAL
Job shop	◊ Back and forth from the point of work to some local or central storage.
Flow	◊ From the beginning of the pipeline through the end.
Partitioned flow	◊ Step by step from those who generate an intermediate output directly to those who need it as an input.
	FLOWS OF INFORMATION
Job shop	◊ Up and down from point of work to a production control (scheduling and monitoring) function.
Flow	◊ From those who need an input back to the beginning of the process.
Partitioned flow	◊ From those who need a particular input back to those directly responsible for providing it.
	LEADERSHIP PRIORITIES
Job shop	◊ Data processing: monitoring what work is in what stage of completion, in what location, to what mechanics, and what state of readiness machinery is in, AND determining what has to go where next and who has to do what next based on demand signals as they drop in.
Flow	◊ Identifying and remediating problems related to safety, cycle time, reliability, yield, quality, etc.
	◊ In unpartitioned flow (i.e., imprecise standards and inadequate stabilization), there are challenges in resolving where a problem originates and how to contain its spread and correct its causes.
	◊ The source is "somewhere in the pipeline" but of indeterminate time and location.
Partitioned flow	◊ Ensuring flows of work are well partitioned.
	◊ Depends on assuring supporting mechanisms are in place, e.g., team leads in support of associates, group leads in support of team leads, etc., so there is enough ingenuity available to develop solutions to problems in planning, testing them in practice, and providing help (stabilization) in performance.
	◊ Leader periodically gets drawn into solving problems that sprawl across several coherent elements.
	◊ That is offset if the leader has developed mechanisms for supporting capability at intermediate levels.

LEADERSHIP CHALLENGES	
Job shop	◊ Tracking everything and everybody all of the time.
Flow	◊ Isolating time and place of problem occurrence and fully engaging the enterprise's distributed wisdom.
Partitioned flow	◊ Creating the partitions by which people can focus on the local issues for which they're uniquely equipped to address and building capability so people can be most fully engaged.
KEY RESPONSIBILITIES	
Job shop	◊ Management as a data-processing problem.
Flow	◊ Management as a search problem of locating symptoms and causes.
Partitioned flow	◊ Management as a system architect and capability development problem.
PRIMARY PROBLEM-SOLVING CHALLENGE	
Job shop	◊ Hard to see their work as part of a larger whole.
	◊ Deficiencies in scheduling and material and information handling mean point of work is under-supported in terms of necessary materials, equipment, and information.
Flow	◊ Problem in another part of the system may escape and be disruptive.
Partitioned flow	◊ Doing work according to the standard, recognize (see) problems when they occur, and call attention to problems so they can be contained and resolved so they don't endure or spread.

The job-shop leader suffers from cognitive overload from having to track everything, everywhere, all the time. They have to create Layer 3 processes that deprive everyone else of their ability to contribute to solving their Layer 1 and 2 problems. The flow leader suffers from less cognitive load, but it's difficult to pinpoint where problems are occurring and it's more difficult to engage their colleagues in distributed problem-solving.

In contrast, the partitioned-flow leader's cognitive capacity is liberated because they've created the Layer 3 wiring that enables problem-solving responsibilities across the enterprise with individuals solving highly localized problems and with small groups addressing factors that affect larger portions of the whole. Therefore, they support those local efforts and still have capacity left to deal with systemic issues for which they have a unique span of responsibility and authority.*

By creating standards around how work flows, how work is done at each step, and, in particular, how work is handed off from one piece to the next, the whole has been broken into coherent units, done to the level of the individual task and task doer.

This would likely be sufficient for a static situation. But with dynamics, there is always the chance that work within those small, coherent units will be more difficult or take longer than typical or expected. That's where stabilization comes in to maintain modularization. Stabilization ensures local problems are less likely to escape and become system problems. Those not directly affected by that local problem can remain focused on their own responsibilities, be that performing current operational tasks or replanning and practicing how to do them in a different fashion.

Simplification and Model Lines

Throughout Chapter 8, we saw examples of simplification being tried out with a model-line approach. In the drug development case, a single program was the platform for piloting linearization. Lessons learned from that one pilot became the model of the fanout to other areas and programs. Similarly, the first attempt at an iPhone was unambitious in scale and scope relative to what Nokia attempted. But it allowed fast, rich learning that could be used for new iterations and new models.

NASA's examples are all of a "start small and local" nature, be it Alan Shepard's fifteen-minute first Mercury flight as a precursor for Armstrong, Aldrin, and Collins's *Apollo 11* milestone, or DART colliding with a relatively small asteroid that was actually orbiting a larger asteroid as a precursor for planetary defense.

With school reopenings after the COVID-19 pandemic, educators in Wisconsin ran small experiments, classroom by classroom, before synthesizing lessons learned and spreading them within a school, then across

---

* This will be further explored in Part IV: Amplification.

individual schools in their district. The Navy also started small when mastering fire controls for turreted gunnery.

Wrapping Up Simplification

The very best performers succeed because they create the conditions in which people's minds can be used more effectively to solve Layer 1 and Layer 2 problems, the solutions to which enable organizations to fulfill their missions. To accomplish this, leaders must wire the social circuitry that integrates individual effort gracefully into collective effort, so people exert less time and energy on Layer 3 problems.

Simplification makes it easier to manage Layer 3 by shifting problems from the *danger zone*'s demands for difficult, complex problems, in which the efforts of each individual have to be constantly coordinated with those of many others, into the *winning zone*'s opportunity to solve simpler problems, for which less coordination is necessary. This means it's easier to:

- Make sense of cause and effect, both in studying the structure of the systems we are designing and diagnosing and interpreting the results of experience (even trial and error) and structured experiments. This is because there are fewer factors in play at any time, and the relationships among those factors are simpler and more obvious (albeit not always easy).
- Accumulate data from which we make sense of cause and effect. Each "coherent piece" is smaller and easier to model, mock-up, simulate, pilot, and so forth, so we can get more iterations per individual element of the larger whole. Also, if the systems are modularized, more experimentation can occur in parallel rather than sequentially.
- Coordinate because interdependencies are both fewer and clearer.

In Part IV, we will focus on the third mechanism of moving an organization from the *danger zone* to the *winning zone*, that of amplification. This mechanism doesn't change the nature of problem-solving, like slowification. Nor does it change the nature of the problems themselves, like simplification. Instead, amplification adds value by making it more obvious we have a problem to solve, even if that problem is unaddressed in early-stage planning, is expressing itself in practice, or is plaguing us in performance.

In the next part, we explore how amplification makes it obvious early and often that we have problems. We'll see how, in performance, knowing this gives us a chance to stabilize systems more quickly and more easily, before they have a chance to become unstable and out of control. This enhances reliability and resilience. Amplification in any phase of work—planning, practice, or performance—is feedback that triggers and informs learning, thereby helping us make progress on knowing what to do, why to do it, and how to get it done well. Amplification is a key dynamic feature of organizations that are wired to win because they are wired so people's minds are put to the best possible use, in the extreme, all of the time.

PART IV

Amplification

CHAPTER 10

Amplification:
A Theory Overview and
Exemplar Case Study

In late December 2022, just in time for winter break, over twenty-eight million people in the US were traveling by air.[1] At the same time, a massive winter storm, named Elliott, blasted parts of Canada and the United States. Its reach extended from the northern Great Plains all the way to the Atlantic, with cold weather effects as far south as Florida. The National Weather Service called Elliott a "once in a generation" storm.[2] Between December 21st and 23rd, airlines cancelled over six thousand flights and delayed another twenty-one thousand due to snow, ice, high winds, and cold temperatures.[3]

As the storm subsided, most airlines began to resume normal operations, getting passengers and their luggage to their intended destinations. However, as the other airlines were recovering, Southwest Airlines' condition continued to degrade. Through December 28th, Southwest cancelled over half of its flights, and the percentage kept increasing.

Southwest was forced to continue cancelling flights because either the planes or the crews assigned to fly them were not in the right place—sometimes both. Southwest ultimately resorted to flying empty planes to get them and their crew repositioned, not allowing customers to book new flights in the meantime.[4]

These adverse effects were due to how Southwest Airlines had wired their crew scheduling system. Among other things, the crew scheduling system assigns flight crews (pilots) and cabin crews (flight attendants) to each flight. When flights were delayed or cancelled because of Elliott, pilots were expected to call the crew-scheduling department, notify them of where they and their plane were as opposed to where they were scheduled (expected) to be. The crew-scheduling department then had to manually update the flight schedules for the following day.

FIGURE 10.1 Percentage of Flights Cancelled by Airlines

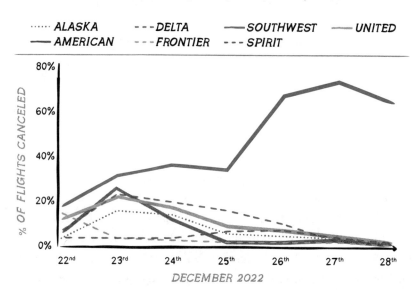

Source: Adapted from Matt Stiles and Christopher Hickey, "How Southwest Failed the Holidays: Four Charts Explaining the Cancellations," CNN.

This system had worked well enough for years. It was able to keep up when there wasn't a high volume of daily updates. However, it was inadequate for Winter Storm Elliott. This event required a large number of schedule corrections all at once. The phoned-in, manually updated system quickly became overwhelmed. So many flights were being cancelled and so many updates were being posted that pilots could not reach the crew scheduling department. Some reported being put on hold for hours (with one pilot reportedly on hold for twenty-two hours).[5]

In short, Southwest Airlines' crew scheduling had lost track of where their pilots were. It was as if Southwest Airlines' operational support system had seized up. They were not able to take any new reservations or operate many of their flights because they were tracking down where their crews and planes were. Then, they were shuttling empty planes and crews around the country. It was as if the system was rebooting itself.

This created enormous hardships for Southwest travelers, more so than those traveling on other airlines at the same time. Across the nation, people saw images of crowds of people stranded in airports and sleeping on floors.

In the aftermath, on February 9, 2023, Southwest's leadership was summoned to testify before the US Senate Committee on Commerce, Science, and Transportation. Andrew Watterson, the airline's chief operating officer, outlined why the airline had to cancel nearly seventeen thousand flights, affecting at least two hundred thousand would-be travelers.

He explained how Southwest had used weather forecasts to develop a precautionary plan for flight delays and cancellations in anticipation of the bad weather (i.e., they'd used offline slow thinking to develop alternatives). However, the speed and severity of operational challenges across multiple airports overwhelmed the speed with which Southwest's operations could keep up in performance.[6]

In the same hearing, Captain Casey A. Murray, president of Southwest Airlines Pilots Association (SWAPA), testified that,

> What SWAPA Pilots saw—and have known for years—is that SWA struggles to manage nearly any disruption, regardless of the cause. Our recent history—and the data—shows a pattern of increasingly disruptive operational failures, misprioritization of resources, and hollow leveraging of our culture to cover up poor management decisions.[7]

He put the three leading causes of failures during Elliott as (1) failure to adequately prepare for Winter Storm Elliott, (2) failure to modernize crew management processes and related IT systems, and (3) failure of leadership and the normalization of drift.[8]

Southwest leadership had purportedly continued to defer modernizing the crew scheduling systems since 1993.[9] For decades, Southwest's operational performance had been celebrated. However, there has been evidence of deteriorating performance, which Southwest leadership and others have attributed to changes in TSA security procedures,[10] weather challenges, and running a more tightly packed schedule that left Southwest's operations more brittle.[11]

Figure 10.2 shows the rank of Southwest in on-time performance compared with the worst in the industry. It clearly shows that Southwest was best in the industry for most of the 1990s, but by the mid-2010s, their on-time performance had dropped to nearly the worst. Captain Murray testified that there had been system failures nearly every eighteen months at Southwest (see Figure 10.2), but they had gone unaddressed.[12]

FIGURE 10.2 Ranking of Southwest On-Time Performance against Worst in Industry (1987–2020)

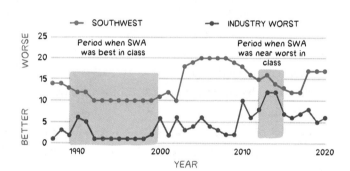

Source: US Bureau of Transportation Statistics, Department of Transportation.

Addressing these problems would have required Southwest's leaders to first slowify their problem-solving. That would have involved creating conditions to find the underlying causes for their problems and developing effective corrective actions. It would also have compelled them to develop corrective actions in a simplified fashion.

Captain Murray highlighted many issues in his congressional testimony. This included baggage-handling problems as Southwest was migrating to a hub-and-spoke approach from its point-to-point heritage or how weather delays in one locale caused problems to spread throughout its network (see Figure 10.3). Leadership could have modularized each issue into their component pieces to better make sense of and solve problems. They could have incrementalized their problem-solving by making changes on the edges of well-validated platforms. They could have tested any changes, small or large, in mock-ups and simulations first before doing a wide-scale deployment. Unfortunately, Winter Storm Elliott showed that such a combination of betterment through slowification and simplification hadn't happened early enough or well enough.

FIGURE 10.3 Southwest Airlines Meltdown History, 2011-2023

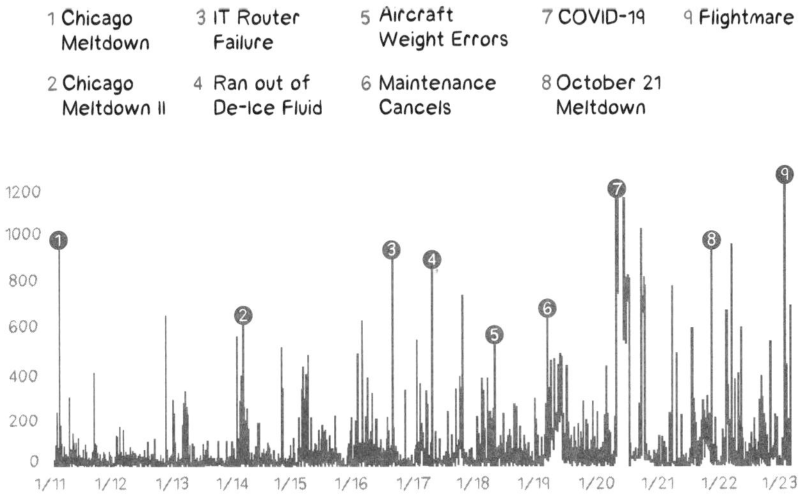
1 Chicago Meltdown
2 Chicago Meltdown II
3 IT Router Failure
4 Ran out of De-Ice Fluid
5 Aircraft Weight Errors
6 Maintenance Cancels
7 COVID-19
8 October 21 Meltdown
9 Flightmare
1200
1000
800
600
400
200
0
1/11
1/12
1/13
1/14
1/15
1/16
1/17
1/18
1/19
1/20
1/21
1/22
1/23

Source: From the Written Testimony of Captain Casey Murray.

One can speculate why this happened. Southwest's leadership might have succumbed to the tyranny of operating tempo (as described in Part II: Slowification) or the normalization of deviance (e.g., "We've had adverse weather events before and crew scheduling didn't fail. So, it's likely okay.").

Regardless of the reasons, Southwest's leadership did not respond sufficiently to these earlier indications about its operational fragility and resilience. The consequent "reboot" required in the aftermath of Winter Storm Elliott illustrates why *amplification*, the third mechanism used by organizations wired to win, is so important.

In December 2022, Southwest's crew scheduling system couldn't keep pace with the rate at which flight crews were trying to provide updates. However, nonresponsiveness to indications of problems and inadequate feedback loops had been characteristic for long periods, not just during day-to-day performance but also during planning. In the absence of these feedback loops, Southwest hadn't been sufficiently self-correcting its operations, either in performance or in offline preparation. Despite evidence that change was warranted, things didn't get better.

Just as in the moving-and-paining vignette where Gene and Steve were initially overwhelmed and unable to get movers and painters where they needed to be, so too, the Southwest crew scheduling system couldn't generate a schedule for planes and crews (the Layer 1 technical object that people were trying to generate and update) accurately or quickly enough. The Southwest staff trying to generate those schedules were hampered by the crew scheduling system (Layer 2 technology) that was inadequate for the task (e.g., telephone calls instead of a mobile phone app). Despite the heroic efforts Southwest employees made with their processes and procedures (Layer 3), these efforts fell far short of compensating for the inadequacies of the technology (Layer 2) given the *danger zone* conditions of fast-moving extremes delivered by Winter Storm Elliott (Table 10.1 outlines this more).

TABLE 10.1 Signals of a Problem at Southwest vs.
Gene and Steve's Hotel Refurbishment

Generate	Transmit	Receive	React	KEY ✳ There was a signal, and it was loud and clear. ☼ There might have been a signal, but it was weak and perhaps ambiguous in its meaning.
GENE AND STEVE: HOTEL REFURBISHMENT				
✳	✳	✳	✳	Commentary: Signals from the movers and painters (e.g., complaints, difficulties, scheduling errors) prompted slowification to plan and practice new approaches that included simplification techniques.
SOUTHWEST				
✳	☼			Commentary: Signals were either not strong enough or not detailed enough to indicate causes of delays (e.g., baggage handling, crew scheduling) or simply went unheard. Consequently, Southwest did not slowify to upgrade its infrastructure to keep pace with the changes in its operating environment.

There is a key difference between Gene and Steve's experience and that of Southwest: amplification. With the hotel, problems managing the assignment of movers and painters to particular rooms prompted a redesign of processes and procedures (Layer 3). Not so with Southwest. Based on all the other meltdowns suffered by the airline, it is clear that signals of significant problems with crew assignment existed, but they were transmitted too weakly or were not received with enough clarity. As a result, they did not trigger improvement. By the time Elliott hit, Southwest was overwhelmed in performance because they'd missed chances to get better in planning and practice.

What Is Amplification?

Earlier, we described *slowification*, where we advocated that the toughest problems be solved in the right conditions, as well as *simplification*, where we advocated that the problems themselves be modified so they are easier to solve, which also makes those systems easier to control. Now we look at the final mechanism to help you wire your organization to win.

Amplification is the act of calling out problems loudly and consistently enough so help is triggered to swarm them. Once the problems are swarmed, they are contained so they neither endure locally nor spread systemically. Then, they are investigated to determine their causes and create corrective actions that prevent recurrence. This requires that the signal of a problem is successfully generated, transmitted, received, and then reacted to.[*]

In the case of Southwest during Winter Storm Elliott, signals could not be adequately amplified during performance because they had not been during previous milestones. When crews were in the wrong location, crew scheduling did not receive the signals the crews transmitted (because the pilots could not get through to them by phone), nor could crew scheduling correctly react to those signals. Consequently, they lost track of where flight and cabin crews actually were. This led to daily operations grinding to a halt as they manually tracked down crews and planes.

---

[*] This corresponds to the "built-in tests" of Capability 1 in *The High-Velocity Edge*, combined with Capability 2 of fast and frequent rigorous problem-solving done close in time and place to where problems occurred and with those affected by the problem.

This inflexibility is not restricted to airline operations. Another example is automobile manufacturing, where material handling changes caused parts to not arrive where and when they were supposed to. In one remarkable case, making six internal changes to production caused a Big Three automobile manufacturing plant to shut down for three days while they re-established what tasks would be done in what work locations. Then, they worked with material handling to assure that parts and materials would arrive properly. In other words, at Southwest, problems were not amplified early enough to trigger slowification, which could have led to redesign and validation of material handling changes, performed in an incrementalized and modularized fashion.

Control and Information Theory

Throughout this chapter, we deliberately use the language of control and information theory, where signals are generated, transmitted, received, and reacted to. This is all part of using feedback loops to stabilize dynamic systems and trigger and inform improvement (see Figure 10.4).

FIGURE 10.4 Amplification of Problems through Feedback Loop

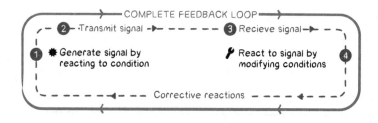

The discipline of control theory is attributed to physicist James Maxwell and his work regulating the velocity of windmills in the nineteenth century.* Control theory addresses a broad variety of situations where no

---

* James Maxwell was a Scottish mathematician and scientist responsible for the classical theory of electromagnetic radiation, which was the first theory to describe electricity, magnetism, and light as different manifestations of the same phenomenon. Maxwell's equations for electromagnetism have been called the second great unification in physics, the first realized by Isaac Newton.

static plan can achieve the desired goal. These are circumstances where, no matter how good the plan is, enough changes occur, both internal to the system and in the environment in which it is operating, that it is unworkable.

Instead, feedback mechanisms are needed to achieve the intended outcomes. These mechanisms assess what is actually going on (versus what the plan predicted) and how that departs from what was expected. This generates a signal that triggers and informs corrective actions to re-steer the situation (as indicated in Figure 10.4).

Control theory is used all around us: in mechanical and electrical engineering, computer science, psychology and sociology, and operations research. Feedback loops are also pervasive in biological systems. For instance, people who have diabetes suffer from a condition where the body either is unable to produce insulin (Type 1 diabetes is failure to signal) or it cannot respond adequately to insulin (Type 2 diabetes is failure to react). In the absence of a reliable control system, the diabetic must manually regulate their exertion and diet to prevent hypo- or hyperglycemia.[*]

For control systems to be effective, the generation, transmission, reception, and reaction to signals must keep pace with the changes going on in and around the system being controlled. This is a point in information theory that was pioneered by Dr. Claude Shannon in his 1948 paper "A Mathematical Theory of Communication." It focuses on the problem of how a sender must encode signals so that they can be understood by the receivers.[13] Even if a control system is complete (i.e., it has mechanisms for generation, transmission, reception, and reaction), it can fail because of delays and imprecision.[14]

In Part II: Slowification, we described how most people have no difficulty driving on an uncongested and well-maintained highway on a clear day. We also described what must happen to retain control when they drive on that same highway during a snowstorm, at night, and with other cars on the road. The environment starts to overwhelm the driver's ability to receive and process information, and it becomes increasingly difficult and even dangerous to drive safely. The corrective action is to slow down so that

---

[*] In effect, during Winter Storm Elliott, Southwest Airlines became a Type 2 diabetic airline.

the driver is better able to process and act upon signals that are fewer and slower arriving.

This need to sense and adjust quickly to the environment will be familiar to many, especially as it is so similar to the OODA loop, a concept that US Air Force Colonel John Boyd first wrote about in 1996. The idea is that to change a course of action, a person or system has to *observe* what is going on (e.g., collect data and information), get *oriented* (e.g., make sense or otherwise interpret what the data means), *decide* what to do based on that sense-making, and then *act* on what has been decided.

In general, one wants to have a fast OODA loop; that is, one can rapidly and effectively respond to changing conditions. In contrast, Winter Storm Elliott created the conditions that required the Southwest Airlines crew scheduling system to observe, orient, decide, and act faster and with greater detail than it was capable of doing.[15]

How Do We Amplify?

We need signals to be generated when we encounter problems in Layer 1 (the work in front of us) or in Layer 2 (the tooling and instrumentation through which we work). The causes and corrective actions for these problem might be expressed as issues of technology or techniques. However, for Layer 3 problems (problems with our social circuitry), causes and corrective actions affect processes, policies, procedures, and routines—the ways by which the work of many individuals is integrated through collective action toward a common purpose.

Our Layer 3 processes and procedures (our social circuitry) must integrate signaling—so that they are generated, sent, received, and effectively reacted to—into our processes and procedures. When amplification happens well, signals are generated and transmitted so that they are received and understood clearly by the receiver and the appropriate corrective actions can be taken.

This requires generating and transmitting signals that are frequent enough, fast enough, precise enough, accurate enough, and *loud enough* to get us to decide to act differently based on what is being observed and understood. When we say a signal is "loud enough," it could be that the signal, once generated, is transmitted loudly and clearly or that when received it is heard and understood clearly.*

Signals also have to be sent with adequate frequency, speed, detail, and accuracy for the reaction to be helpful. For control systems to work well, they must be designed well and deliberately. Design of the informational overlay can't be an after thought, as the control system must be significantly faster and more reliable than the object being controlled. As we mentioned earlier in this book, the Nyquist-Shannon Sampling Theorem, first introduced in 1928, demonstrates that the receiver must sample at least twice the rate of the sender to accurately reconstruct the message that is required to measure and control a system. This theorem forms the basis of all things digital, including telecommunications, medical imaging systems, astronomy, quantum computing, and more.

Nyquist-Shannon sets a theoretical minimum for how much faster the control system must be relative to the system being controlled. However, in reality, controlling a complex engineered or biological system means that ratio has to be multiples, even orders of magnitude, faster for systems to be both resilient *and* agile. For instance, aircraft flight control systems are orders of magnitude faster than turbulence that affects the altitude of an aircraft; otherwise, there is a risk of losing control.

This leads to a stark implication for top-down management. For example, if reports are generated and reviewed once a week, they can only be used to control (or manage) changing situations no faster than every two weeks. Any changes that occur more frequently will be uncontrollable, hence the emphasis on persistent shop floor leadership at Toyota (as we'll see later in this chapter) and elsewhere.

Amplification in the Case Studies

When we examine the cases previously presented in this book, we can see how important amplification was in getting the full effect from slow-ification and simplification. In general, amplification does not change the

---

* This framing of generation-transmission-reception-reaction is based on Shannon and Weaver's "The Mathematical Theory of Communication."

problem-solving experience (as does slowification), nor does it change the problems themselves (as does simplification). Amplification tells us it's time to move from the *danger zone* to the *winning zone*. Then we can trigger either slowification (so solving problems is easier) or simplification (so problems are easier to solve). That signal, if properly generated, delivered, received, and reacted to, can occur during planning, practice, or performance. It can also be in any system, regardless of how much it's been incrementalized, modularized, or linearized.

FIGURE 10.5 Using Amplification to Move from the
Danger Zone to the *Winning Zone*

In the remainder of this chapter, we will revisit and analyze the case studies that we presented earlier in this book through the lens of amplification. By doing this, we will show how amplification was either effective or ineffective through the presence or absence of these six steps of amplification:

1. Sender generates signal.
2. Sender transmits signal.
3. Receiver receives signal.
4. Corrective reaction is started.
5. Corrective reaction is completed.
6. Sender confirms that reported problem has been solved, otherwise they send another signal.

We will then describe factors that either help or hinder each of these six steps. Finally, we'll present an exemplar case study that shows how slowification, simplification, and amplification come together to create a dynamic and adaptive system that is market-leading and continually pushing the frontiers of performance.

FIGURE 10.6 The Six Steps of the Amplification Feedback Loop

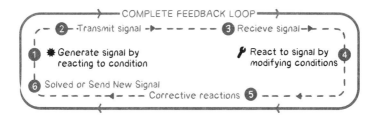

A note for leaders here: If you somehow diminish amplification, you put whatever you are trying to accomplish at grave risk. If you create conditions in which feedback loops work well, you are likely to generate wonderful outcomes for both the people in the organization and the people they serve. On the other hand, if you create conditions in which feedback loops don't work well, you are likely to generate disappointing outcomes for both the people in the organization and the people they serve.

Success and Failure of Amplification
in the Case Studies

Throughout the case studies we can see various degrees of successful ampli-fication. For example, with the MIT Sloan sailing team, the crew's captain and pilot established the norm that when something was confusing to any member of the crew, they would raise a signal. The reaction would be to pause performance. They would stop sailing in order to shifting problem-solving from the fast-thinking domain of performance to the slower-think-ing realm of (re)planning and new practice before rejoining the race. This was the combination of reception and reaction in their feedback loop. It was both complete and also operating with sufficient frequency, speed, detail, and accuracy to make notable progress in performance.

In contrast, consider the habitualness with which problems were worked around or unheeded in the Mrs. Morris/Ms. Morrison case study. There is a strong indication that leaders there hadn't established mecha-nisms for staff to call out moments of confusion (e.g., identifying the correct patient) or of outright error (e.g., no consent form, patient is protesting). Nor did they establish their own commitment to swarming problems once they were called out and seen.

This pattern of perform-problem-pause-(re)plan-new practice is mod-eled directly on Toyota's andon cord. How such andon cords are deployed illustrates the characteristics of well-amplified feedback versus not. Harvard Business School doctoral student Marcelo Pancotto contrasted two plants. Both had andon cords hanging over workstations, which asso-ciates could pull to generate a request for help if they had a problem. One of these plants was among the best in the world; the other, not.

Pancotto found that in the best plant, mechanics pulled the cord twelve times a shift. Also, there were enough capable team leaders to consistently provide help. In the other plant, mechanics hardly ever pulled the andon cord because there were far too few team leaders to respond reliably, and on the chance they did, the reaction was often accusatory, not supportive.

In the first plant, the feedback loop was frequent (more than once an hour), fast (immediate reaction by the team leader), detailed, and accurate (responding to each particular associate one by one about specific problems and supportive of incredible industrial effectiveness). In the other, plant the feedback loop was infrequent, slow, and imprecise. The plant's overall performance was consistent with individuals' experiences.

Amplification was also a critical factor for the success of the US space program. As described, Neil Armstrong and Buzz Aldrin were well prepared to land on the moon. When they discovered a boulder-strewn landing zone, they knew what to do because of the immense amount of practice they had completed with land-based simulators and training vehicles. Feedback helped astronauts become better prepared when they trained, and feedback helped mission controllers on how to manage the missions. Feedback from another simulation made chief flight director Gene Kranz realize he and his team didn't understand well enough how to respond to a "1201 alarm code."

Again, we see effective amplification occurring in a well-designed feedback loop. It was able to generate and transmit the signal that something is amiss, and the receiver (Kranz) reacted decisively. After all, he might have insisted that the astronauts keep trying harder to avoid creating the conditions that triggered the alarm, or he could have insisted on continuing to react to it in an unchanged way.

This dynamic was pervasive throughout the US space program in the 1960s. Alan Shepard's first flight in the Mercury program was atop a Redstone rocket (the increment being tested). Feedback from the experiences using the astronaut's capsule led to lessons learned, which fed forward into the design of controls for subsequent missions. Much of the Gemini program's missions were designed to test ideas and generate feedback that would inform how to conduct the Apollo missions more confidently.

In many cases throughout the program, systems were deliberately designed so each experience (in the extreme) was configured to be an experiment: generating feedback about what was surprising or not, triggering and informing changes, and having those changes tested in feedback-rich, highly amplified conditions.

In contrast, the fundamental critique about the root causes of the *Challenger* and *Columbia* catastrophes wasn't that they were caused by problems in NASA's science, engineering, and technology work (Layers 1 and 2). The failure was in the social circuitry (Layer 3), where policies, procedures, processes, and routines were oblivious to feedback. Problems weren't sufficiently amplified to generate corrective reactions. And that resulted in two tragic disasters.

Table 10.2 outlines how amplification has been present (or not) in all the previous case studies we've explored in the book. Next, we'll take a look at the factors that allow for or impede successful amplification.

TABLE 10.2 Amplification's Presence or Absence in Cases We've Reviewed

SWA MELTDOWN HISTORY 2011–2023

AMPLIFICATION IN SLOWIFICATION

Generate	Transmit	Receive	React	KEY
				✳ There was a signal, and it was loud and clear. ✩ There might have been a signal, but it was weak and perhaps ambiguous in its meaning.
MIT SLOAN SAILING TEAM				
✳	✳	✳	✳	Difficulty during performance triggered immediate pause for (re)planning and new practice.
MORRIS / MORRISON				
✳	✩			Confusion ignored ("where's the patient?"). Patient's protests dismissed ("you've got the wrong patient"). No pause to reset and correct the situation or to fix and prevent recurrence.
APOLLO 11				
✳	✳			Steady and relentless feedback from practice to modify plans for lunar landing (e.g., how to respond to a 1201 error code).
COLUMBIA SPACE SHUTTLE				
✳	✩			Evidence that the thermal system didn't perform as designed existed, but it wasn't reacted to (i.e., deviances were normalized).

AMPLIFICATION IN SLOWIFICATION

Generate	Transmit	Receive	React	
				KEY ✹ There was a signal, and it was loud and clear. ☆ There might have been a signal, but it was weak and perhaps ambiguous in its meaning.
JAPANESE NAVY LEADERSHIP (LEAD-UP TO JUNE 1942 BATTLE)				
☆	☆			Feedback during war games was dismissed as failure by subordinates to execute, rather than recognized as flaws in the battle plan.
US NAVY LEADERSHIP (1923–1940)				
✹	✹	✹	✹	Feedback during Fleet Problems was encouraged, informing development of superior operating concepts for US naval aviation.
UA232				
✹	✹	✹	✹	CRM was the result of feedback from many airline disasters and helped the flight crew slow its thinking, despite fast-moving and catastrophic circumstances. This enabled the crew to engage sound OODA loop feedback, incorporating everyone's efforts and experiences.
UA173				
☆	☆			Lack of CRM meant the crew did not have practiced slow-thinking routines to help them solve their problem, resulting in loss of situational awareness and important signals either not being transmitted or being ignored, resulting in a crash when they ran out of fuel.
GOOGLE AND AMAZON				
✹	✹	✹	✹	Use of stress tests during offline drills (practice) fed lessons learned into performance.
NETFLIX				
✹	✹	✹	✹	Chaos Monkey stress tests during performance (of a modularized system) generated lessons to be fed forward into system redesign and practiced routines.
BOSTON MASS CASUALTY PREPARATION				
✹	✹	✹	✹	Drills, exercises, and previous mass casualty events found flaws in existing procedures and informed improvements.

AMPLIFICATION IN SIMPLIFICATION

Generate	Transmit	Receive	React	
				KEY ✳ There was a signal, and it was loud and clear. ☆ There might have been a signal, but it was weak and perhaps ambiguous in its meaning. *I*: Incrementalization, *M*: Modularization, *L*: Linearization
				DART
✳	✳	✳	✳	Key point: Partitioning makes signals easier to generate, receive, interpret, and react to. *I*: Feed forward lessons from previous missions into the DART mission. *M*: Partition the DART mission into components, which were assigned to different parties.
				WRIGHT BROTHERS
✳	✳	✳	✳	*M*: Break the problem of powered flight into many problems to create feedback around each experiment quicker and clearer to incorporate into the next iteration. *I*: Small, fast, frequent experiments (e.g., wind tunnel, Kitty Hawk) increase speed of feedback to improve understanding.
				MONET AND PICASSO
✳	✳	✳	✳	*M*: (Monet) Isolated single-variable experiments in his various series to get quicker, easier feedback from changes in technique. *I*: (Picasso) Used small-scale "pilots" to get fast feedback on changes in composition.
				MENOMONEE FALLS SCHOOL REOPENINGS
✳	✳	✳	✳	*M*: Partitioned the reopening problem from county-level through district, school, and then classroom. Quicker, easier to learn relevant lessons; apply those locally and incorporate those into collective lessons learned. *I*: Daily trials increased the frequency of seeing and solving problems + weekly sharing of lessons learned.
				NAVY GUNNERY: CDR SIMS
✳	✳	✳	✳	*M*: Partitioning fleet to ships to gun crews made clearer what had been changed to improve or diminish results. *I*: Isolating the novel from the known increased clarity of the signal that a change in an approach was effective or not.

AMPLIFICATION IN SIMPLIFICATION

Generate	Transmit	Receive	React	
				KEY ✳ There was a signal, and it was loud and clear. ☆ There might have been a signal, but it was weak and perhaps ambiguous in its meaning. *I*: Incrementalization, *M*: Modularization, *L*: Linearization
				**IBM SYSTEM/360**
✳	✳	✳	✳	*M:* Partitioning behind modular interfaces meant components could be developed with independence of action. Clarity at the interfaces made clear when adjacent designs would create compatibility issues.
				AMAZON E-COMMERCE SOFTWARE before
☆	☆			*M:* The tight coupling of so many functions limited independence of action and impeded understanding the source of problems and the construction and testing of corrective actions. Evidence of problems might be "transmitted," but ability to receive and react is compromised by complexity. *L:* Dev and Ops silos being separate created a slow feedback loop back to developers, and tight coupling further slowed down the pace at which tests of change could be conducted.
				AMAZON E-COMMERCE SOFTWARE after
✳	✳	✳	✳	*M:* Partitioning into modules meant problems could be seen and solved locally with significant independence of action. *L:* Elimination of "Dev vs. Ops" silos meant that every module team was responsible for their entire feedback loop (e.g., running their systems in production and interacting with their customers).
				DRUG DEVELOPMENT before
☆	☆			*L:* Having to integrate work by lab and program leaders left individual contributors disconnected from the whole without the ability to see when and how their work was or was not syncing with larger objectives and efforts.
				DRUG DEVELOPMENT after
✳	✳	✳	✳	*L:* Made clear where individual efforts fit into the larger whole. During planning, collaboration could occur across boundaries about exchanges during performance; content and format of outputs-inputs was clear.

AMPLIFICATION IN SIMPLIFICATION

Generate	Transmit	Receive	React	
				KEY ✸ There was a signal, and it was loud and clear. ☆ There might have been a signal, but it was weak and perhaps ambiguous in its meaning. *I:* Incrementalization, *M:* Modularization, *L:* Linearization
PRATT & WHITNEY before				
☆	☆			*L:* Disconnect of individual engineers from a larger situational awareness made it slower and harder to see when and where problems were occurring that needed resolution.
PRATT & WHITNEY after				
✸	✸	✸	✸	*L:* Working across functions rather than up and down silos fed faster, more frequent feedback on design of components and how they fit into larger systems.
TEAM OF TEAMS before				
☆	☆			*L:* Poor integration of individual efforts through collective action toward a common purpose meant that information realized in one function wasn't transmitted or received quickly and clearly enough to trigger a productive reaction to what had been learned.
TEAM OF TEAMS after				
✸	✸	✸	✸	*L:* Direct linkages across different military, intelligence, and diplomatic units moved information through systems faster and more frequently and allowed greater clarity about what signals meant and how they should be reacted to.
MANNED MOON MISSIONS				
✸	✸	✸	✸	*I:* Validate man, machine, and methods on one flight (a signal of an effective approach) and build upon that foundation with novelty (increasing clarity of signal of effectiveness or ineffectiveness). *M:* Partitioning of the entire system into components (e.g., capsule separate from booster in Mercury, command and service module different from landing module in Apollo, simulators assigned to different contractors than operational components) made signals easier to see and react to. *L:* "System engineering" gave clearer definition to the pattern of interdependencies (potential interferences) among component systems, allowing collaboration about interface design and independent design behind interface; ensured that important signals were received by everyone who needed them.

AMPLIFICATION IN SIMPLIFICATION

Generate	Transmit	Receive	React	
				KEY ✹ There was a signal, and it was loud and clear. ✧ There might have been a signal, but it was weak and perhaps ambiguous in its meaning. *I*: Incrementalization, *M*: Modularization, *L*: Linearization
				SOUTHWEST
✹	✧			Signals weren't strong enough or detailed enough to indicate causes of delays (e.g., baggage handling, crew scheduling) or simply went unheard. As a result, Southwest did not slowify to upgrade its infrastructure to keep pace with the changes in its operating environment.

Factors That Help or Hinder Amplification

There are many factors that help or hinder amplification. In this section, we'll break down many of those factors at each of the six steps of amplification, as well as the corrective actions being started, completed, and validated. (As a reminder, Figure 10.7 shows the six steps of Amplification.)

FIGURE 10.7 The Six Steps in the Amplification Feedback Loop

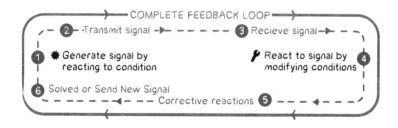

(1) Factors Affecting Signal Generation

When people point out problems that are never fixed, or help is requested but never arrives, people can become indifferent to them. They accept problems as normal and resort to daily workarounds and just "make do." People can become desensitized. They no longer see problems as something they can do anything about. They don't call out problems when they are seen.

We can see how leaders create the opposite of this dynamic in the NASA Apollo space program. On January 27, 1961, NASA suffered a huge tragedy when three *Apollo 1* astronauts, Gus Grissom, Ed White, and Roger Chaffee, died on the launchpad during a launch test rehearsal.

The following Monday, Gene Kranz, chief flight director of the NASA Mercury, Gemini, and Apollo programs, convened his entire branch and flight control team in an auditorium.

In his speech was the following:

> Spaceflight will never tolerate carelessness, incapacity, and neglect. Somewhere, somehow, we screwed up. It could have been in design, build, or test. Whatever it was, we should have caught it....Every element of the program was in trouble and so were we....The simulators were not working, Mission Control was behind in virtually every area, and the flight and test procedures changed daily....Not one of us stood up and said, 'Dammit, stop!'
>
> We are the cause! We were not ready! We did not do our job. We were rolling the dice, hoping that things would come together by launch day, when in our hearts we knew it would take a miracle....[16]

Kranz later wrote that during this moment, his remarks "were received with silence, no movement, no shifting in the seats. The controllers, each and every one, knew what I meant. I was just putting their thoughts into words."[17] Kranz continually spoke about the need to speak fearlessly; to call out and examine anything anomalous or unexpected that happened. Each anomaly was then studied until it could be explained.

He viewed each anomaly that was not investigated and explained as a potential divergence of the mental model of the flight crew and the actual reality, which could potentially kill an astronaut. This encouraged signal generation of potential problems. Each could trigger improvement through slowification or simplification or both. This continual learning eventually enabled their successes, sending twelve Apollo astronauts to land on the moon and return.

Leaders of an organization, whether deliberately or inadvertently, set and reinforce the organizational values, norms, and expectations through their actions. Audit, accounting, and ethics experts have long observed that the "tone at the top" predicts the likelihood of fraud and other unethical practices. We believe that "tone at the top" also determines what signals are generated or not generated.

Leaders can set expectations for everyone to strive to achieve perfect understanding and performance of the system, calling out anomalies and things they don't understand. Or they can do the opposite. Through their actions or words, they can encourage everyone to "go with the flow" and can ignore imperfections in the system and their own understanding. They ignore everyone's talents, experiences, ingenuity, and creativity, making them passive participants in the system. By doing this, leaders are complicit in the dismal outcomes that follow.

(2) Factors Affecting Signal Transmission

A well-known risk that impedes important signals from being generated is when people recognize a problem but do not feel safe calling it out, fearful of the reaction that it will create. We have all likely seen situations where people are afraid to speak up, even if it puts their own lives at risk. This was the case in the United Airlines Flight 173 crash and what researchers observed in many other airline disasters. This concept has been popularized as psychological safety by Dr. Amy Edmondson.[18]

Dr. Ron Westrum described information flow as a "prime variable in creating safety, but also it is an indicator of organizational functioning."[19] This was based on studying human factors in system safety in complex and risky industries, including aviation and healthcare. Westrum asserted that "When information does not flow, it imperils the safe and proper functioning of the organization...and second, information flow is a powerful indicator of the organization's overall functioning."[20]

The State of DevOps research found that this model was one of the top predictors of software delivery and organizational performance. Respondents were asked to what extent their organization had high cooperation, that people were "trained to tell bad news," that risks were shared, that bridging between functional groups was encouraged, that failures lead to genuine inquiry, and that novelty was encouraged.

Organizations that rated highly on these characteristics performed better on every technical performance measure (as measured by code-deployment frequency, code deployment lead times, change failure rates, and mean time to restore service) often by orders of magnitude. They also performed better on every organizational performance measure (exceeding profitability, market share, and productivity goals). Employees in these organizations also reported high job satisfaction and were more and more likely to recommend their organization to their colleagues and friends.

These findings are also consistent with Amy Edmondson's research on psychological safety. As she describes it, leaders create psychological safety that creates "felt permission for candor."[21]

In 2012, researchers at Google also found Edmondson's model of psychological safety to be predictive of performance. This was part of a research initiative, called Project Aristotle, that wanted to find what made teams effective at Google.[22] They studied 180 teams, reviewing a combination of attributes and dynamics, and found that the interactions between team members mattered more than who was on the team.[23] The top predictor was psychological safety.[24]*

The State of DevOps research also revealed the contrasting ways that organizations deal with failures and accidents. The lower-performing organization with poor information flow:

> [looked] for a "throat to choke": Investigations aim to find the person or persons "responsible" for the problem, and then punish or blame them. But in complex adaptive systems, accidents are almost never the fault of a single person who saw clearly what was going to happen and then ran toward it or failed to act to prevent it. Rather, accidents typically emerge from a complex interplay of contributing factors. Failure in complex systems is, like other types of behavior in

---

* For more on Google culture and Project Aristotle, check out the book *The Power of Habit* by Charles Duhigg.

such systems, emergent (Perrow 2011). Thus, accident investigations that stop at "human error" are not just bad but dangerous. Human error should, instead, be the start of the investigation. Our goal should be to discover how we could improve information flow so that people have better or more timely information, or to find better tools to help prevent catastrophic failures following apparently mundane operations.[25]

Leaders must model the behaviors to make this work. To those suffering problems, whether regular inconveniences or episodic threats, leaders have to model how to call out problems when and where they occur. While this is necessary, alone it is insufficient. Leaders also have to model to those with supervisory authority and supporting responsibility how to respond quickly, respectfully, and effectively, so calling out problems is proven to be worthwhile and appreciated.

(3) Factors Affecting Signal Reception

No matter how well or loudly a signal is transmitted, it may not be effectively received. We suspect Dr. Claude Shannon, who created information theory, would agree with author Simon Sinek, who wrote, "Communication is not about speaking what we think. It's about ensuring others hear what we mean."[26]

It might disappear into a report. It might have to travel up a functional or departmental silo to be acted on at the very top. Or, it might become diluted or dissipate before it reaches someone with the capability, responsibility, and authority to act upon it. Furthermore, leaders may not react, despite clear indications that something is wrong. Leaders consumed with maintaining operational tempo can't pause long enough to develop new approaches, validate them, and then use them in practice.

Southwest's leadership seems to have been afflicted by one or both of these factors. Even if the signal was generated, transmitted, received, and reacted to, it was not with enough frequency, speed, precision, or accuracy to be good enough. The result was leaders had to "reboot" the system.

The signal might also need to carry more information than can be accommodated through the channel it is being transmitted. We saw this earlier in the book, when Gene and Steve were moving a couch. In one scenario, we introduced so much background noise that Gene and Steve couldn't communicate directly with each other. They even tried to solve the problem by introducing a helpful friend to serve as an intermediary, passing messages between them. Regardless of how much the friend tried, the needed information flow could not be conveyed, failing due to some combination of frequency, speed, precision, or accuracy, or even all of them.

As a leader, you must ensure that there is a sufficiently coherent environment for information that must be conveyed. In some cases, introducing a structured form can help (perhaps a mobile app that allows pilots to convey precisely and easily what city they're in). In other cases, a free-flowing, face-to-face conversation is needed to enable joint problem-solving.

An example can be seen in the Apollo space program. Mission Control needed to effectively communicate with astronauts in space during highly consequential situations when radio communication was unreliable but also critical. NASA needed to maximize the probability that joint problem-solving could happen between them when it mattered the most. Their solution reminded us of the following (paraphrased) adage: when there is an immense amount of information that exceeds the bandwidth of the communications interface, you cannot just send a message—instead, you send a messenger.

During Apollo missions, the only people allowed to communicate with astronauts in space were the five to ten designated capsule communicators, known as CAPCOMs. The CAPCOMs were themselves astronauts, and also served as the backup crew to the astronauts in space or were the team who trained them. Therefore, CAPCOMs had the same training and the same shared experiences with those they were communicating with.

This enabled the CAPCOMs on Earth and the astronauts in space to develop and use a highly efficient code to transmit needed information between the sender and receiver. When a catastrophe hit *Apollo 13* on April 13, 1970, important messages were sent with confidence that the other side would understand, such as astronaut James Lovell saying, "Houston, we have a problem. We are venting something out...into space." Or the CAPCOM astronaut Jack Lousma saying, "We'd like you to go down that power-down procedure until you get a delta of 10 amps."*

The lesson here is that leaders must understand the nature of what signals need to be communicated. This may dictate who does the sending and receiving to enable the necessary coherence. As we've seen in the linearization section, when information needs are high, that information cannot travel to the top of a functional silo. Instead, we must make direct connections across functional specialties to enable joint problem-solving at the frequency and speed, and with the detail and accuracy, necessary.

(4) Factors Affecting Corrective Action Beginning

Another failure mode is when signals for help are received but no actions are taken in response. An example of such a failure can be found in organizations that espouse having an alert system (e.g., an andon cord) but one that is in name only. The cord or button is put in place for people to call out problems when and where they occur, but there is no one who receives the signal, or no one reacts to it quickly and well enough. Thus, calling out the problem in the first place is not worth the while. (Recall Marcelo Pancotto's research of automobile assembly plants presented earlier in this chapter.)

Another danger is that the signals arrive too late to enable effective corrective action. The Nokia case study was presented as a failure of incrementalization, but it also serves as a remarkable example of amplifying a weak failure signal. When Risto Siilasmaa, then a board member, was dismayed to learn about the two-day compile times for the Symbian OS, he interpreted it as an existential risk and took decisive action, resulting in a new CEO taking over the company.

---

* *Team of Teams* describes a similar situation where having an expert at the interface between two organizations was critical for signals to be transmitted with clarity and problems to be amplified reliably. For the Joint Special Operations Command, this required reassigning "our best operators from the battlefield" to be liaisons with diplomatic and intelligence organizations (a counterintuitive action).[27]

Gene asked him in an interview, "Why and how did you interpret that problem, which could be interpreted as such a tactical issue, as something so important that it led to bringing in a new CEO?" He answered,

> In any environment, you have people doing the most important work of the organization. Leaders must ask to what extent is it easy or difficult for them to do their job? And when I heard that engineers had to endure the two-day compile times to know whether their change worked or not, I knew that it was nearly impossible for tens of thousands of engineers to do their jobs well.[28]

This shows the importance of enabling people to get fast feedback on their work so they can be productive, get in the flow, and be focused on the problems in Layers 1 and 2. Nokia correctly identified a vulnerability in Layer 3. Alas, their corrective action was too late.

Leaders must model the behaviors that ensure actions are taken quickly and decisively. This helps solve problems before they snowball into larger (and potentially existentially threatening) ones.

(5) Factors Affecting Corrective Action Completion

Another failure mode is when corrective action is taken but never completed. The Nokia case study illustrates this, but there is more to the story. Siilasmaa described how the two-day-compile-time problem indicated very deep problems in Layer 3, as well as Layers 1 and 2. He noted that there were two possibilities: (1) senior leaders did not know about the two-day-compile-time problem, or (2) they knew about it but didn't act decisively to address the problem.

He wrote,

> Nokia's problem wasn't just a technology issue or a leadership issue. It was a cultural issue that pervaded the entire organization. Bad news wasn't percolating up from the bottom, and the top-down process of fact-finding and problem-spotting didn't work, either. This

indicated a lack of courage in the former and a complete misunderstanding of a critical aspect of good leadership by the latter...When no one cares, the only resort is to change the people at the top—starting with the CEO.[29]

As mentioned, the State of DevOps research showed that one of the top predictors of performance in technology environments is to what extent important information can be shared, how messengers of bad news are trained to tell bad news, how responsibilities are shared across functional specialties, how bridging between teams is rewarded, and how failure causes genuine inquiry.[*]

(6) Factors Affecting Corrective Action Validation

Amplification, as a mechanism, is fundamentally about feedback, about the generation of signals specifically to validate or refute what we assume to be true. This way, when we are wrong, we know early and often and can react.

This creates a single feedback loop, where signals are generated, transmitted, received, and reacted to. While this is necessary, it is not sufficient. We must also ensure that the reaction actually addresses the problem, as opposed to leaving it unresolved or, worse, actually exacerbating it. All too often, a reaction to the signal was generated, but no one validated that the problem was actually solved.

There are myriad possible reasons, including:

- Pressure to maintain operational tempo (to get on to the next task), thereby not leaving time to follow up before moving on.
- Conviction that we've got the correct solution without actual evidence.

---

[*] Many technologists might recognize this as the Westrum organizational typology model. We will discuss this even further in the Conclusion of the book.

- Lags between when actions are taken and when effects can be felt.*
- Lack of continuity between those who took actions and those who are in a position to follow up.†
- And other separations, such as time, distance, or actor affected, that make connecting action, outcome, and assessment effective.

Corrective action and validation form one of the key parts of the Plan-Do-Study-Act cycle, from Dr. W. Edwards Deming.‡

- Plan: the conceptualization of new ideas and actions to rectify or improve a situation.
- Do: the substantiation of those ideas in action.
- Study: the deliberate and rigorous assessment of what had happened versus what was expected and an attempt to explain causally the reasons for those inaccuracies.
- Act: the new behaviors informed by what was discovered during study; the validation and correction part of the feedback loop.

---

* During 2022 and 2023, the Federal Reserve and other central bankers were trying to use monetary policy to control inflation. Inflation had spiked as COVID-19 restrictions were eased and consumer demand increased, but supply chains were slow to activate, as Russia's war with Ukraine and other factors increased petroleum prices and as shifting technologies drove demand for other natural resources like lithium for batteries, etc. The problem for central bankers was that the policies they were using to tighten money supply and bring down inflation weren't mechanistically causal, nor were they fast. Rather, there were "long and variable lags" between when action was taken and when its effects could be measured and assessed.[30] This concept links back to an article by Milton Friedman, "The lag in effect of monetary policy."[31] These long and variable effects lags were the reason given by head US central banker Jerome Powell for why the Federal Reserve was pausing interest rate hikes, despite persistent inflation. They needed time to validate the effects of earlier actions.[32]

† This becomes an issue where the cycle times between action and outcome are long, the cycle times with which personnel are replaced in billets are short, and there is insufficient continuity of action and intent between predecessors and successors.

‡ This cycle was based on Walter Shewhart's Plan-Do-Check-Act cycle. One can see how Deming's simple word change from Plan-Do-CHECK-Act to Plan-Do-STUDY-Act might increase the vigor with which gaps between predicted and actual outcomes are sought out and the rigor with which they are explained.

Exemplar Case Study:
Bringing Slowification, Simplification, and Amplification Together at Toyota

We've discussed the factors that can help or hinder each of the six steps of amplification. Now, let's turn to a final exemplar case study that shows how slowification, simplification, and amplification come together to create a dynamic, adaptive system that is both market leading and continually pushing the frontiers of performance.

A recent visit to Toyota's San Antonio truck plant TMMTX (Toyota Motor Manufacturing, Texas), one of the outstanding industrial sites in the world, reinforced the criticality of amplification in outstanding organizations. It also highlighted how the interplay of amplification with slowification and simplification wires an organization to win.

The case outlines the complexity of an operating system in terms of production volume; the variety and sheer number of people and things that have to move gracefully and fluidly for the system not to crash, let alone produce outstanding results; and the rigors under which the system operates in terms of its expected output. This case sets the stage to explain how and why amplification helps resolve the contradiction between complexity/operating demands and outstanding outcomes.

An Outstanding Industrial Site

TMMTX is wildly complex, producing both Tundra pickup trucks and Sequoia SUVs on a single production line. Both the Tundra and the Sequoia are available in several configurations of power trains, suspensions, and trim options. The Tundra also offers different sized cabins and different length beds, while the Sequoia offers a hybrid version. Every minute, a completed vehicle drives off the line, resulting in nearly one thousand vehicles ready for distribution to their sales network each day.

Accomplishing this volume, variety, and complexity of work requires several thousand employees working in fabrication and assembly operations, like stamping and welding, paint and plastics, final assembly, material handling, production engineering, and so forth.

In addition to Toyota's workforce, there are some two dozen first-tier suppliers on site. The size and difficulty of packaging some components efficiently makes shipping them uneconomical. In addition, some components have to arrive in sequence and made to order, so inventorying them is not an option. Even for smaller, more generic items, compressing the time and distance between their production and their use creates faster feedback between customer and supplier.

When suppliers are close, feedback can be supplied in minutes or hours. When suppliers are far away, this feedback can take days or weeks, as items must be shipped over land or sea. Keeping suppliers nearby reflects Toyota's policy of "global localization": in other words, building where it sells and buying where it builds. So, while the plastic that might become a truck's fuel tank comes from far away, the tanks themselves are molded nearby. This is just one example of creating more local, geographic coherence in production, which makes amplification easier to achieve.

For instance, on-site supplier Avanzar Interior Technologies (Avanzar) makes seat sets (front and rear for the Tundra, three rows for the Sequoia), which are tailored for each vehicle. These are built one-by-one, just in time for the vehicle in which they will be installed. A two-row seat set can have 922 parts and component pieces sourced from 152 vendors located in twenty-two countries.* Avanzar also produces the headliners, which are the multi-material panels that line the inside of the roof. They are infused with sensors, microphones, speakers, and all sorts of electronics and attendant wiring. They are also made to order and delivered in sequence for the vehicle in which they will be installed.

The choreography to support just seat installation is complex and demanding, with little margin for error. There are only three and a half hours from when a vehicle body leaves the paint shop to when seats are installed. (This is the 65% completion point of the entire assembly process.) It takes about an hour and a half to convey the finished seat to installation, so Avanzar only has about two hours to complete each seat set. The headliners have even less lead time, only one hour and thirty-five minutes until

---

* And this is just a fraction of the thirty thousand components that must be put into a typical vehicle.

they are picked up and delivered to where they're installed five minutes later. If Avanzar doesn't get it right, they threaten to starve the system.

Amplification is critical to achieving and maintaining high performance amid such complexity and demanding conditions, both for Toyota and suppliers like Avanzar.

Anywhere we look at TMMTX, there is an intricate, fluid, and choreographed ballet on display. Large components are carried in overhead conveyors one by one to points of installation. Smaller assemblies and component parts are loaded at pickup points and ferried by tugs to be dropped off where they'll be installed. The margins of acceptable error for arrival times can be as little as a few seconds, since there is no "line side store" for large items or ones that arrive one by one for specific vehicles (like headliners and seats), and the goal is no wasted motion.

On the final assembly line alone, hundreds of associates perform individually choreographed steps of retrieving components from racks, taking the prepositioned tools and other equipment they need, replacing it when they're done, stepping here, lifting there, all while installing or fastening an item to the vehicle and moving it one step closer to completion. It's an engrossing performance of moving and interacting people, machines, and parts—all of which must be in exactly the positions they need to be at exactly the right moment to start the next motion.

To perform this ballet gracefully, there is, of course, the need for practice, to develop smooth and effective routines before production begins. Slowification, using feedback-rich planning and practice to prepare for performance, is used here energetically, perhaps more so than elsewhere in industry.

We saw such discipline in the preparations for *Apollo 11*'s lunar landing. NASA ran the routines over and over and over again, first to find out their failure points so they could be corrected and then to ensure the performers were capable and comfortable. Once performance begins, most potential errors have already been debugged and people have become familiar and comfortable with the routines.

As important as all that preparation is during the feedback-rich and improvement-laden environments of planning and practice, the dynamics during performance makes possible smooth and reliable operations and that enables associates to be productive without injury. This is also why the myriad tugs and parts ferries can navigate their various routes so fluidly at the TMMTX plant. Everything works well because feedback loops allow for real-time adjustment, providing stabilization in the short term and correction in the long term. This is where simplification techniques like linearization (with its attendant steps standardization and stabilization) interplay with amplification for powerful results.

However, this is not a top-down approach. As we mentioned earlier, the Nyquist-Shannon Theorem shows us that an operating system's "control overlay" has to sense and react with speed and detail greater than the speed and detail with which the actual operating system operates. In biological systems, for instance, cells, tissues, and organs have to be this agile for healthy functioning. Without this, transmission to, processing by, and reactions from the brain would be too slow to keep up with all that is going on in the body: balance, heart and breathing rates; pupil dilation; blood sugar control; manual dexterity; heating and cooling; etc.

To account for the Nyquist-Shannon Theorem, technical systems have controllers distributed throughout, sensing and reacting quickly and with high frequency, rather than having everything centrally processed, least of all by the most remote leader.

Amplification and feedback loops make this possible—from those closest to the work to those with responsibility over ever greater spans of the enterprise. At TMMTX, for example, for every four or so associates doing the direct work of fastening, installing, or attaching material, there's a team leader providing them with support (and for every five or so team leaders, there's a group leader who provides support to them).*

In part, this is to offset the periodic extra effort required on particular vehicles (e.g., an extended version of the pickup truck requires the installation of an extra-long headliner). However, the primary job of team leaders is to help associates when they encounter problems (e.g., a part hasn't been replenished or a power tool stops operating properly).

---

* We're deliberate in saying "four or so" for the associate to team leader ratio or "five or so" for the team leader to group leader ratio. As explained later, these are not fixed ratios but flexible depending on the situation.

Remember, the customer experiences the vehicle only when they finally drive it off the lot. That experience, however, is determined by the work of the associates who created the vehicle. To ensure high customer experiences, anyone in a leadership role must be supportive of the associates and the work they are doing.

For example, due to the frequency with which support is needed directly to the line, the number of associates per team leader is kept low. Likewise, due to the intensity with which additional support is needed, continuing through the most senior members of the organization, there are few team leaders per group, few groups per manager, and so forth. Thus, the organizational structure is layered versus flat.

When Kevin Voelkel, president of TMMTX and group vice president of North America Truck Manufacturing, was asked about the leadership model, he gestured with his hands facing each other, wrists touching, his fingers apart to form a "V". He was emphasizing that each leader's job was to support those right above them, each layer of support one closer to where associates actually did the work that created the products that formed customers' experiences. This was a deliberate inversion of who was responsible to whom compared with the typical hierarchical structure of the head honchos on top and everyone answering to them.

It is important to note here that organizations must do more than simply invert their structure. Stabilizing support is necessary, even in a system that is arguably one of the best engineered in the world. The ratios of people supported to people supporting are small, a few associates per team leader, a few team leaders in a group, and so on. This might seem contrary to what some might wrongly think of (i.e., industrial operations being easily codifiable or "push and play"). Recall how even Gene and Steve moving a couch has a substantial brain element to it.

The second point is that there is no fixed ratio of associates to team leaders, team leaders to group leaders, etc. Those ratios are driven by the technical sophistication of the work and by the frequency, severity, and technical difficulty with which problems occur. So, assembly, with its fast pace of production, might have an team-leader-to-associate ratio of 1:4, with one group leader for every five team leaders and one manager for every four group leaders. The paint shop may be 1:5 and welding 1:4. Stamping, which is highly technical, has a first-level ratio of associates to team leaders of only 1:3, and in the back shops, which are responsible for equipment mainte-nance and repair, the ratios can be 1:1 in some situations (see Figure 10.8).

The right ratio is determined by whether amplification is working; that is, if problems are being seen often and early enough and solved quickly and reliably enough that their effects don't spread and they don't recur. In fact, depending on the experiences on a shift one day, there may be slight adjustments the next.

Creating such reliable, agile, and flexible support requires disciplined linearization of production and supporting processes. Sequentialization allows for clean partitions, defining what it means for one task to be done and what has to be in place for the next to start.

This clarity makes for easier standardization. That delivers several ben-efits. Reliable standards make accomplishing tasks easier; there's already a validated "script" of the best-known approach, and there are clear boundar-ies of when and where work begins, how it should progress, and where and how it should end.

FIGURE 10.8 Leadership to Supporting Ratios at Toyota Plant

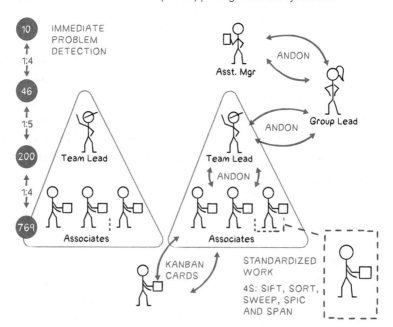

But, there's more to it than that. Not only do standards make succeeding easier; they make it more obvious that something is difficult or even wrong. Problems are made visible.

If it is declared what is expected to occur, when, where, and how, it's easier for associates and team leaders to realize something is going astray. In fact, with sufficient clarity, team leaders can recognize issues even without associates calling attention to the problems. And, if not, the associate can give a quick tug to an andon cord to signal that help is needed.

In the majority of cases, the team lead and associates will contain the issue, dealing with the temporary overburden of a more complex job or preventing the problem from escaping the local area. If the problem cannot be contained, the signal is transmitted to a group leader, who is triggered to react and respond with help.

These feedback loops are everywhere and involve everyone. Stabilization and improvement responsibilities extend through all layers of the supporting structure, from associate to team leader to group leader to area manager and so forth. Issues can even escalate to Susann Kazunas, the vice president of manufacturing at TMMTX. She can step in to help stabilize and lend expertise and resources. But it doesn't just stop there.

During our tour, Kevin Voelkel was asked how much time he's on the shop floor in a typical day. His answer was several hours. Regardless of the plant he's at, this time on the floor helps him see the nuance and detail of what is actually occurring.

The answer was a bit staggering to the leaders on the tour, given their own daily experiences. Most of these visiting leaders are so busy with reports about the shop floor, that they are lucky to get a few hour per week to actually "go and see" the shop floor. It was probably even more surprising to some of the visitors when Voelkel added that when his colleagues from other sites and executive leaders from the broader Toyota enterprise visit, even more time is spent in production to observe what is happening first hand.

Kazunas offered that she is on the floor several hours a day so that the support she provides around problems is rooted in the nuanced reality of the people working with the processes on products and not diluted by distillation and aggregation into charts and tables.

The heads of the major production centers—stamping and welding, plastics and paint, and final assembly—reported that it'd be easier to count the minutes they were *off* the shop floor than *on*.

Of course, amplification is never perfect at fully stabilizing a system. Sometimes there are disruptions that can't be well contained. Even then, how people respond is a sign of how integrated amplification is in normal operations. For instance, while we were visiting TMMTX, an associate had difficulty with a task and a team leader responded. However, the problem was too difficult, which triggered a group leader to assist. That didn't resolve the issue either (because of its difficulty), so the line segment stopped moving.

What happened next was telling. There was no freak-out. There was no frenzy or panic. The stoppage was routine. Associates and team leaders in adjacent workstations spent the time tidying up their areas, stretching, walking around, chatting with colleagues, etc., all while those drawn into the issue dealt with it. When the problem was resolved minutes later, the line started moving and everyone stepped back into their roles.

Only a few minutes later, the line stopped again. Why? It was time for a scheduled break. This scheduled break was not delayed or skipped to "make up" for the lost production time. After all, seeing and swarming was as routine as making outstanding vehicles in the first place.

It's important to note that the activities associates engage in during these stoppages are quite deliberate. If it is just for a minute or two, those in adjacent areas might be idled. If the problem appears more serious and will take more time to resolve, there are preplanned activities. The complexity of these tasks is matched to the duration of the interruption. For instance, with a short pause, associates might tidy the work area. For longer interruptions, teams might resume improvement activities, or a team leader might use the pause as an opportunity to do training with an associate.

In effect, work is not designed with a single play, where everything stops when the play is interrupted. There's more deliberateness to how unplanned interruptions are managed. For instance, during a stoppage, associates first complete the standard work for the task in which they were engaged. That way, they get to the end of that piece, and when the line resumes running, they restart at the beginning of the next module as opposed to having to pick up somewhere mid-cycle.

This deliberate planning for stoppage of work is similar to *Apollo 11's* ready-to-run plays (developed in the planning and practice phases) that are available if circumstances are different from first expected.

However, there was even more to this. While final assembly associates were taking a break, back-shop teams were using the stoppage of the assembly line to do maintenance and repairs. They had already planned, practiced, and debugged the work offline so it could be executed quickly and reliably in a short period. Extreme partitioning into smaller cohesive blocks of work created the opportunity to slot pieces in and out without disrupting the larger system as a whole.

All of this is impacted by amplification, not just for stabilization in performance but to bring feedback into planning and practice as well. Having each leader support a few associates or teams creates benefits that extend outside of performance. It allows problem-solving to occur within teams (to improve the experience of individual associates) and within groups (to improve the balance, flow, and performance of work across teams).

Just as stabilization during performance happened everywhere and all the time at TMMTX, so too did problem-solving and improvement. For instance, in final assembly, there were nearly eighteen problem-solving stations, part of the Floor Management Development System (FMDS). (There are sixty-two of these FMDSs in the plant as a whole.) Each FMDS station encompasses the associates in a group, both on first and second shift, and each is focused on some aspect of the work that, if resolved, would improve safety, quality, cycle time, and so forth.

Sharing a single board across shifts allows big problems to be collaborated on continually, from one shift to the next, and with clear visibility. Hence, no redundancy and no gaps in coverage. Within groups, individual teams had their own workstations to run offline problem-solving on improving work standards, the organization, or work areas, and so forth.

This amount of online and offline amplification and escalation had obvious benefits for associates at TMMTX. Compared with counterparts in similarly challenging industrial settings, these associates could say they were prepared to succeed, and, if not, that they'd be better prepared the next day. Furthermore, the experience of leaders was quite different from their counterparts elsewhere (and those of the plant visitors).

Consider the plight of Gene and Steve when they first tried to help renovate the old Victorian hotel. They were constantly reacting to problems, firefighting, and unable to create enduring solutions. They were chasing data, generating schedules, and hectoring people to expedite and reprioritize, but they contributed little to actually making things better.

After slowifying, simplifying, and amplifying their system, they were less harried and spent less time firefighting. They were more effective in lending their creative energies to solve problems, improve performance, and be useful to others.

This is what happens in the "real world" too. Leaders who wire their organizations to win create social circuitry (Layer 3 conditions) like those at TMMTX. These leaders are able to appreciate, understand, and support the work being done in Layers 1 and 2, take the effort to make that work quicker, and make it easier for that work to be safer and better.

On our way out of the factory, Voelkel showed off a detail on a recently produced truck. There was film on each window frame, a styling element. Aligning the film from the front door to the rear door was tricky. The film was hard to handle and manipulate, leaving a misalignment of a millimeter or less. Fixing this alignment problem required redesigning the film so it was easier for associates to manipulate and affix properly. What was striking was that someone of Kevin's seniority was involved in resolving such a detailed problem because of the span of coordination needed—redesigning this film meant coordinating with product engineering, production engineering, material handling, and parts of the supply chain. He didn't have authority over those groups, but he did have peer-to-peer influence to get engagement.

In effect, this film problem couldn't be solved without Kevin Voelkel's involvement because this problem didn't fall within a coherent module that was part of the normal partitioning of responsibilities. Rather, part of the problem was one group's responsibility and parts of the problem were the responsibility of other groups. What Voelkel did was temporarily repartition the enterprise, creating a coherent module around the window frame film problem so it could be resolved.

Of course, had he been busy scheduling, rescheduling, expediting, hectoring employees and suppliers, demanding accountability, and all the rest, he never would have had time to facilitate this complex collaboration across departments. Fortunately, because of the combination of process lineariazation with substantial amplification, minute problems were regularly being seen and solved. As a result, he could be focused on the intricacies of improving the window frame films, improving the end product, and improving the work experience of the associates.

Wrapping Up Amplification

As we have illustrated, amplification helps wire our organization to move from the *danger zone* to the *winning zone* by making it easier for people to solve hard problems individually and have their creative collaborations be more productive. Critical to amplification are (1) the ease of generating and transmitting signals that something is amiss and (2) the act of those signals being received and reacted to quickly. In performance, it's a significant stabilization mechanism. In planning and practice, amplification within the nested modularization of teams and groups allows for significant independence of action in improvement.

The TMMTX case study shows how critical leaders are to making amplification feedback loops effective, even reducing the number of teams or associates they support to do their job well. Contrast this with the common practice of stripping out middle management for cost savings, which has negative consequences by depleting the systemic ability to see and solve problems.

Part of wiring an organization to win is to ensure that leaders at all levels are able to create conditions in which people can give the fullest expression to their problem-solving potential, both individually and through collective action toward a common purpose.

QUESTIONS FOR THE READER

1. As someone responsible for the social circuitry in which people work, have you and the people with whom you work made sure there's enough clarity about what "right" looks like that it is possible to rec-

ognize "wrong"? If not, you have no signal to generate to start the self-corrective feedback loop.

2. When "wrong" is evident, how does someone experiencing it call it out from inside one of these partitioned, coherent elements of the larger system? Is there a means for transmitting in a way that the message is received?

3. To whom and how is the signal that attention is needed transmitted and received? Does it land with someone able and available to respond with adequate frequency, speed, detail, and accuracy? Or is there such latency and imprecision built in that the signal is lost?

4. When reactions do occur, are they by the right person, at the right time and place, with the right capabilities, so that the frequency, speed, detail, and accuracy of response stabilize the situation immediately and inform their improvement continuously? Or are their reactions so mis-synced that they just make matters worse?

CONCLUSION

Our goal in writing *Wiring the Winning Organization* was to present a simple and robust theory of performance that explains why and how exemplary teams, companies, and groups from a broad range of situations, in many sectors, across different disciplines, and from different points in the value-creation process can deliver amazing and ever-improving performance. And why and how the mediocre organizations are unable to do so.

As we have presented, these differences in performance are dependent on the ease with which people can solve the difficult problems associated with generating and delivering products and services of great value. This difference is a consequence of how leaders create the social circuitry (Layer 3) of processes, procedures, and routines. How leaders can unlevel otherwise level playing fields through using (or ignoring) slowification, simplification, and amplification, which either enable their organizations to compete in the *winning zone* or constrain them to struggle in the *danger zone*.

Winners win because they have superior approaches for designing, operating, and improving the social circuitry by which individual efforts are harmonized through collective action toward a common purpose.* The best social circuitry simply makes it easier for individuals to put their minds to good use, to give fullest expression to their innate creativity, and to solve

---

* In effect, we're saying that competitive strategy shouldn't just be oriented around finding or creating defensible positions, those with barriers to entry or exit, as Michael Porter's *Competitive Strategy* would have it. Rather, it should be oriented around velocity and even acceleration, finding ever better ways to do things of ever greater value.

the difficult problems in front of them. As a result, leaders liberate their colleagues from worrying about or being worn out by Layer 3 problems, so they can direct their attention where it's actually needed, to the Layer 1 and Layer 2 problems, solutions for which have great value for organizations and society.

In contrast, organizations with poor wiring have Layer 3 problems. People are unable to do their work because they can't get the information, equipment, and materials they need. Or, there's ambiguity on what they're supposed to do, for what reason, when, and on behalf of whom. Collectively, these Layer 3 problems prevent people from doing great technical work in Layers 1 and 2, preventing individual effort from harmonizing into an effective whole.

The value of creating excellent wiring in Layer 3 is clear in the cross-sectional case studies we presented among organizations and their peers and near-peers. We saw this in competing organizations such as Apple and Nokia.* The argument becomes even clearer in longitudinal comparisons, which contrast the experiences of the same organization before and after it rewired its social circuitry: for example, with the case study on Amazon's e-commerce software, there was no shift in mission and no dramatic change in their resources, talent pool, operating conditions, and so forth. The result was vast improvements in their experiences and outcomes. The only thing they changed were their management systems, the social circuitry by which collaboration and coordination occur.

In fact, when leadership effectively employs the three mechanisms of slowification, simplification, and amplification, successes are fantastic, yet often without obvious evidence of leadership involvement. Consider the experience of student pilot Maggie Taraska (discussed in Chapter 2), who found herself alone in the cockpit of an airplane that had lost its landing gear. What could have been a tragedy wasn't. Habituated amplification from a fellow pilot enabled quick reporting that Maggie's plane had gone into distress, broadcasting it immediately and clearly to the controller, who could receive the signal and react appropriately. Air traffic control simplified the situation by creating a coherent, modular communication bubble around the situation, so Maggie, the controller, and her instructor

---

* It's an ongoing comparison in the manufacturing sector between Toyota and other automakers.

could work through the problem without being interrupted by other air-to-ground communication. Maggie's instructor broke the norms of terse, coded communication to provide reassurance, anchoring her back in her training. This created the necessary time and space to arrive at a solution creatively and deliberately, without resorting to impulsive, fast-thinking habits (i.e., they shifted to the simplified, slowified conditions needed to rescue the situation).

So, in all of this, where was leadership? In short, the answer is, nowhere. At least, not in performance. But leadership was everywhere in planning and practice. The performance environment was in the *danger zone*, with fast-moving, complex, high-hazard situations. However, because of the previous cycles of planning and preparation, the flight instructor knew how to coach a student out of a precarious situation over the radio because there'd been opportunity to practice and build that capability. Air traffic control knew when and how to switch the boundaries around who was communicating with whom, about what, in what way. They knew how to flip from normal operations to emergency operations, which had been planned and practiced to the point of great proficiency. Leaders aren't obvious in the midst of performance, but their fingerprints are all over the planning and preparatory practice.

In this conclusion, we will show how many management concepts you're likely familiar with map onto the three mechanisms of slowification, simplification, and amplification. This is to make clearer why and how each helps—so it's more obvious which to use in what circumstances—how they all fit in the greater whole. We will also describe how leading an organization that is wired to win is quite different in beliefs and behaviors when compared with organizations that are less well wired. Finally, this conclusion will also help you understand the choices you have, as a leader responsible for the conditions in which your colleagues work and the experiences that they have in trying to generate and deliver value.

Connecting the Dots

In the beginning of the book, we noted that you almost certainly recognize familiar concepts such as agile, DevOps, Deming, the Toyota Production System (TPS), OODA loops, improvement katas, and Lean startup. Or you may have heard of system dynamics, learning organizations, double-loop learning, psychological safety, the Westrum organizational typology model, empowerment and participative management, enabling front-line workers, and the normalization of deviance. And you may be using terms such as "gemba walks," Team Topologies, cognitive load, software architecture, Conway's Law, modularity, resilience engineering, and paying down technical debt.

We had promised to explain how these concepts are all incomplete expressions of a far greater whole and how they fit together. Both Figure C.1 and Table C.1 (see page 276) show how these bodies of knowledge are expressed through the three mechanisms of slowification, simplification, and amplification.

For example, when done well, DevOps employs all three mechanisms. TPS—as used in actual practice at Toyota, its best suppliers, and those organizations that have been high-fidelity learners—also employs all three mechanisms. There's process simplification by way of linearization. This is not just for assembly line operations but, in the extreme, all processes, such as onboarding of new employees, ramp-up production in new products, and standby of entirely new facilities. There's amplification through the use of tools that draw attention to problems when and where they occur. And that amplification both triggers and informs regular and rigorous problem-solving by individuals, teams, groups, and larger aggregations. Slowification is also used regularly to develop, test, and introduce new ideas when problem-solving is triggered by amplified signals that something is amiss.[1]

Similarly, DevOps codifies the principles and practices used in the best-performing technology organizations, which enable them to deliver applications and services quickly and safely. This enables rapid experimentation and innovation and the fastest delivery of value to their customers while preserving world-class security, reliability, and stability.[2] This is achieved through technical practices (linearization, amplification, slowification), architectural practices (modularization), and cultural norms (amplification, which should trigger slowification or simplification).

On the one hand, the fact that DevOps and TPS employ similar mechanisms might be surprising, given their apparent differences in inspiration and origins. Yet, perhaps this should not be surprising. Designing and producing automobiles reliably and effectively designing and implementing the processes by which the vehicles will be produced and delivered require enormous intellectual and physical effort, far beyond the capability of any small group. Similarly, for DevOps, the creation of new software systems and their design, development, deployment, and operations are staggering in their immensity and difficulty, requiring a vast number of functional specialties that must be integrated into the whole.

Therefore, as different as they might initially appear, both DevOps and TPS have the commonality of being developed to create conditions in which it's easier for individuals to succeed at what they do and have their efforts contribute seamlessly to a much larger whole. That there is "convergent evolution" of management systems across different situations is encouraging. Designing and operating software services pre-DevOps, in the 2000s, is different from the work done designing and producing automobiles at Toyota in the 1950s and 1960s, both in Layers 1 and 2. However, the Layer 3 problems are very similar between those two very different domains (and others that have shown a similar coevolution).

We find it exciting that in both of these disparate domains, a similar solution was independently derived, indicating that there is indeed a common underlying mechanism.*

In Table C.1 (on page 274), you will note groups of management practices are very similar in how they rely on a combination of slowification, simplification, or amplification despite the apparent dissimilarities in their origins and the domains in which they are applied. For instance, consider the similarities in the following practices: "Gemba walks" are encouraged, in part, so that what might get missed in reports becomes amplified in clarity, frequency, and speed to those who actually go and see. This is to encourage deliberate reflection on what's been observed and to inform a rigorously generated corrective action[3] using amplification to trigger slowification. The concept of "single-loop learning" describes how experiences often go without reflection on why things went differently than expected or desired.

---

* This characterization is actually not entirely coincidental—the domains most cited in the earliest DevOps talks and papers (circa 2009) were Deming, the Toyota Production System, and Lean thinking.

On the other hand, double-loop learning describes how the signal should be received and reacted to, with self-reflective assessment that informs an improved understanding and better approaches for next iterations.[4]

Here, again, we observe different advice from different sources and motivated by different experiences, but all advise on amplification (by seeing or hearing), ideally leading to slowification (in the form of slow-thinking reevaluation and (re)planning). Other practices have the shared emphasis of increasing the likelihood of seeing and believing something is amiss (amplification) and reacting to it thoroughly and deliberately, as opposed to responding haphazardly and in haste.

Another group of practices are a combination of incrementalization and amplification. For example, Agile software development practices were created in response to waterfall approaches, where everything was sequentially designed, developed, tested, and then delivered to the user. The first opportunity to test the integrated whole was after all the software was written (likely too late to make meaningful changes). Similarly, the first opportunity to get user feedback on the tested software was at the very end of the process (again, too late to make changes). These contributed to massive rework, driving projects over deadline and over budget.[5] Agile methods advocate developing the smallest possible version of something that can be tested and getting user feedback on its features, functionality, and fit to inform the next development iteration. Doing this enabled incrementalization in the development and deployment of capabilities, as amplified signals from testing and user feedback.[6]

The Lean startup methodology has a similar combination of incrementalization and iteration for amplification, applied not just to products but to the entire business model supporting them. The initial motivation was similar to that which prompted Agile. So much was being invested in business model planning, but the plans failed too often. Too much was assumed and too little was discovered when ideas were piloted in the field.[7]

Here's one more example of a cluster of practices that have a common theme: avoiding the suppression of signals that something is amiss. Researchers from both psychological safety (Dr. Amy Edmondson) and safety culture (Dr. James Reason, Dr. Ron Westrum) emphasize the importance of not "shooting the messenger of bad news." Doing so discourages people from generating signals of problems and dangers, ensuring that those who could fix them will never learn of them, and the problems will go unaddressed.

Dr. Diane Vaughan's concept of "normalization of deviance" similarly highlights the risks of diminishing signals that something is amiss. In her work, it's not so much someone with more authority deliberately silencing those with less; it's more people becoming conditioned to accept as normal what once was not. Nevertheless, the effect is the same: suppression of signal generation and transmission and weakening of reception and reaction.

Additionally, research studies have repeatedly demonstrated that amplification of signals is critical for high performance in software delivery. In 2012, a team of researchers at Google found that psychological safety was the top predictor of team effectiveness.[8] Similarly, in the State of DevOps research, a high-trust culture, which includes psychological safety, predicted software delivery and organizational performance in technology value streams, as measured by the Westrum organizational typology model, which divided organizations into pathological, bureaucratic, and generative.[9]

These are just a few examples that show how different practices, emerging from different situations, nevertheless converge on similar conclusions about how to manage the complex interaction of people working toward a common purpose. However, when we consider that the most precious resource in any organization is people's ingenuity and creativity, the most common risk is cognitive overload. Given that, perhaps it is very logical and encouraging that luminary thinkers from both practice and research have come to similar conclusions about how to protect those precious resources so they can be put to the best possible use.

Table C.1 (on page 276) shows a variety of commonly known practices. We display how we believe they are best characterized by slowification, simplification, and amplification. The Venn diagram (Figure C.1) shows a different representation: our best effort to place the practices on which of the mechanisms most characterizes them. The intent of both the table and the diagram is to help you navigate among the alternatives available when you recognize a situation is in need of being slowified to make problem-solving easier, simplified to make the problems themselves easier to solve, or amplified to make it more obvious there are problems to be addressed.

FIGURE C.1 Venn Diagram of How Different Practices
Slowify, Simplify, or Amplify

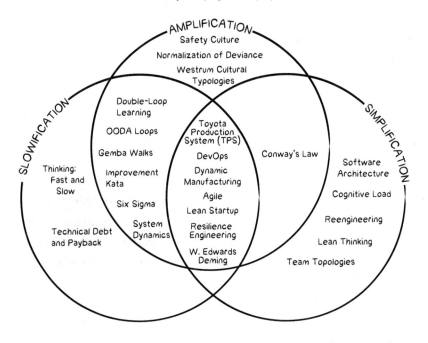

TABLE C.1 Common Practices Compared to Slowification,
Simplification, and Amplification

PRACTICE OR THEORY	Slowification	Simplification			Amplification	KEY I: Incrementalization, M: Modularization, L: Linearization
		I	M	L		COMMENTS
Toyota Production System Ohno, Liker, Spear	✓	✓	✓	✓	✓	When done at its highest levels, TPS is characterized by flow, linearization, standardization (simplification), and tests built in to work to reveal problems (amplification), which trigger offline, disciplined problem-solving (slowification).

| PRACTICE OR THEORY | Slowification | Simplification | | | Amplification | KEY I: Incrementalization, M: Modularization, L: Linearization |
		I	M	L		COMMENTS
DevOps *Debois, Forsgren, Humble, Kim, Willis*	✓	✓	✓	✓	✓	Set of architectural practices (modularization, linearization), technical practices (incrementalization), and cultural norms (slowification, amplification) that enable software delivery performance and organizational performance.
W. Edwards Deming	✓			✓	✓	Championed a number of approaches for increasing the clarity of feedback in systems. Control charts to make it clearer sooner whether a process was in control or not. Shewhart problem-solving cycles to make clearer what hypotheses are being tested and whether or not they are being refuted. These and other methodologies make possible the steady generation and accumulation of "profound knowledge" that allows for ever better performance.
Agile Software Development	✓	✓			✓	Emerged as an attempt to build through a process of discovery, aiming to deliver higher-quality software more quickly, through small, fast, and frequent iterations. By encouraging developers to interact with users, user feedback was amplified.
Lean Startup *Blank, Ries*	✓	✓			✓	Feedback-rich cycling of incrementally improved products, sales and marketing processes, etc., so the entirety of the business model is discovered iteratively and dynamically.
Resilience Engineering *Hollnagel, Woods, Leveson, Allspaw*	✓		✓		✓	Studies how systems and organizations can absorb and adapt to shocks and disruptions, recognizing that complex systems are inherently unpredictable and that failure is inevitable, but that systems can be designed and managed to prevent these failures from leading to catastrophic outcomes.

| PRACTICE OR THEORY | Slowification | Simplification | | | Amplification | KEY *I*: Incrementalization, *M*: Modularization, *L*: Linearization |
		I	*M*	*L*		COMMENTS
System Dynamics *Forrester, Sterman*	✓				✓	Key point: how systems are structured determines the patterns of feedback in them, and thus determines their dynamic behavior over time.
Double-Loop Learning *Argyris, Schön*	✓				✓	Recognizing that something has gone awry and reacting to that by changing how one understands situations. In contrast to single-loop learning, which doesn't trigger appropriate learning reactions.
Improvement Kata *Rother*	✓				✓	Emphasizes a structured, disciplined approach to problem-solving that makes clear and tests hypotheses (understand direction, set a challenge, grasp the current condition, set the next target condition, and conduct experiments to achieve the target condition).
"Gemba Walks," Empowerment, Participative Management	✓				✓	When done faithfully, promotes a culture of openness, collaboration, and continuous learning and active involvement and decision-making authority at all levels of an organization to enhance performance and problem-solving.
Conway's Law			✓	✓		Organizations design and build systems that mirror their communication structure.
Cognitive Load *Sweller, Reason*			✓	✓		Cognitive load is associated with how much information someone needs to know and understand in order to get their work done. High cognitive load can lead to mistakes, slow progress, and poor decision-making.
Team Topologies *Skelton, Pais*	✓		✓	✓		Uses cognitive load to inform team structures and architectures, noting that the organization of teams directly affects the software systems created.

| PRACTICE OR THEORY | Slowification | Simplification | | | Amplification | KEY I: Incrementalization, M: Modularization, L: Linearization |
		I	M	L		COMMENTS
Technical Debt *Cunningham, Cagan*	✓					Term used in software to delay slowification, leading to problems that get increasingly more difficult to fix over time, continually reducing our available options in the future, increasing our cost of change over time.
Software Architecture *Brooks, Parnas*			✓			Described properties of encapsulation (the ability to make changes to one module without changing other modules), high cohesion, low coupling, interchangeability, and reuse.
Normalization of Deviance *Vaughan*					✓	What were once considered defects and errors become accepted as normal, so feedback diminishes (weaker generation and transmission) that problems exist, and even if they are called out, they are less acknowledged as being worthy of attention (weakened reception and reaction).
Lean Thinking *Womack, Jones*				✓		Emphasis on value stream, flow, and pull as actions to improve efficiency (remove waste) and improve quality.
Psychological Safety *Edmondson*					✓	Social, psychological, and professional impediments to calling out problems (squelching of generation and transmission of useful feedback) diminishes the ability of individuals and groups to learn and improve.
Cultural Typologies *Westrum*					✓	Described information flow as a prime variable in creating safety, but also an indicator of organizational functioning. Defined three categories of organizations: pathological, bureaucratic, and generative.

Leadership Beliefs and Behaviors

The differences in leadership mindset and actions are evident in how Gene and Steve thought and acted in the beginning of refurbishing the old Victorian hotel and in the end. They started with elaborate schedules and expediting. In effect, movers and painters were being treated as "resources," scarce ones at that, who had to be assigned where they could be put to best possible use. Gene and Steve were doing what markets do. They were using the best information they had to allocate scarce resources among competing needs and putting those resources where they thought they had the greatest value.

Or we could think about this slightly differently. They were treating the schedule as an operations research optimization problem: assign resources, the supply of which is "constrained," across competing objectives to algorithmically maximize on some objective function. Either way, they were trying to figure out how to get the movers and painters to best fit into the Layer 3 management system they had created.

What's telling is what they *weren't* doing. By treating the painters and movers as objects, they weren't engaging them as colleagues and collaborators—active contributors to solving important problems.* Moreover, Gene and Steve had a very static view of their experience and that of the people for whom they were responsible. Refurbishing the hotel required lifting, moving, and repositioning furniture and prepping and painting the different rooms. Gene and Steve had an implicit assumption of what was achievable, given "the resources" available to them, limited by their own ability to schedule and optimize.

Contrast that to how the situation ended. Gene and Steve were no longer treating the movers and painters whose help they had enlisted as "objects" to be assigned or otherwise told where to be and what to do. They'd switched from what was essentially a transactional approach to

---

* Dr. Alistair Cockburn made this same observation in the study of software engineering; the most often overlooked, but most important, active components of complex software systems are...the people working within the system. The wonderful title of his paper describes people as the opposite of automatons: "Characterizing People as Non-Linear 1st Order Components in Software Development."[10]

management—in which resources were being swapped from one use to another—to one that was more developmental or learning oriented. With this developmental orientation, Gene and Steve increasingly focused on creating conditions in which people's minds could be put to better use discovering solutions to difficult problems.

To do this, they collaborated to determine where and when it made sense to partition work so more people could contribute to solving problems. And those problems largely revolved around making it easier for painters and movers to do outstanding work, safer, quicker, easier, and better than they had been doing it.

Focusing on the experiences of the front-line worker and rewiring the overlay of processes and procedures to make it easier to do those jobs well is paralleled throughout the various cases. The MIT Sloan School sailing team captains were working with their classmates to make it easier to be an outstanding novice sailor. In the drug development case, those with leadership responsibilities worked with their colleagues to make it easier to be outstanding chemists, biologists, technicians, supply-chain experts, or facilities managers.

The Navy's leadership (1900–1945) worked with sailors of different ranks to figure out how they could contribute to a more effective Navy. To reopen schools after the COVID-19 lockdowns, the leadership in Waukesha County, Wisconsin, worked with their district counterparts to figure out how to create conditions in which principals and teachers could be more effective in solving the problems that would impact them and their students.

In effect, Gene and Steve started by thinking that their job was to get the movers and painters to fit into and support the system. By the end, they were trying to figure out, with the help of the movers and painters, how to get the system to be as centered around the movers and painters as possible as well as be supportive of their efforts. Such a worker-centric mindset is reflected in the practices of the exemplar factory, showcased at the end of Chapter 10. There, leaders' roles were to support those for whom they were responsible during performance. Then, between rounds of performance, their job was to support (re)planning and new practice to make the system even more conducive to success.

That mindset and the behaviors associated with it—of slowification, simplification, and amplification—weren't static. They didn't imply that because "resources" were scarce, achievement was limited. Rather, by designing work so that it was easier for people to solve more problems, easier, quicker, and better, they were, in effect, implying that their situation wasn't limited permanently by some conservation of mass and energy or some other natural law. The work was limited only temporarily by what they knew and by what they still did not understand. But, structure the situation to allow a productive learning dynamic, and those limitations will be short lived. This is the essential difference between transactional and developmental mindsets (which you can explore in more detail in Appendix B). And it is vital to note, that approaching leadership with a developmental mindset is essential to wiring your organization to win. Without it, you and your organization can never experience the full effects of slowification, simplification, and amplification.

Final Thoughts

In the Preface, we described the magic of being part of a winning organization. Some of us have been lucky enough to experience this at least once in our careers. Hopefully this is something you experience every day. In winning organizations, leaders are able to liberate the full creativity and problem-solving capabilities of everyone in their organization, resulting in delight and appreciation from the customers they serve. In dismal organizations, leaders constrain, or maybe even fully extinguish, the creativity and problem-solving capabilities of everyone in their organization, resulting in customers being disappointed and frustrated.

The magic of winning organizations can be explained by how those organizations are wired. Conversely, when an organization is miswired, the result is not just dismal outcomes, but drudgery, frustration, misery, cynicism, loss of dignity, and maybe even danger.

As we stated at the beginning of this book, leadership matters. But leadership requires more than being inspirational, motivational, direction setting, and so forth. Leaders must manage the social circuitry of their organization as well.

As a leader, you set the conditions that dictate the extent to which people in the organization are able to do work well. And these conditions determine whether we experience misery or delight, boredom or engagement, abysmal failure or stunning success. This, in turn, dictates the ability of the organization to achieve any metric that matters, such as resilience, agility, time to market, quality, profitability, and so forth.

To put these theories into practice in your own organizations and liberate the full potential of your people, you can start by asking three simple questions:

1. Are we solving our toughest problems in planning and practice, where we can iterate and learn? Or are we being forced to solve them in the unforgiving environment of performance?
2. Are we shaping our problems so that they are easier to solve because they are simple, low risk, controllable, and easy to understand and iterate and learn from? Or are we solving problems that are complex, high stakes, high risk, and fast moving, with many intertwined factors, where it's difficult to iterate and learn?
3. Are we calling out problems loudly and consistently so that they can be swarmed, contained, solved, and prevent future occurrences? Or are important signals of problems unable to be generated, transmitted, received, acted upon, and corrected, and are people suffering from problems, working around them, with problems snowballing?

If you answered yes to the first question in each of these pairs, you are making it possible for everyone to do their job well and enabling them to use their full skills and talents to solve important and meaningful problems for themselves and others. Moreover, as a leader, you are able to spend less time reacting and firefighting and instead create enduring solutions that help push the frontiers of performance, both for your organization and the customers you serve.

If you answered yes to the second question in each of these pairs, we challenge you to answer the following questions to help you think about where best to start:

1. What part of your organization is experiencing the problem?
2. Why is this problem important? Whom does it affect, and how does it affect them?
3. Who will help you, as the leader, improve your ability to slowify, simplify, and amplify?
4. When will you start?

Answering these questions gives you what you need to start a model line, which will be the basis for moving that part of your organization from the *danger zone* to the *winning zone*. This will then serve as the basis for even more improvements faster, better, easier, at a larger scale, and with even more impact.

We sincerely hope that *Wiring the Winning Organization* has provided you with the principles and practices that will enable you to replicate the amazing and inspiring achievements that have been described in this book. The rewards for doing so are enormous, for the people in the organization, as well as for the customers and the members of society you serve.

Remember, as Winston Churchill said, "We shape our buildings and afterwards our buildings shape us."[11] So too the social circuitry of processes, procedures, routines, and the like determine how we do our work individually and how we do it collaboratively and collectively.

We wire our organizations to win through the three mechanisms of slowification, simplification, and amplification. This moves our organization out of the *danger zone* and into the *winning zone*. This is evident in the cases we shared—and hopefully in the many other cases and experiences that came to mind as you read this.

Remember, you have the potential to change the conditions in which you and your colleagues work, so please take advantage of it.

Influences: Authors, Thinkers, and Leaders

We want to take a moment to explain the substantial number of influences and theories that inform this book, which draws on management, engineering, and mathematics. For the avid reader and thoughtful practitioner (and academics) who have spent time studying these areas, you may find the lineage of ideas interesting and surprising.

§

What is novel about our theory is that it directly addresses the mechanisms of the social circuitry that enables organizations to achieve these performance advantages. And it recognizes that coordinating and synchronizing various specialties is an information problem to support creative collaboration. The concept of *circuitry* will be familiar to those concerned with how machines connect to and communicate with other machines. We apply it here to how people and groups communicate and coordinate with each other.

Wiring the Winning Organization asserts that outsized performance doesn't come merely from reorganizing the shop floor or from adjusting how materials pass through machines (literally or figuratively). Doing so still leaves people spending time and energy on heroics to get things they need to succeed (e.g., information, approvals, requirements, time), navigating often bewildering and byzantine work conditions, processes, procedures, policies, politics, rules, and regulations in their daily work (what we call the *danger zone*).

Instead, the most successful organizations are those that create conditions in which people can fully focus their intellects on solving difficult problems collaboratively and toward a common purpose, delivering solutions that have great societal value (conditions that we call the *winning zone*).

Creating such conditions requires developing and engaging three mechanisms to get out of an operating *danger zone* and into a contemplative *winning zone*:

1. slowification of the environment in which the problem-solving occurs to make problem-solving easier;
2. simplification of products, processes, and systems through the use of modularization, incrementalization, and linearization to make the problems themselves easier; and
3. amplification to make it more obvious that problems are occurring so they can be seen and solved.

This book explored each of these concepts at length. These insights build on and are informed by streams of research in management theory and adjacent areas that are worth breaking down briefly. We'll start with *slowification*.

There are distinctions between fast and slow thinking, as explained by Dr. Daniel Kahneman and Dr. Amos Tversky, that we lean heavily into throughout Part II of the book. Their work distinguishes between slower conditions (in which people can be deliberate, reflective, and creative) versus faster-moving, higher-stakes conditions (in which people must depend upon the "muscle memory" of practiced habits and routines because there is neither sufficient time nor emotional or psychological safety to consider if new approaches might be warranted).[1]

Slowification expands upon this concept by placing an emphasis on creating opportunities to absorb feedback that fosters self-reflection and self-correction. This connects to the literature on organizational learning from systems scientist Dr. Peter Senge's *The Fifth Discipline*, business theorist Dr. Chris Argyris's *Organizational Learning*, and work by philosopher Dr. Donald Schön.

Simplification may be the most difficult of the three mechanisms because there are three distinct techniques to engage it—modularization, incrementalization, and linearization.

- Modularization simplifies problems by partitioning *large, complex systems* (the elements of which have highly intertwined interdependencies) into systems that are more modular in structure, with each module having clearly defined boundaries and established conventions for interactions with other modules. Clarity around modularization was influenced by Dr. Steve Eppinger's design structure matrix concepts, Dr. Carliss Baldwin and Dr. Kim Clark's book *Design Rules*, Dr. Charles Perrow's ideas around complexity and coupling in *Normal Accidents*, and the wealth of architectural practices around APIs, containers, domain-driven design, and so forth.
- Incrementalization simplifies problem-solving by converting a *few, complex experiments* (in which many factors are being tested simultaneously) into *many smaller, faster, simpler experiments* (in which fewer factors are being tested individually). It does this by partitioning what is already known and validated from what is novel and new, and by adding to the novelty in many small bits rather than in a few large bites. This simplification method is informed by agile processes for product development, and, for the enterprise more generally, by work about the "lean launchpad," as explained by Steve Blank's *The Four Steps to the Epiphany* and by Eric Ries in *The Lean Startup*.
- Linearization *sequences* tasks associated with completing a larger set of work so that they flow successively, like a baton being passed from one person to the next. What follows is *standardization* for those sequences, for exchanges at partition boundaries, and for how individual tasks are performed. This creates opportunities to introduce *stabilization*, so that when a problem occurs, it triggers a reaction that contains the problem and prevents it from enduring and from its effects from spreading. This allows for *self-synchronization*, so the system is self-pacing without top-down monitoring and

direction. Linearization (as well as amplification and slowification) draws from the teachings of the Toyota Production System and Taiichi Ohno; Hammer and Champy's book *Reengineering the Corporation* (which championed a process view for organizing enterprises in lieu of an overly functionalized approach); Dr. Bob Hayes, Dr. Steve Wheelwright, and Dr. Kim Clark's *Dynamic Manufacturing* (which also speaks to a process view of organizing versus a functional, metric-driven approach); Dr. Eliyahu Goldratt and Jeff Cox's *The Goal*; Dr. James Womack, Dr. Daniel Jones, and Dr. Daniel Roos's *The Machine that Changed the World*; and, of course, Dr. Jeffrey Liker's monumental *The Toyota Way*.

The science around the *amplification* (or suppression) of small problems includes "normalization of deviance," as explained by Dr. Diane Vaughan in *The Challenger Launch Decision*, and feedback as critical for stability and progress, as explained by Dr. Jay Forrester and the systems dynamics community. The common link is that in the absence of fast, frequent, and useful feedback, systems of any type—technological, biological, social, psychological—will experience instability and even collapse. Systems with reliable feedback that triggers appropriate reactions are stable, resilient, and agile in even the most arduous situations. In the long term, systems that have adequate feedback and are capable of adaptation will improve, sometimes in dramatic ways, both by direction and magnitude.

Amplification also draws heavily on the work about control systems of Dr. Harry Nyquist and Dr. Claude Shannon in "Communication in the Presence of Noise," and Shannon and Dr. Warren Weaver's 1948 book *The Mathematical Theory of Communication*.

There's a meta-acknowledgment necessary here, and that is from Steve to mentors Dr. Clay Christensen and Dr. H. Kent Bowen for pushing so hard on developing a bona fide theory that explains competitive success. Both emphasized, supported, and coached the "inductive" element of theory building—observation, description, categorization, classification, and finally, declaration of causality. They were both wildly supportive of the "deductive" element of theory testing by creating hypotheses that could be refuted or not in practice. Neither Gene nor Steve would have been so obsessive in creating a "simple" theory of learning-based operational excellence without having this thinking in mind.

Last, we don't want to understate how strongly we argue against the static transactional notions of management and leadership that have so relentlessly gripped theory and practice. Decades ago, economist Dr. Michael Porter compared industrial sectors. He found that those in which competition was less perfect—due to the firms' ability to lock in customers and suppliers and lock out rivals—offered higher returns than those in which competition was more perfect—due to the ruthlessness of challenge and the greater difficulty of differentiating one's own offerings from those of rivals.[2]

However, by having the "unit of analysis" of the industrial sector, Porter's theory of differentiation by positioning couldn't explain the sustained heterogeneity of outcomes, even within highly competitive sectors. In other words, competitive advantage alone couldn't explain Toyota's outlandish successes, overcoming whatever barriers to entry existed to newcomers and beating rivals in an otherwise level playing field, once it was established in the sector.

Yet, obsessiveness about grand strategic vision has, it seems, blinded too many manager/leaders to the opportunity to take a developmental approach, as we saw throughout the book. That developmental approach is not one of incessantly figuring out what transactions will yield the highest reward from existing resources in already established ways. While the transactions may be many, the mindset is not sufficiently dynamic. Rather, the developmental approach requires designing and improving the social circuitry by which people can best apply their creative energies to find new and better things to do with their time and the resources they have, and by developing new and better ways to do so.

Similarly, agency theory, as credited to economists Dr. Michael Jensen and Dr. William Meckling, takes the general notion that people respond to incentives in motivating their actions and creates a reductionist view of characterizing enterprises as primarily a collection of contractual relationships.[3] Get the metrics and incentives right, it would suggest, and people will behave accordingly. Again, this is a rather transactional notion of people's efforts, one that leaves little consideration for collaboration or coordination.

The problem is, of course, that the right metrics vary by degree of aggregation, phase, type of value creation, and so forth. How one measures performance in pharmaceutical research and development is different from measuring performance in clinical trials or production. So, you'd either have to measure everything by the same standards (so measure everything poorly) or you'd have to create metrics and rewards that are too impossibly diverse to monitor effectively.

And, of course, there's an implied assumption that you know well enough about what needs to be done individually and collectively, and you know well enough about how to get it done that contracts can be well written. So, organizations trying to create metrics, accountability, and incentives to drive performance—rather than designing systems that are able to harness the investment people are already willing to make in achieving great things together—miss the developmental opportunities that create the chance for greatness.

In contrast, we present slowification, simplification, and amplification as the mechanisms by which a developmental approach of creating new and better things in new and better ways can be most fully expressed.

Transactional vs. Developmental Leadership

To better see the contrast between transactional and developmental leadership mindsets, let's revisit NASA's experience with the *Apollo 11* landing (and the missions that preceded it) and that of Boston's medical community on the day of the marathon bombing.

When asked about what limitations hinder their ability to create and deliver value, transactional leaders will likely be concerned about constraints (row *a* in Table A.1). They will point out that they have limited resources, which restrict the alternatives available to which those resources can be put to use. For them, the corrective action is to improve resource allocation, either by transactions in a market to get more or better people and more or better resources or by some algorithm (e.g., assign them better for more productive uses), (row *c*), to achieve some "optimal" outcome as measured by productivity, efficiency, profitability, utility, and so forth, (row *d* in Table A.1).

The result is that they are stuck operating within a frontier, constantly weighing what to do with what they have, and why to do it, based on costs and benefits. That is also reflected in Figure A.1. Those with a transactional mindset are constantly doing cost-benefit analysis, trying to determine how much of Need 1 to satisfy at the expense of not meeting all of Need 2, and vice versa. For transactional leaders, their only relief is to add more resources.

We must acknowledge that almost everyone, at some point, is forced into transactional cost-benefit analyses. However, those with a developmental mindset are able to create much better alternatives to choose from than they would have had otherwise. In contrast to transactional leaders, developmental leaders constantly expand the frontier to expand the possibilities (i.e., possible choices) available to them and their colleagues.

FIGURE A.1 Transactional vs. Developmental Attitudes

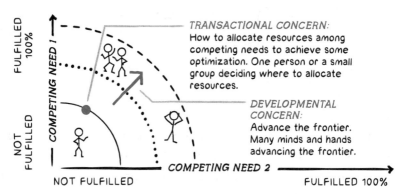

Optimizing on the frontier or advancing it (collaboratively).

Consider how developmental leaders responded to the following *danger zone* situations of fast-moving, unforgiving, uncontrollable, high-stakes, and nonrepeatable conditions in which they simply had to do the best that they could with the resources that were immediately available. On July 20, 1969, Neil Armstrong and Buzz Aldrin had a limited set of backup alternatives from which to choose (including aborting their mission) when they discovered that the designated lunar landing zone was strewn with boulders. On Patriots' Day 2013, Boston-area hospitals had limited alternatives as to what to do with patients already in their emergency departments when they found that trauma patients from the marathon bombing were on the way, who would need half or more of the capacity typically available.*

---

* Escort commanders had to make terrible choices during the early months of 1943, when the Battle of the Atlantic was in full fury. German U-boat submarine "wolf packs" were exacting huge tolls on convoys crossing from East Coast ports to bolster Britain with men and materials. They could scout ahead for the enemy, head back to protect the flocks of slower-moving cargo ships, or stay even farther back to pick up survivors of ships that had already been torpedoed. The resources were few, the demands were many, and the choices were terrible.

In those situations, developmental leaders were able to create far better choices in those *danger zone* situations. Aldrin and Armstrong had an alternative landing spot and a way to land safely because NASA had invested so heavily in preparatory, feedback-rich planning and practice that tested people, systems, and processes. NASA had created *winning zone* conditions of greater simplicity, lower risk, more controllability, and repeatability to build a repertoire of possibilities. NASA invested in building the skills to solve the difficult problems that might have imperiled the successful lunar landing of *Apollo 11*'s crew and expanded the number of possible alternatives available to the crew. In doing so, they were using the same developmental mindset that characterized NASA's management of itself and its university and corporate partners from the early days of the Mercury program, through the Gemini missions, and those Apollo flights that had preceded *Apollo 11*.

On the day of the marathon bombing, Boston-area emergency departments had routines they could employ to get patients already in the emergency department admitted into other units of the hospital (or quickly discharged) to clear space and allow attention to the trauma casualties. This was because they'd done so many drills and other rehearsals to expand their set of alternatives.

Similarly, leaders at Amazon were faced with thousands of software engineers with little independence of action, having increasing difficulties making changes within a tightly coupled software system, often resulting in global outages. Instead of hiring more managers to coordinate the work being done on Layer 1 and Layer 2 problems, Amazon focused instead on creating *winning zone* conditions by re-architecting their Layer 3 wiring, which brought back independence of action to software teams. This enabled them to push the frontiers of performance, from twenty risky software deployments per year in 2011 to doing 136,000 routine deployments per day in 2015.

Those specific examples highlight the mindset that distinguishes developmental leaders from ones who are always transactional. For developmental leaders, the limitations are not resources but useful knowledge about what to do with the resources that are available and how and why to get it done. In other words, the limitation is lack of knowledge (ignorance), (row *a* in Table A.1), for which the corrective action is creating and utilizing conditions in which it's far easier for people individually and collaboratively to solve difficult problems quicker, easier, and better (row *b*).

The objective for them is not finding an optimal solution along a fixed frontier. It is advancing the frontier of what solutions are possible (row *c*). And that leads them in the direction of creating systems in which people can succeed, so that they can generate great solutions to difficult problems, and then bring those ideas into action (row *d*). In the longer term, the developmental leader is not constantly lobbying for more resources, which would otherwise be used in much the same fashion for the same purposes as the resources that are already available. Instead, developmental leaders are always trying to figure out how to improve the problem-solving capabilities of the people for whom they are responsible.[*]

Therefore, as shown in the Figure A.1, developmental leaders' concerns are different from transactional ones. They are not constantly recalculating how much of Need 1 to satisfy at the expense of Need 2 or how much of Need 2 to satisfy in trade-off with Need 1. Rather, they're trying to figure out how to engage the minds of more people pushing together to advance the frontier of what is possible.

We've seen distinctions between the transactional and developmental mindset throughout the various cases. The developmental mindset is one of relentless and iterative experimentation. That is why designers in any field, who have such a developmental mindset, are always looking to increase the number and speed of iterations from which we might learn. Their desks will be covered by (the equivalent of) drawings and they are marked by mock-ups and prototypes. Then they will construct scale models and increasingly realistic models before committing to the final design, which can be constructed and released.

---

[*] In the book *Engineers of Victory*, it is shown that while in the short term, commanders had to make terrible transactional decisions for every convoy, the good fortune was that, in parallel, a developmental effort was also occurring: development of better code breaking to anticipate where U-boats might be lurking, development of better sonar to detect U-boats, and better long-range aircraft to destroy the U-boats once they'd been detected. Yes, in the short term, leaders were limited to short-term, transactional decisions. But the developmental engine behind them meant that the frontier of possibilities was being pushed out and the set of alternatives was improving.

TABLE A.1 Contrasting Transactional and Developmental Leadership

		TRANSACTIONAL ORIENTATION	DEVELOPMENTAL ORIENTATION
a	What limits our ability to create and deliver value?	Scarce resources and the limited alternatives for which they can be used.	Useful understanding of resources' best possible use: the range of alternatives that might be pursued and how to use the resources most effectively in pursuit of those possibilities.
b	What actions can we take to meet our goals?	"Optimization": allocation of scarce resources to best possible use (by transaction [in a market] or reassignment [by algorithm]).	Slowification, simplification, and amplification make it quicker and easier to solve difficult problems better.
c	What are we trying to achieve?	Achieve some optimal point on the frontier of what is achievable, given the resources available.	Advance the frontier of what is achievable by bringing new and useful knowledge into practice.
d	What is primary and what has to adapt?	The system is primary, and people have to adapt to it.	The people are primary, and the system has to be adapted to fit people and the work they have to do individually and collaboratively, so more value is created quicker and easier.
e	What is needed to increase output?	More resources.	Better problem-solving.

Literally or figuratively, projects for them are crumpled-up sketches overflowing from a wastebasket, foam-core models scattered on a desk, and drawing sets that are numbered by their double-digit revisions. Of course, if not for those iterations, subject to strong (self-)critical review, code wouldn't run, medications wouldn't work, planes wouldn't fly, cars would underperform, articles and books would be unreadable, and buildings would leak and be poorly lit.

Transactional vs. Developmental Mindset in Improving Layer 3 Processes

We see such a developmental mindset come into play when it comes to designing new or improving existing processes. Transactional leaders focus on the process itself. They believe that by carefully calculating and developing a solution, they can effectively impose it on the individuals responsible for executing it. This approach stems from the belief that limited resources are the primary constraint and the appropriate course of action is to allocate them optimally.

Contrast that to leaders with a developmental mindset. Their starting assumption is that their limitation is insufficient understanding about how to use the resources available to them; that better understanding has to be discovered. So, they don't try to fix everything all at once. They partition a microcosm model line from the larger whole of the enterprise.

This presents an opportunity for individuals to collaborate with their colleagues, identify areas that are not functioning effectively, propose new approaches, rapidly test them in real-world scenarios, learn from the outcomes, and iterate for further discoveries. In practice, the model line serves as the practical equivalent of sketches and scale models used by designers, who are focused on continuous development.

How We Teach Layer 3 Skills: Model Lines and Developmental Leadership

The model line can be used to build Layer 3 skills in much the same way that it can be used for problems in Layers 1 and 2. It facilitates a rapid comprehension of processes, but it also becomes a platform in which more people can build the skills for being great Layer 3 designers, operators, and improvers. The model line is a small piece of the larger whole. It is more controllable; fewer people are involved, so coordination is easier, less disruptive, and less costly; and the consequences of it not working are manageable. Furthermore, there's more opportunity to pause, plan again, and practice anew.

When learning how to solve problems in Layers 1 and 2, professionals are first trained to understand the underlying principles and science of their domains. As first principles are being introduced, small problems are being offered—preferably with feedback and coaching—and work is often completed on paper. Then they explore and iterate to solve increasingly larger problems. As skill is demonstrated, less work is on paper and more is practical problem-solving with small projects. If successful, they then become responsible for increasingly larger, more complex, and more consequential projects that might require more collaboration.

So too with building great Layer 3 skills. The model line can not only serve as the platform for piloting and validating new ideas of social circuitry, but it can also be the training ground for those who need exposure to, practice with, and mastery of the mechanisms of slowification, simplification, and amplification.

FIGURE A.2 Transactional vs. Developmental Mindsets:

Improving Processes Directly or through the Minds and Hands of Colleagues

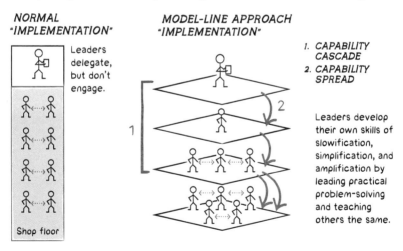

The model line yields multiple outputs. It generates lessons learned about problems in Layers 1 and 2. It identifies how to better use the technical and administrative apparatuses available to create the products and services for which the enterprise is responsible. It yields insights into better Layer 3 designs for processes, procedures, and routines. And, model lines increase the number of people creating better conditions for themselves and for those for whom they are directly responsible.

In organizations, we are all likely, at some point, to be responsible for teaching someone something that is important. The transactional mindset is to focus on grading the learner, whereas the developmental mindset will be focused on building capability.

Transactional and developmental mindsets are also found throughout education, from primary school through professional training. For instance, we can see this with how a high school teacher might handle a quiz. A transactional teacher might focus on the graded outcomes without allowing for opportunities to learn from the wrong answers. A developmental teacher might focus on the opportunity wrong answers give for more practice and learning.

Those wrong answers might be recognized as amplification of what students didn't yet know and what they still needed to learn. The response to those signals would be to focus on teaching students how to correctly do problems of the types that each had gotten wrong.

BIBLIOGRAPHY

4Sammich. "I Have Friends in CS...." Reddit (comment). *R/Flying*, December 27, 2022. www.reddit.com/r/flying/comments/zw5lsl/southwest_pilots_hows _it_going/j1tne9z/.

"17-Year-Old Student Pilot Lands Her Plane Without A Wheel!" YouTube video, 3:27, posted by VASAviation, posted on September 11, 2018. https://www .youtube.com/watch?v=B229-KLudTo.

"Adapter, Gemini." National Air and Space (website). Accessed July 7, 2023. https://airandspace.si.edu/collection-objects/adapter-gemini/nasm_A1 9700287000.

Adler, Paul S., and Robert E. Cole. "Designed for Learning: A Tale of Two Auto Plants." *MIT Sloan Management Review*. Spring 1993. https://sloanreview .mit.edu/article/designed-for-learning-a-tale-of-two-auto-plants/.

"The Wright Brothers at Kitty Hawk." National Air and Space (website).June 23, 2022. https://airandspace.si.edu/stories/editorial/wright-brothers-kitty -hawk.

"Airline On-Time Tables." Bureau of Transportation Statistics (website). Accessed July 7, 2023. https://www.bts.gov/topics/airline-time-tables.

"Amazon Annual Net Sales 2022." Statista (website). Accessed July 7, 2023. https://www.statista.com/statistics/266282/annual-net-revenue-of-amazoncom/.

"Amazon.Com Revenue (Annual)." YCharts (website). Accessed July 7, 2023. https://ycharts.com/companies/AMZN/revenues_annual.

"Amazon Web Services Revenue Growth 2022." Statista (website). Accessed July 7, 2023. https://www.statista.com/statistics/422273/yoy-quarterly-growth -aws-revenues/.

Apple Newsroom. "Apple Reports Fourth Quarter Results." Apple.com (website). Accessed July 6, 2023. https://www.apple.com/newsroom/2007/10/22 Apple-Reports-Fourth-Quarter-Results/.

Argyris, Chris, and Donald A. Schön. *Organizational Learning: A Theory of Action Perspective*. Reading, Mass: Addison-Wesley, 1978.

Armstrong, Benjamin F. "Continuous-Aim Fire: Learning How to Shoot." *Naval History Magazine* 29, no. 2 (April 2015). https://www.usni.org/magazines /naval-history-magazine/2015/april/continuous-aim-fire-learning-how -shoot.

"Arrival Procedures." FAA.gov (website). Accessed July 6, 2023. https://www.faa .gov/air_traffic/publications/atpubs/aim_html/chap5_section_4.html.

Ars OpenForum. "The Audacious Rescue Plan That Might Have Saved Space Shuttle Columbia," *Ars Technica*. February 26, 2014. https://arstechnica.com /civis/threads/the-audacious-rescue-plan-that-might-have-saved-space -shuttle-columbia.1236031/.

Atchison, Lee. "Coding Over Cocktails: How to Archtect Your Applications to Scale with Lee Atchison." Coding over Cocktails (website). Accessed July 7, 2023. https://www.torocloud.com/podcast/lee-atchison.

"Ault, Frank Willis." Naval History and Heritage Command (website). Accessed July 6, 2023. https://www.history.navy.mil/research/library/research-guides /modern-biographical-files-ndl/modern-bios-a/ault-frank-willis.html.

Baldwin, Carliss Y., and Kim B. Clark. *Design Rules, Volume 1: The Power of Modularity*. Cambridge, MA: The MIT Press, 2000.

Baranek, David "TOPGUN: The Navy's First Center of Excellence." *Proceedings: US Naval Institute*, September 2019. https://www.usni.org/magazines/pro ceedings/2019/september/topgun-navys-first-center-excellence.

Bell, T. E., and T. A. Thayer. "Software Requirements: Are They Really a Problem?" In *Proceedings of the 2nd International Conference on Software Engineering*, 61–68. ICSE '76. Washington, DC, USA: IEEE Computer Society Press, 1976.

Benington, Herbert D. "Production of Large Computer Programs." *Annals of the History of Computing* 5, no. 4 (October 1983): 350–61. https://doi.org /10.1109/MAHC.1983.10102.

Bernstein, Larry. "Characterizing People as Non-Linear, First-Order Components in Software Development, Is Written by Alistair A.R. Cockburn and Published in Humans and Technology, HaT Technical Report 1999.03, Oct 21, 1999." *ACM SIGSOFT Software Engineering Notes* 35, no. 4 (July 20, 2010): 33–34. https://doi.org/10.1145/1811226.1811241.

Bhattacharya, Ananya. "A 'Once-in-a-Generation' Winter Storm Is Causing Thousands of Flight Cancellations." Quartz. December 23, 2022. https://qz.com /winter-storm-elliott-flight-cancellations-christmas-tra-1849926058.

Biddinger, Paul D., Aaron Baggish, Lori Harrington, Pierre d'Hemecourt, James Hooley, Jerrilyn Jones, Ricky Kue, Chris Troyanos, and K. Sophia Dyer. "Be Prepared—The Boston Marathon and Mass-Casualty Events." *New England Journal of Medicine* 368, no. 21 (May 23, 2013): 1958–60. https://doi.org/10.1056/NEJMp1305480.

Blank, Steve. "No Plan Survives First Contact With Customers—Business Plans versus Business Models." *Steve Blank* (blog), April 8, 2010. https://steveblank.com/2010/04/08/no-plan-survives-first-contact-with-customers-%e2%80%93-business-plans-versus-business models/.

———. *The Four Steps to the Epiphany: Successful Strategies for Products That Win.* 1st edition. Hoboken, NJ: Wiley, 2020.

Bomey, Nathan. "How Barnes & Noble Pulled off an Unlikely Turnaround." Axios. March 1, 2023. https://www.axios.com/2023/03/01/barnes-and-noble-james-duant-ceo.

Boston Trauma Center Chiefs' Collaborative. "Boston Marathon Bombings: An after-Action Review." *The Journal of Trauma and Acute Care Surgery* 77, no. 3 (September 2014): 501–3. https://doi.org/10.1097/TA.0000000000000397.

Boyer, Chuck. "The 360 Revolution." IBM (website). April 2004. http://archive.computerhistory.org/resources/text/IBM/ibm_%20360_revolution_story_102634496.pdf.

"Brooklyn Museum—Open Collection." Brooklyn Museum (website). Accessed July 6, 2023. https://www.brooklynmuseum.org/opencollection/exhibitions/1188.

Bureau, US Census. "Nearly 93% of Households With School-Age Children Report Some Form of Distance Learning During COVID-19." Census.gov(website). Accessed July 6, 2023. https://www.census.gov/library/stories/2020/08/schooling-during-the-covid-19-pandemic.html.

Bushard, Brian. "Winter Storm Elliott: Nearly 2,000 U.S. Flights Canceled As Mega Storm Disrupts Holiday Travel." *Forbes*. Accessed July 7, 2023. https://www.forbes.com/sites/brianbushard/2022/12/22/winter-storm-elliott-nearly-2000-us-flights-canceled-as-mega-storm-disrupts-holiday-travel/.

Byyny, Richard L. "Cognitive Bias: Recognizing and Managing Our Uncon-scious Biases." *The Pharos* (Winter 2017): 2–6.

Cagan, Marty. *Inspired: How to Create Tech Products Customers Love*. 2nd edition. Hoboken, NJ: Wiley, 2017.

Carpenter, Dick, and Joshua Dunn. "We're All Teachers Now: Remote Learning During COVID-19." *Journal of School Choice* 14, no. 4 (October 1, 2020): 567–94. https://doi.org/10.1080/15582159.2020.1822727.

Charles, John. "The Space Review: Adapter in the Rough." *The Space Review*. January 30, 2017. https://www.thespacereview.com/article/3158/1.

Cheng, A. F., A. G. Santo, K. J. Heeres, J. A. Landshof, R. W. Farquhar, R. E. Gold,and S. C. Lee. "Near-Earth Asteroid Rendezvous: Mission Overview." *Journal of Geophysical Research: Planets* 102, no. E10 (October 25, 1997): 23695–708. https://doi.org/10.1029/96JE03364.

Cheng, Andrew F., Andrew S. Rivkin, Patrick Michel, Justin Atchison, Olivier Barnouin, Lance Benner, Nancy L. Chabot, et al. "AIDA DART Asteroid Deflection Test: Planetary Defense and Science Objectives." *Planetary and Space Science* 157 (August 2018): 104–15. https://doi.org/10.1016/j.pss.2018 .02.015.

Christensen, Clayton M., Steven King, Matt Verlinden, and Woodward Yang."The New Economics of Semiconductor Manufacturing." *IEEE Spectrum*45, no. 5 (May 2008): 24–29. https://doi.org/10.1109/MSPEC.2008.4505308.

"Columbia Accident Investigation Board Report." NASA (website). Accessed July 6, 2023. https://history.nasa.gov/columbia/CAIB_reportindex.html.

"Consumer Price Index, 1800- | Federal Reserve Bank of Minneapolis." Federal Reserve Bank of Minneapolis (website). Accessed July 6, 2023. https://www .minneapolisfed.org/about-us/monetary-policy/inflation-calculator/ consumer-price-index-1800-.

"Control Theory." *Wikipedia* (website). July 5, 2023. https://en.wikipedia.org/w /index.php?title=Control_theory&oldid=1163522462.

"Controller Gives Pilot Terrible News."YouTube video, 2:26, posted by 74 Gear, posted on May 29 2022. https://www.youtube.com/watch?v=RZ0Qr3l8 UPM.

Cortada, James W. "Change and Continuity at IBM: Key Themes in Histories of IBM." *Business History Review* 92, no. 1 (April 2018): 117–48. https://doi .org/10.1017/S0007680518000041.

"Crash Course: The Decisions That Brought Down United Flight 173-ProQuest." ProQuest (website). Accessed July 6, 2023. https://www.proquest.com/doc view/1698504019/.

Cunningham, Ward. "The WyCash Portfolio Management System." OOPSLA '92 Experience Report. March 26, 1992. https://c2.com/doc/oopsla92.html

"DART Impactor Spacecraft." DART (website). Accessed July 6, 2023. https://dart .jhuapl.edu/Mission/Impactor-Spacecraft.php.

"DART Team." DART (website). Accessed July 6, 2023. https://dart.jhuapl.edu /Team/.

"David Silverman, Coauthor of 'Team of Teams: New Rules of Engagement for a Complex World.'" DevOps Enterprise Summit (video). 2022. https://www.youtube.com/watch?v=OCsTBo8QN2w.

"Dawn." NASA (website). Accessed July 6, 2023. https://nssdc.gsfc.nasa.gov/nmc/spacecraft/display.action?id=2007-043A.

"December 1, 1913 | Ford's Assembly Line Starts Rolling." History (website). Accessed July 6, 2023. https://www.history.com/this-day-in-history/fords-assembly-line-starts-rolling.

"Deep Space 1."NASA (website). Accessed July 6, 2023. https://nssdc.gsfc.nasa.gov/nmc/spacecraft/display.action?id=1998-061A.

"Digest of Education Statistics, 2021." National Center for Education Statistics. Accessed July 6, 2023. https://nces.ed.gov/programs/digest/d21/tables/dt21_203.10.asp.

"Double Asteroid Redircetion Test (DART)." NASA (website). Accessed July 6, 2023. https://nssdc.gsfc.nasa.gov/nmc/spacecraft/display.action?id=2021-110A.

Dupor, Bill. "Examining Long and Variable Lags in Monetary Policy." Federal Reserve Bank of St. Louis. May 4, 2023. https://www.stlouisfed.org/publications/regional-economist/2023/may/examining-long-variable-lags-monetary-policy.

Eagle, James. "Animation: The Most Popular Websites by Web Traffic (1993-2022)." Visual Capitalist (website). September 9, 2022. https://www.visualcapitalist.com/cp/most-popular-websites-by-web-traffic/

Edmondson, Amy C. *The Fearless Organization: Creating Psychological Safety in the Workplace for Learning, Innovation, and Growth.* 1st edition. Hoboken, New Jersey: Wiley, 2018.

EdWeek Research Team. "Survey Tracker: Monitoring How K-12 Educators Are Responding to Coronavirus." *Education Week.* April 28, 2020. https://www.edweek.org/teaching-learning/survey-tracker-monitoring-how-k-12-educators-are-responding-to-coronavirus/2020/04.

Finlay, Mark. "The Various Factors That Downed United Airlines Flight 173 On This Day In 1978." *Simple Flying.* January 1, 2023. https://simpleflying.com/united-airlines-flight-173-crash-anniversary/.

Forsgren, Nicole, Jez Humble, and Gene Kim. *Accelerate: The Science of Lean Software and DevOps: Building and Scaling High Performing Technology Organizations.* 1st edition. Portland, Oregon: IT Revolution Press, 2018.

Friedman, Milton. "The Lag in Effect of Monetary Policy." *Journal of Political Economy* 69, no. 5 (1961): 447–66.

Furfaro, Emily. "NASA's DART Data Validates Kinetic Impact as Planetary Defense Method." NASA (website). February 28, 2023. http://www.nasa.gov/feature /nasa-s-dart-data-validates-kinetic-impact-as-planetary-defense-method.

Gates, Jonathan D., Sandra Arabian, Paul Biddinger, Joe Blansfield, Peter Burke, Sarita Chung, Jonathan Fischer, et al. "The Initial Response to the Boston Marathon Bombing." *Annals of Surgery* 260, no. 6 (December 2014): 960–66. https://doi.org/10.1097/SLA.0000000000000914.

Gist. "Stevey's Google Platforms Rant." GitHub (website). Accessed July 7, 2023. https://gist.github.com/chitchcock/1281611.

Glass, Ira. "This American Life Episode 561: NUMMI (2015)." This American Life. December 14, 2017. https://www.thisamericanlife.org/561/transcript.

Goldratt, Eliyahu M., and Jeff Cox. *The Goal: A Process of Ongoing Improvement - 30th Anniversary Edition*. 30th Anniversary Edition. Great Barrington, Mass: North River Press, 2014.

Goodfriend, Marvin, and John McDermott. "The American System of Economic Growth." *Journal of Economic Growth* 26, no. 1 (March 1, 2021): 31–75. https://doi.org/10.1007/s10887-021-09186-x.

Goralnick, Eric, and Jonathan Gates. "We Fight Like We Train." *New England Journal of Medicine* 368, no. 21 (May 23, 2013): 1960–61. https://doi.org/10.10 56/NEJMp1305359.

Goralnick, Eric, Pinchas Halpern, Stephanie Loo, Jonathan Gates, Paul Biddinger, John Fisher, George Velmahos, et al. "Leadership During the Boston Marathon Bombings: A Qualitative After-Action Review." *Disaster Medicine and Public Health Preparedness* 9, no. 5 (October 2015): 489–95. https://doi.org /10.1017/dmp.2015.42.

Hadaway, Stuart. "The Real Top Gun: History of the US Navy Pilot School." LiveScience (website). March 29, 2022. https://www.livescience.com/real-top-gun.

Hammer, Michael. "Reengineering Work: Don't Automate, Obliterate." *Harvard Business Review*, July 1, 1990. https://hbr.org/1990/07/reengineering -work-dont-automate-obliterate.

Hammer, Michael, and James Champy. *Reengineering the Corporation: A Manifesto for Business Revolution*. Illustrated edition. New York: Harper Business, 2006.

"Hayabusa." NASA (website) Accessed July 6, 2023. https://nssdc.gsfc.nasa.gov /nmc/spacecraft/display.action?id=1998-061A.

Hayes, Robert H., Steven C. Wheelwright, and Kim B. Clark. *Dynamic Manufacturing: Creating the Learning Organization*. New York: Free Press, 1988.

Haynes, Al. "The Crash of United Flight 232." Transcript. Edwards, California: Ames Research Center, Dryden Flight Research facility, May 24, 1991. http://clear-prop.org/aviation/haynes.html.

Hearing before the Committee on Homeland Security and Governmental Affairs. "Lessons Learned from the Boston Marathon Bombings: Preparing for and Responding to the Attack." US Government Publishing Office, July 10, 2013. https://www.govinfo.gov/content/pkg/CHRG-113shrg82575/html/CHRG -113shrg82575.htm.

Henderson, Rebecca M., and Kim B. Clark. "Architectural Innovation: The Reconfiguration of Existing Product Technologies and the Failure of Established Firms." *Administrative Science Quarterly* 35, no. 1 (1990): 9–30. https://doi .org/10.2307/2393549.

Hickey, Matt Stiles, Christopher. "How Southwest Failed the Holidays: Four Charts Explaining the Cancellations | CNN Business." *CNN*. December 29, 2022. https://www.cnn.com/2022/12/29/business/southwest-cancellations -history-charts-dg/index.html.

Hiltzik, Michael. "The Real Story behind the Collapse in Southwest's on-Time Performance." *Los Angeles Times*. October 14, 2014. https://www.latimes.com /business/hiltzik/la-fi-mh-southwest-air-20141014-column.html.

"History of the Royal Society." Royal Society (website). Accessed July 6, 2023. https://royalsociety.org/about-us/history/.

Hone, Trent. *Learning War: The Evolution of Fighting Doctrine in the U.S. Navy, 1898–1945*. Illustrated edition. Naval Institute Press, 2018.

Hounshell, David. *From the American System to Mass Production, 1800-1932: The Development of Manufacturing Technology in the United States*. Baltimore, Md.: Johns Hopkins University Press, 1985.

"House of Commons Rebuilding (Hansard, 28 October 1943)." Accessed July 7, 2023. https://hansard.millbanksystems.com/commons/1943/oct/28/house -of-commons-rebuilding.

IBM. "Explore the 2022 IBM Annual Report Today." IBM (website). March 7, 2023. https://www.ibm.com/annualreport/index.html.

Itazaki, Hideshi. *The Prius That Shook the World: How Toyota Developed the World's First Mass-Production Hybrid Vehicle*. Translated by Albert Yamada and Maasako Ishikawa. The Nikkan Kogyo Shimbun, Ltd., 1999.

Jaspan, Caitlin, Edward Sadowski, Alex Aftandilian, Liam Eagle, and Ciera Miller-Cushon. "Lessons from Building Static Analysis Tools at Google." *Communications of the ACM* 61, no. 4 (April 2018): 58–66. https://doi.org/10.1145 /3188720.

Jensen, Michael C., and William H. Meckling. "Theory of the Firm: Managerial Behavior, Agency Costs and Ownership Structure." SSRN Scholarly Paper. Rochester, NY, July 1, 1976. https://doi.org/10.2139/ssrn.94043.

Johnson, Stephen B. *The Secret of Apollo: Systems Management in American and European Space Programs*. Baltimore, MD: Johns Hopkins University Press, 2006.

Kahneman, Daniel. *Thinking, Fast and Slow*. 1st edition. New York: Farrar, Straus and Giroux, 2013.

Killalea, Tom. "A Second Conversation with Werner Vogels: The Amazon CTO Sits with Tom Killalea to Discuss Designing for Evolution at Scale." *Queue* 18, no. 5 (November 10, 2020): Pages 10:67–10:92. https://doi.org/10.1145/34345 71.3434573.

Kim, Gene. "The Idealcast: Episode 11: David Silverman and Jessica Reif." Accessed July 7, 2023. https://itrevolution.com/podcast/the-idealcast-episode-11/.

———. "The Idealcast: Episode 13: David Silverman & Jessica Reif (Part 2)." Accessed July 7, 2023. https://itrevolution.com/podcast/the-idealcast-episode-13/.

Kim, Gene, Jez Humble, Patrick Debois, John Willis, and Nicole Forsgren. *The DevOps Handbook: How to Create World-Class Agility, Reliability, & Security in Technology Organizations*. Second edition. Portland, OR: IT Revolution Press, 2021.

King, David Richard, Andreas Larentzakis, Elie P. Ramly, and Boston Trauma Collaborative. "Tourniquet Use at the Boston Marathon Bombing: Lost in Translation." *The Journal of Trauma and Acute Care Surgery* 78, no. 3 (March 2015): 594–99. https://doi.org/10.1097/TA.0000000000000561.

Klein, Gary. *The Power of Intuition: How to Use Your Gut Feelings to Make Better Decisions at Work*. New York: Doubleday, 2003.

Klein, Gary. *Sources of Power, 20th Anniversary Edition: How People Make Decisions*. Cambridge, MA: MIT Press, 1999.

Kocienda, Ken. *Creative Selection: Inside Apple's Design Process During the Golden Age of Steve Jobs*. Illustrated edition. New York: St. Martin's Press, 2018.

"Kohelet - Ecclesiastes - Chapter 10." Chabad.org (website). Accessed July 6, 2023. https://www.chabad.org/library/bible_cdo/aid/16471/jewish/Chapter-10.htm.

Kranz, Gene. *Failure Is Not an Option: Mission Control From Mercury to Apollo 13 and Beyond*. New York: Simon & Schuster, 2009.

Krishnan, Kripa. "Weathering the Unexpected: Failures Happen, and Resilience Drills Help Organizations Prepare for Them." *Queue* 10, no. 9 (September 16, 2012): 30–37. https://doi.org/10.1145/2367376.2371516.

Landman, Adam, Jonathan M. Teich, Peter Pruitt, Samantha E. Moore, Jennifer Theriault, Elizabeth Dorisca, Sheila Harris, Heidi Crim, Nicole Lurie, and Eric Goralnick. "The Boston Marathon Bombings Mass Casualty Incident:

One Emergency Department's Information Systems Challenges and Opportunities." *Annals of Emergency Medicine* 66, no. 1 (July 2015): 51–59. https://doi.org/10.1016/j.annemergmed.2014.06.009.

"Langley Aerodrome A." National Air and Space Museum (website). Accessed July 6, 2023. https://airandspace.si.edu/collection-objects/langley-aerodrome/nasm_A19180001000.

Legacy User. "Battle of Lexington Reenactment, Patriots Day 2013." Boston.com (website). April 15, 2013. https://www.boston.com/uncategorized/noprimarytagmatch/2013/04/15/battle-of-lexington reenactment-patriots-day -2013/.

———. "Patriots Day Celebrations in Lincoln, Acton, Lexington, And Concord." Boston.com (website). April 11, 2013. https://www.boston.com/uncategorized/noprimarytagmatch/2013/04/11/patriots-day-celebrations-in-lincoln -acton-lexington-andconcord/.

Leone, Dario. "The Story of United Airlines Flight 173, the Plane Crash That Launched the Crew Resource Management Revolution in Airline Training." The Aviation Geek Club (website). June 23, 2021. https://theaviationgeek club.com/the-story-of-united-airlines-flight-173-the-plane-crash-that -launched-the-crew-resource-management-revolution-in-airline-training/.

"Lessons Netflix Learned from the AWS Outage." Netflix Technology Blog. April 18, 2017. https://netflixtechblog.com/lessons-netflix-learned-from-the -aws-outage-deefe5fd0c04.

Levy, Steven. "Google Throws Open Doors to Its Top-Secret Data Center." *Wired.* Accessed July 6, 2023. https://www.wired.com/2012/10/ff-inside-google -data-center/.

Lewis, Michael. *The Undoing Project: A Friendship That Changed Our Minds.* First Edition. New York: W. W. Norton & Company, 2016.

Loff, Sarah. "Apollo 11 Mission Overview." NASA (website). April 17, 2015. http://www.nasa.gov/mission_pages/apollo/missions/apollo11.html.

Marcus, Leonard, Eric McNulty, and Richard Serino. "Swarm Leadership in Times of Crisis." Harvard Kennedy School Center for Public Leadership (website). October 4, 2017. https://cpl.hks.harvard.edu/news/swarm-leadership-times -crisis.

McChrystal, General Stanley, Tantum Collins, David Silverman, and Chris Fussell. *Team of Teams: New Rules of Engagement for a Complex World.* Illustrated edition. New York, New York: Portfolio, 2015.

McCullough, David. *The Wright Brothers.* Simon & Schuster, 2016.

McGregor, Douglas. *The Human Side of Enterprise, Annotated Edition.* New York: McGraw Hill, 2006.

Meyer, Marc H. "IBM Rises from the Ashes." In *The Fast Path to Corporate Growth: Leveraging Knowledge and Technologies to New Market Applications*, edited by Marc H. Meyer. Oxford: Oxford University Press, 2007. https://doi.org/10 .1093/acprof:oso/9780195180862.003.0002.

"Microsoft Mobile." *Wikipedia*. Accessed July 1, 2023. https://en.wikipedia.org/w /index.php?title=Microsoft_Mobile&oldid=1162880214.

Milwaukee Journal Sentinel. "Wisconsin Public and Private Schools Are Canceling Classes; Here's an Updating List." *Milwaukee Journal Sentinel*. March 13, 2020. https://www.jsonline.com/story/news/education/2020/03/13 /wisconsin-schools-district-closed-closings-because-coronavirus-illness -full-list/5042213002/.

"Monet and Chicago." The Art Institute of Chicago (website). Accessed July 6, 2023. https://www.artic.edu/exhibitions/9036/monet-and-chicago.

Murray, Casey. "Strengthening Airline Operations and Consumer Protections: Written Testimony of Captain Casey Murray, President, Southwest Airlines Pilots Association (SWAPA)." Committe on Commerce, Science, & Transportation, United States Senate, February 9, 2023. https://www.commerce. senate.gov/services/files/B8D729EC-5F96-4E8D-A902-F43DA29F2E08.

Nadworny, Daniel, Katherine Davis, Cynthia Miers, Tyler Howrigan, Eileen Broderick, Kirsten Boyd, and Garry Dunster. "Boston Strong—One Hospital's Response to the 2013 Boston Marathon Bombings." *Journal of Emergency Nursing* 40, no. 5 (September 1, 2014): 418–27. https://doi.org/10.1016/j .jen.2014.06.007.

National Aeronautics and Space Administration. "Rosetta." Accessed July 6, 2023. https://nssdc.gsfc.nasa.gov/nmc/spacecraft/display.action?id=2004-006A.

National Transportation Safety Board. "Aircraft Accident Report: United Airlines, Inc. McDonnell-Douglas, DC-8-61, N8082U." Washington, DC: United States Government, December 28, 1978. https://www.ntsb.gov/investigations /AccidentReports/Reports/AAR7907.pdf.

Naval Air Systems Command. "Report of the Air-to-Air Missile System Capability Review, July - November 1968 (a.k.a. The Ault Report)," January 1, 1969.

"NEAR Shoemaker." eNational Aeronautics and Space Administration. (website). Accessed July 6, 2023. https://nssdc.gsfc.nasa.gov/nmc/spacecraft/display .action?id=1996-008A.

Nofi, Albert. "HM 18: To Train the Fleet for War: The U.S. Navy Fleet Problems, 1923-1940." *Historical Monographs*. January 1, 2010. https://digital -commons.usnwc.edu/historical-monographs/18.

Not a Blue Check Mark [@FlyingTigress]. "Evidently the @SouthwestAir Debacle Is Due to a Software Issue? Holy… @ElShanerino. https://T.Co/3jCDgHJwJ6." Tweet. *Twitter*, December 27, 2022. https://twitter.com/FlyingTigress/status/1607739070687371268.

NWS Buffalo [@NWSBUFFALO]. "A Once-in-a-Generation Storm Will Produce High Winds East of Lake Ontario Thursday Night into Friday Morning, Then over a Larger Coverage of Our Region Friday into Saturday. Winds Could Gust over 65 Mph, Leading to at LEAST Scattered Power Outages, If Not Widespread Outages. https://T.Co/G5EXx1TVNf." Tweet. *Twitter*, December 21, 2022. https://twitter.com/NWSBUFFALO/status/16055429438798 27458.

O'Hanlon, Charlene. "A Conversation with Werner Vogels: Learning from the Amazon Technology Platform: Many Think of Amazon as 'that Hugely Successful Online Bookstore.' You Would Expect Amazon CTO Werner Vogels to Embrace This Distinction, but in Fact It Causes Him Some Concern." *Queue* 4, no. 4 (May 1, 2006): 14–22. https://doi.org/10.1145/1142055.1142065.

Ohno, Taiichi. *Toyota Production System: Beyond Large-Scale Production*. 1st Edition. Cambridge, Mass: Productivity Press, 1988.

"Origins of the IBM System/360 : History of Information." History of Information (website). Accessed July 7, 2023. https://historyofinformation.com/detail .php?entryid=2703.

Pancotto, Marcelo. "Underlying Dynamics of Organizational Learning from a Problem Solving Perspective: Quality Improvement Efforts and Problem Population Dynamics - ProQuest." Harvard University. (Thesis). 2007. https://www.proquest.com/openview/1dc95e10e62c9cc4d0a31cbf29 44c97f/1?pq-origsite=gscholar&cbl=18750.

Parshall, Jonathan, and Anthony Tully. *Shattered Sword: The Untold Story of the Battle of Midway*. Illustrated edition. Washington, DC: Potomoc Cooks, 2007.

"Participation." Boston Athletic Association (website). Accessed July 6, 2023. https://www.baa.org/races/boston-marathon/results/participation.

Pascale, Richard, Jerry Sternin, and Monique Sternin. *The Power of Positive Devi-ance: How Unlikely Innovators Solve the World's Toughest Problems*. American First edition. Boston, Mass: Harvard Business Review Press, 2010.

Phorn, Bopha. "Teen Pilot on First Solo Flight 'freaked out a Little Bit' While Preparing to Land Damaged Plane." *ABC News*. September 12, 2018. https:// abcnews.go.com/US/teen-pilots-mom-describes-nerve-wracking-minutes -watching/story?id=57745039.

Porter, Michael E. *The Competitive Strategy: Techniques for Analyzing Industries and Competitors*. Export edition. New York: Free Press, 2003.

Press Center. "Amazon.Com Announces Financial Results for First Quarter 1998," April 27, 1998. https://press.aboutamazon.com/1998/4/amazon-com -announces-financial-results-for-first-quarter-1998.

Ralston, Katherine, and Alisha Coleman-Jensen. "USDA's National School Lunch Program Reduces Food Insecurity." *US Department of Agriculture: Economic Research Service*, August 7, 2017. https://www.ers.usda.gov/am- ber-waves/2017/august/usda-s-national-school-lunch-program-reduces -food-insecurity.

Redgap, Curtis, "Who Was That Guy? The Great American Automobile Pioneers." AllPar (website). November 16, 2020. https://www.allpar.com/threads/ who-was-that-guy-the-great-american-automobile-pioneers.229372/# post-1085223470

Reinertsen, Donald G. *The Principles of Product Development Flow: Second Gener- ation Lean Product Development*. 1st edition. Redondo Beach, California: Celeritas Pub, 2009.

"Re:Work Guide: Understanding Team Effectiveness." Accessed July 7, 2023. https://rework.withgoogle.com/print/guides/5721312655835136/.

Rhoades, Brady. "Meet The 'Godfather of Top Gun' | U.S. Veterans Magazine." US Veterans and Military Magazine | A US Veterans News Resource (blog), April 28, 2022. https://usveteransmagazine.com/2022/04/godfather -top-gun-story/.

Richards, Chet. *Certain to Win: The Strategy of John Boyd, Applied to Business*. Xlibris, Corp., 2004.

Ries, Eric. *The Lean Startup: How Today's Entrepreneurs Use Continuous Innovation to Create Radically Successful Businesses*. First Edition. New York: Currency, 2011.

Robbins, Jesse, Kripa Krishnan, John Allspaw, and Thomas A. Limoncelli. "Re- silience Engineering: Learning to Embrace Failure: A Discussion with Jesse Robbins, Kripa Krishnan, John Allspaw, and Tom Limoncelli." *Queue* 10, no. 9 (September 12, 2012): 20–28. https://doi.org/10.1145/2367376.2371297.

Rooney, Ben. "Apple Profits Surge 67%, Shares Soar." *CNN Money*. October 22, 2007. https://money.cnn.com/2007/10/22/technology/aapl_earnings/ index.htm?source=yahoo_quote

Rubinstein, Joshua S., David E. Meyer, and Jeffrey E. Evans. "Executive Control of Cognitive Processes in Task Switching." *Journal of Experimental Psychology: Human Perception and Performance* 27, no. 4 (2001): 763–97. https://doi .org/10.1037/0096-1523.27.4.763.

Sanchez, Czarina E., and Leon D. Sanchez. "Case Study: Emergency Department Response to the Boston Marathon Bombing." *Operational and Medical Management of Explosive and Blast Incidents* (July 2020): 363–367.

Scannell, Jack W., Alex Blanckley, Helen Boldon, and Brian Warrington. "Diagnosing the Decline in Pharmaceutical R&D Efficiency." *Nature Reviews Drug Discovery* 11, no. 3 (March 2012): 191–200. https://doi.org/10.1038/nrd3681.

Shannon, Claude E., and Warren Weaver. *The Mathematical Theory of Communication.* 16th Printing edition. Urbana: The University of Illinois Press, 1971.

Shannon, Richard P., Diane Frndak, Naida Grunden, Jon C. Lloyd, Cheryl Herbert, Bhavin Patel, Daniel Cummins, Alexander H. Shannon, Paul H. O'Neill, and Steven J. Spear. "Using Real-Time Problem Solving to Eliminate Central Line Infections." *Joint Commission Journal on Quality and Patient Safety* 32, no. 9 (September 2006): 479–487. https://doi.org/10.1016/s1553-7250(06)32 063-6.

"Share of K-12 Schools in the United States Teaching in-Person Due to the COVID-19 Pandemic from September 2020 to Febraury 2021." Statista (website). Accessed September 3, 2023. https://www.statista.com/statistics /1220611/covid-19-share-k-12-schools-in-person-teaching-us/

Sheth, Joann S. Lublin And Niraj. "Nokia Conducting Search for New CEO." *Wall Street Journal*, July 20, 2010, sec. Tech. https://www.wsj.com/articles/SB100 01424052748703720504575377750449338786.

Siilasmaa, Risto. *Transforming NOKIA: The Power of Paranoid Optimism to Lead Through Colossal Change.* 1st edition. New York: McGraw-Hill, 2018.

Skelton, Matthew, and Manuel Pais. *Team Topologies: Organizing Business and Technology Teams for Fast Flow*. Illustrated edition. Portland, OR: IT Revolution Press, 2019.

Skinner, Wickham. "The Focused Factory." *Harvard Business Review*. May 1, 1974. https://hbr.org/1974/05/the-focused-factory.

Smith, R. Jeffrey. "NASA Was Warned on Foam Question." *Washington Post.*July 28, 2005. https://www.washingtonpost.com/archive/politics/2005/07/28/ nasa-was-warned-on-foam-question/50056275-eef3-4a64-9b3b-e62d399 aee09/.

"Space Shuttle *Columbia* Disaster." *Wikipedia*. Accessed June 20, 2023. https:// en.wikipedia.org/w/index.php?title=Space_Shuttle_Columbia_disaster&ol did=1161017429.

"Space Shuttle Flights by Orbiter." NASA (website). Accessed July 6, 2023. https:// www.nasa.gov/mission_pages/shuttle/launch/orbiter_flights.html.

Spear, Steven. "Frequency Domain Quantification of Manufacturing Process Reso-
    lution." Massachusetts Institute of Technology (thesis). September 24, 2013.
    https://dspace.mit.edu/bitstream/handle/1721.1/80915/28358943-MIT
    .pdf;sequence=2

Spear, Steven J. "The Essence of Just-in-Time: Embedding Diagnostic Tests
    inWork-Systems to Achieve Operational Excellence." *Production Planning &
    Control* 13, no. 8 (November 1, 2002): 754–767. https://doi.org/10.1080/09
    53728031000057307.

———. "Fixing Health Care from the Inside, Today," *Harvard Business Review*,
    September 2005. https://hbr.org/2005/09/fixing-health-care-from-the
    -inside-today.

———. *The High-Velocity Edge: How Market Leaders Leverage Operational Excellence
    to Beat the Competition.* 2nd edition. New York: McGraw-Hill, 2010.

Spear, Steven J., and Mark Schmidhofer. "Ambiguity and Workarounds as Con-
    tributors to Medical Error." *Annals of Internal Medicine* 142, no. 8 (April 19,
    2005): 627–630. https://doi.org/10.7326/0003-4819-142-8-200504190
    -00011.

Spear, Steve, and Trent Hone. "Succeeding in Periods of Change," US Naval Insti-
    tute Magazine. March 1, 2022. https://www.usni.org/magazines/proceed
    ings/2022/march/succeeding-periods-change.

"Special Message to Congress on Urgent National Needs, 25 May 1961 | JFK Li-
    brary." JFK Library (website). Accessed July 6, 2023. https://www.jfklibrary
    .org/asset-viewer/archives/JFKWHA/1961/JFKWHA-032/JFKWHA-032.

"State of Devops Report 2017." Puppet, DORA. 2017. https://services.google.
    com/fh/files/misc/state-of-devops-2017.pdf.

St. George, Donna. "National Test Scores Plunge, with Still No Sign of Pandemic
    Recovery." *Washington Post.* June 20, 2023. https://www.washingtonpost.com
    /education/2023/06/21/national-student-test-scores-drop-naep/.

Stone, Brad. *The Everything Store: Jeff Bezos and the Age of Amazon.* Reprint edition.
    New York, NY: Back Bay Books, 2014.

Svigals, Jerry. "IBM's Gamble, Part I, September 1966," September 4, 1966. Com-
    puterHistory.org (website). http://archive.computerhistory.org/resources
    /access/text/2011/10/102713231-05-01-acc.pdf.

Sweller, John. "Cognitive Load during Problem Solving: Effects on Learning." *Cog-
    nitive Science* 12, no. 2 (April 1, 1988): 257–85. https://doi.org/10.1016
    /0364-0213(88)90023-7.

"Tenerife Airport Disaster." *Wikipedia.* Accessed July 1, 2023. https://en.wikipedia
    .org/w/index.php?title=Tenerife_airport_disaster&oldid=1162860047.

Tink, Andrew. "'They Nailed It': How a Little Dish in Australia Broadcast the Moon Landing to the World." *The Guardian*. July 18, 2019. https://www.the guardian.com/science/2019/jul/19/they-nailed-it-how-a-little-dish-in -australia-broadcast-the-moon-landing-to-the-world.

"Transcript: Fed Chief Powell's Postmeeting Press Conference." *Wall Street Journal*. June 14, 2023. https://www.wsj.com/articles/transcript-fed-chief -powells-postmeeting-press-conference-fa29e77e.

"Transforming Software Development." YouTube video, 40:58, posted by Amazon Web Services, posted on April 10, 2015. https://www.youtube.com/watch ?v=YCrhemssYuI.

Trottman, Melanie. "Vaunted Southwest Slips In On-Time Performance." *Wall Street Journal*. September 25, 2002. https://www.wsj.com/articles/SB103 289713522832313.

Tversky, Amos, and Daniel Kahneman. "Judgment under Uncertainty: Heuristics and Biases." *Science* 185, no. 4157 (1974): 1124–1131.

"United Airlines Flight 173." *Wikipedia*. Accessed on June 24, 2023. https://en .wikipedia.org/w/index.php?title=United_Airlines_Flight_173&oldid =1161748923.

"United Airlines Flight 232 | Facts & History | Britannica." Britannica (website). Accessed July 6, 2023. https://www.britannica.com/event/United-Airlines -Flight-232.

US Senate Committee on Commerce, Science, & Transportation. "Executive Session & Hearing: Strengthening Airline Operations and Consumer Protections," February 9, 2023. https://www.commerce.senate.gov/2023/2 /executive-session.

Vaughan, Diane. *The Challenger Launch Decision: Risky Technology, Culture, and Deviance at NASA*. First Edition. Chicago: University of Chicago Press, 1996.

"Velocity 2011: Jon Jenkins, 'Velocity Culture,'" YouTube video, 15:13, posted by O'Reilly, posted on June 20, 2011. https://www.youtube.com/watch?v= dxk8b9rSKOo.

"Vendors' Market Share of Mobile Phone Unit Sales Worldwide 1997-2014." Statista (website). Accessed July 6, 2023. https://www.statista.com/ statistics/271574/global-market-share-held-by-mobile-phone-manufactur ers-since-2009/.

Von Hippel, Eric. "'Sticky Information' and the Locus of Problem Solving: Implications for Innovation." In *The Dynamic Firm: The Role of Technology, Strategy, Organization, and Regions*, edited by Alfred D. Chandler, Peter Hagstrom, and Örjan Sölvell. Oxford University Press, 1999. https://doi.org/10.1093/0198 296045.003.0004.

Wakelin, Nicole. "How Many Parts Are in a Car?" NAPA (blog). July 2, 2021. https://knowhow.napaonline.com/how-many-parts-are-in-a-car/.

Wall, Mike. "NASA's Shuttle Program Cost $209 Billion - Was It Worth It?"Space. com (website). July 5, 2011. https://www.space.com/12166-space-shuttle -program-cost-promises-209-billion.html.

Walls, Ron M., and Michael J. Zinner. "The Boston Marathon Response: Why Did It Work So Well?" *JAMA* 309, no. 23 (June 19, 2013): 2441–2442. https:// doi.org/10.1001/jama.2013.5965.

Ward, Allen, Jeffrey K. Liker, John J. Cristiano, and Durward K. Sobek Ii. "The Second Toyota Paradox: How Delaying Decisions Can Make Better Cars Faster." *MIT Sloan Management Review*, April 15, 1995. https://sloanreview.mit.edu /article/the-second-toyota-paradox-how-delaying-decisions-can-make -better-cars-faster/.

Watkins, Michael D. "How Managers Become Leaders." *Harvard Business Review*. June 2012. https://hbr.org/2012/06/how-managers-become-leaders.

Waugh, Alice C. "MIT Sloan Team Wins International MBA Regatta." *MIT News | Massachusetts Institute of Technology*. October 7, 2014. https://news.mit .edu/2014/mit-sloan-team-wins-international-mba-regatta-1007.

"Weather in April 2013 in Boston, Massachusetts, USA." Time and Date (website). Accessed July 6, 2023. https://www.timeanddate.com/weather/usa/boston /historic?month=4&year=2013.

"What Happens When You Declare An Emergency With ATC?" Bold Method (website). Accessed July 6, 2023. https://www.boldmethod.com/learn-to-fly /regulations/what-happens-when-you-declare-an-emergency-with-atc/.

Wheelwright, Steven C. *Leading Product Development: The Senior Manager's Guide to Creating and Shaping the Enterprise*. New York: Free Press, 2007.

"Where Were You? Watching the Apollo 11 Moon Landing," *NY Post*. July 18, 2019. https://nypost.com/2019/07/18/readers-share-their-memories-of -the-apollo-11-moon-landing/.

"Wilbur and Orville." National Park Service (website). Accessed September 3, 2023. https://www.nps.gov/daav/learn/kidsyouth/wilburandorville.htm.

Womack, Jim, and John Shook. *Gemba Walks Expanded 2nd Edition*. 2nd ed. edition. Lean Enterprise Institute, Incorporated, 2019.

Wouters, Olivier J., Martin McKee, and Jeroen Luyten. "Estimated Research and Development Investment Needed to Bring a New Medicine to Market, 2009-2018." *JAMA* 323, no. 9 (March 3, 2020): 844–53. https://doi.org/10.1001 /jama.2020.1166.

Yamamoto, Kat, Mallory Milstead, and Robert Lloyd. "A Review of the Develop-
    ment of Lean Manufacturing and Related Lean Practices: The Case of Toyota
    Production System and Managerial Thinking" 15, no. 2 (2019).
Younkin, George, and Erling Hesla. "Origin of Numerical Control [History]." *IEEE
    Industry Applications Magazine* 14, no. 5 (September 2008): 10–12. https://
    doi.org/10.1109/MIAS.2008.927525.
Zaleznik, Abraham. "Managers and Leaders: Are They Different." *Harvard Business
    Review*. Janaury 2004. https://hbr.org/2004/01/managers-and-leaders
    -are-they-different

NOTES

Chapter 1

1. "Where Were You? Watching the Apollo 11 Moon Landing."
2. Loff, "Apollo 11 Mission Overview," 11.
3. Johnson, *The Secret of Apollo*.
4. Kranz, *Failure Is Not an Option*, 252.
5. Tink, "'They Nailed It.'"
6. "Special Message to Congress on Urgent National Needs."
7. Porter, *The Competitive Strategy*.
8. Yamamoto, Milstead, and LIoyd, "A Review of the Development of Lean Manufacturing and Related Lean Practices."
9. Ward et al., "The Second Toyota Paradox."
10. Itazaki, *The Prius That Shook the World*.
11. Adler and Cole, "Designed for Learning."
12. Christensen et al., "The New Economics of Semiconductor Manufacturing."
13. Robbins et al., "Resilience Engineering."
14. McChrystal et al., *Team of Teams*.
15. Spear, "Fixing Health Care from the Inside, Today"; Shannon et al., "Using Real-Time Problem Solving to Eliminate Central Line Infections."

Chapter 2

1. "Arrival Procedures."
2. "What Happens When You Declare An Emergency With ATC?"
3. Phorn, "Teen Pilot on First Solo Flight 'Freaked Out a Little Bit' While Preparing to Land Damaged Plane."
4. "Controller Gives Pilot Terrible News"; Phorn, "Teen Pilot on First Solo Flight 'Freaked Out a Little Bit' While Preparing to Land Damaged Plane"; "17-Year-Old Student Pilot Lands Her Plane Without A Wheel!"

5. *"Controller Gives Pilot Terrible News"*; Phorn, "Teen Pilot on First Solo Flight 'Freaked Out a Little Bit' While Preparing to Land Damaged Plane"; "17-Year-Old Student Pilot Lands Her Plane Without A Wheel!"

Chapter 3
1. Pascale, Sternin, and Sternin, *The Power of Positive Deviance*, 57–58.

Chapter 4
1. Rhoades, "Meet The 'Godfather of Top Gun' | U.S. Veterans Magazine."
2. Naval Air Systems Command, "Report of the Air-to-Air Missile System Capability Review, July - November 1968 (a.k.a. The Ault Report)."
3. Naval Air Systems Command, "Report of the Air-to-Air Missile System Capability Review, July - November 1968 (a.k.a. The Ault Report)."
4. Hadaway, "The Real Top Gun."
5. Baranek, "TOPGUN."
6. Klein, *The Power of Intuition*; Klein, *Sources of Power*.
7. Tversky and Kahneman, "Judgment under Uncertainty."
8. Byyny, "Cognitive Bias: Recognizing and Managing Our Unconscious Biases."
9. Lewis, *The Undoing Project*, 192.
10. Lewis, *The Undoing Project* 270.
11. Tversky and Kahneman, "Judgment under Uncertainty."
12. "Kohelet - Ecclesiastes - Chapter 10."
13. Cagan, *Inspired*, Kindle loc. 469.
14. Cunningham, "The WyCash Portfolio Management System."

Chapter 5
1. Based on conversations with the participants; Waugh, "MIT Sloan Team Wins International MBA Regatta."
2. Spear and Schmidhofer, "Ambiguity and Workarounds as Contributors to Medical Error."
3. Shannon et al., "Using Real-Time Problem Solving to Eliminate Central Line Infections."
4. Shannon et al., "Using Real-Time Problem Solving to Eliminate Central Line Infections."
5. Author interview with clinicians.
6. Author interview with center representatives.
7. Kranz, *Failure Is Not an Option*, 287.
8. Kranz, *Failure Is Not an Option*, 287.
9. Kranz, *Failure Is Not an Option*, 21.

10. Kranz, *Failure Is Not an Option*, 263.
11. Kranz, *Failure Is Not an Option*, 265.
12. Kranz, *Failure Is Not an Option*, 269.
13. Kranz, *Failure Is Not an Option*, 269.
14. Kranz, *Failure Is Not an Option*, 271.
15. Kranz, *Failure Is Not an Option*, 271.
16. "Columbia Accident Investigation Board Report."
17. Ars Open Forum, "The Audacious Rescue Plan That Might Have Saved Space Shuttle Columbia."
18. Ars Open Forum, "The Audacious Rescue Plan That Might Have Saved Space Shuttle Columbia."
19. Ars Open Forum, "The Audacious Rescue Plan That Might Have Saved Space Shuttle Columbia."
20. Ars Open Forum, "The Audacious Rescue Plan That Might Have Saved Space Shuttle Columbia."
21. Wall, "NASA's Shuttle Program Cost $209 Billion."
22. "Space Shuttle Flights by Orbiter."
23. Vaughan, *The Challenger Launch Decision*.
24. Smith, "NASA Was Warned on Foam Question"; "Space Shuttle *Columbia* Disaster."
25. "Space Shuttle *Columbia* Disaster."
26. Parshall and Tully, *Shattered Sword*.
27. Nofi, "HM 18."
28. "United Airlines Flight 232 | Facts & History | Britannica."
29. Haynes, "The Crash of United Flight 232."
30. Haynes "The Crash of United Flight 232."
31. Haynes "The Crash of United Flight 232."
32. "United Airlines Flight 232 | Facts & History | Britannica."
33. "United Airlines Flight 232 | Facts & History | Britannica."
34. Haynes, "The Crash of United Flight 232."
35. Haynes "The Crash of United Flight 232."
36. Haynes "The Crash of United Flight 232."
37. "United Airlines Flight 173"; Leone, "The Story of United Airlines Flight 173, the Plane Crash That Launched the Crew Resource Management Revolution in Airline Training"; Finlay, "The Various Factors That Downed United Airlines Flight 173 On This Day In 1978."
38. "United Airlines Flight 173."
39. National Transportation Safety Board, "Aircraft Accident Report: United Airlines, Inc. McDonnell-Douglas, DC-8-61, N8082U."

40. "Crash Course."
41. National Transportation Safety Board, "Aircraft Accident Report: United Airlines, Inc. McDonnell-Douglas, DC-8-61, N8082U."
42. "Tenerife Airport Disaster."
43. Eagle, "Animation: The Most Popular Websites by Web Traffic (1993-2022)."
44. Krishnan, "Weathering the Unexpected."
45. Robbins et al., "Resilience Engineering."
46. Krishnan, "Weathering the Unexpected."
47. Robbins et al., "Resilience Engineering."
48. Robbins et al., "Resilience Engineering."
49. Levy, "Google Throws Open Doors to Its Top-Secret Data Center."
50. "Amazon.Com Revenue (Annual)"; "Amazon.Com Announces Financial Results for First Quarter 1998."
51. Robbins et al., "Resilience Engineering."
52. Robbins et al., "Resilience Engineering."
53. "Lessons Netflix Learned from the AWS Outage."
54. "Lessons Netflix Learned from the AWS Outage."
55. "Lessons Netflix Learned from the AWS Outage."

Chapter 6
1. "Weather in April 2013 in Boston, Massachusetts, USA."
2. Gates et al., "The Initial Response to the Boston Marathon Bombing."
3. Goralnick et al., "Leadership During the Boston Marathon Bombings."
4. Biddinger et al., "Be Prepared — The Boston Marathon and Mass-Casualty Events."
5. Biddinger et al., "Be Prepared — The Boston Marathon and Mass-Casualty Events."
6. Sanchez and Sanchez, "Case Study: Emergency Department Response to the Boston Marathon Bombing."
7. Goralnick and Gates, "We Fight Like We Train."
8. Biddinger et al., "Be Prepared — The Boston Marathon and Mass-Casualty Events."
9. Goralnick and Gates, "We Fight Like We Train."
10. Walls and Zinner, "The Boston Marathon Response."
11. Sanchez and Sanchez, "Case Study: Emergency Department Response to the Boston Marathon Bombing."
12. Biddinger et al., "Be Prepared — The Boston Marathon and Mass-Casualty Events."

13. Nadworny et al., "Boston Strong—One Hospital's Response to the 2013 Boston Marathon Bombings."
14. Hearing before the Committee on Homeland Security and Governmental Affairs, "Lessons Learned from the Boston Marathon Bombings."
15. Walls and Zinner, "The Boston Marathon Response."
16. Biddinger et al., "Be Prepared — The Boston Marathon and Mass-Casualty Events."
17. Nadworny et al., "Boston Strong—One Hospital's Response to the 2013 Boston Marathon Bombings."
18. Hearing before the Committee on Homeland Security and Governmental Affairs, "Lessons Learned from the Boston Marathon Bombings"; Marcus, McNulty, and Serino, "Swarm Leadership in Times of Crisis."
19. Landman et al., "The Boston Marathon Bombings Mass Casualty Incident."
20. Goralnick and Gates, "We Fight Like We Train."
21. King et al., "Tourniquet Use at the Boston Marathon Bombing."
22. Boston Trauma Center Chiefs' Collaborative, "Boston Marathon Bombings."
23. Hounshell, *From the American System to Mass Production, 1800-1932.*
24. Goodfriend and McDermott, "The American System of Economic Growth."
25. Von Hippel, "'Sticky Information' and the Locus of Problem Solving"; Henderson and Clark, "Architectural Innovation."
26. Younkin and Hesla, "Origin of Numerical Control [History]."
27. Based on the authors' conversations, observations, and interviews.

Chapter 7
1. "Double Asteroid Redircetion Test (DART)"; Furfaro, "NASA's DART Data Validates Kinetic Impact as Planetary Defense Method."
2. Sweller, "Cognitive Load during Problem Solving."
3. Rubinstein, Meyer, and Evans, "Executive Control of Cognitive Processes in Task Switching."
4. Wheelwright, *Leading Product Development.*
5. Wheelwright, *Leading Product Development.*
6. "NEAR Shoemaker."
7. "Deep Space 1."
8. "Hayabusa."
9. "Rosetta."
10. "Dawn."
11. Bell and Thayer, "Software Requirements"; Benington, "Production of Large Computer Programs."

12. Kim et al., *The DevOps Handbook*.
13. Ward et al., "The Second Toyota Paradox."
14. Kim et al., *The DevOps Handbook*.
15. Blank, "No Plan Survives First Contact With Customers – Business Plans versus Business Models."
16. "DART Team."
17. "DART Impactor Spacecraft."
18. Skinner, "The Focused Factory."
19. Reinertsen, *The Principles of Product Development Flow*.
20. Reinertsen, *The Principles of Product Development Flow*, 57. (We replaced Reinertsen's use of the word "lean" with "linearized," to more precisely describe the causal mechanism at work.)
21. Hounshell, *From the American System to Mass Production, 1800-1932*.
22. Redgap, "Who Was That Guy?"; " December 1, 1923 | Ford's Assembly Line Starts Rolling."
23. Goldratt and Cox, *The Goal*.
24. Hayes, Wheelwright, and Clark, *Dynamic Manufacturing*.
25. Hammer, "Reengineering Work"; Hammer and Champy, *Reengineering the Corporation*.
26. Ohno, *Toyota Production System*.
27. Spear, *The High-Velocity Edge*.

Chapter 8
1. McCullough, *The Wright Brothers*.
2. "Consumer Price Index, 1800- | Federal Reserve Bank of Minneapolis."
3. "Wilbur and Orville"
4. "The Wright Brothers at Kitty Hawk."
5. "Langley Aerodrome A | National Air and Space Museum."
6. "Langley Aerodrome A | National Air and Space Museum."
7. "Brooklyn Museum - Open Collection."
8. "Monet and Chicago."
9. Explanatory plaque at the museum.
10. "Apple Reports Fourth Quarter Results."
11. Rooney, "Apple Profits Surge 67%, Shares Soar."
12. Kocienda, *Creative Selection*, 178–179.
13. Kocienda, *Creative Selection*, 178–179.
14. Kocienda, *Creative Selection*, 178–179.
15. Kocienda, *Creative Selection*, 178–179.
16. Kocienda, *Creative Selection*, 178–179.

17. Kocienda, *Creative Selection*, 178–179.
18. Siilasmaa, *Transforming NOKIA*.
19. Sheth, "Nokia Conducting Search for New CEO."
20. "Vendors' Market Share of Mobile Phone Unit Sales Worldwide 1997-2014"; Siilasmaa, *Transforming NOKIA*.
21. "Microsoft Mobile."
22. "Digest of Education Statistics, 2021."
23. "Wisconsin Public and Private Schools Are Canceling Classes; Here's an Updating List."
24. George, "National Test Scores Plunge, with Still No Sign of Pandemic Recovery."
25. Ralston and Coleman-Jensen, "USDA's National School Lunch Program Reduces Food Insecurity."
26. E-mail correspondence between Steve Spear and Dale Shaver, senior county administrator, June 27, 2023.
27. Bureau, "Nearly 93% of Households With School-Age Children Report Some Form of Distance Learning During COVID-19."
28. Carpenter and Dunn, "We're All Teachers Now."
29. "Survey Tracker."
30. "Share of K-12 Schools in the United States Teaching in-Person Due to the COVID-19 Pandemic from September 2020 to Febraury 2021."
31. "Share of K-12 Schools in the United States Teaching in-Person Due to the COVID-19 Pandemic from September 2020 to Febraury 2021."
32. Hone, *Learning War*; "Succeeding in Periods of Change."
33. Armstrong, "Continuous-Aim Fire."
34. Armstrong, "Continuous-Aim Fire."
35. Bomey, "How Barnes & Noble Pulled off an Unlikely Turnaround."
36. "Amazon.Com Revenue (Annual)"; "Amazon.Com Announces Financial Results for First Quarter 1998."
37. Killalea, "A Second Conversation with Werner Vogels."
38. Jesse Robbins, interview with Gene Kim, May 2, 2023.
39. Atchison, "Coding Over Cocktails: How to Archtect Your Applications to Scale with Lee Atchison."
40. Skelton and Pais, *Team Topologies*, 17.
41. Jesse Robbins, interview with Gene Kim, May 2, 2023.
42. Stone, *The Everything Store*, Kindle loc. 2486.
43. Stone, *The Everything Store*, Kindle loc. 2486.
44. Stone, *The Everything Store*, Kindle loc. 2486.
45. "Stevey's Google Platforms Rant."

46. O'Hanlon, "A Conversation with Werner Vogels."
47. "Velocity 2011"; "Transforming Software Development."
48. Kim et al., *The DevOps Handbook.*
49. "Amazon Annual Net Sales 2022."
50. "Amazon Web Services Revenue Growth 2022."
51. "Explore the 2022 IBM Annual Report Today"; Boyer, "The 360 Revolution."
52. "Origins of the IBM System/360 : History of Information"; Svigals, "IBM's Gamble, Part I, September 1966," September 4, 1966; Boyer, "The 360 Revolution."
53. Baldwin and Clark, *Design Rules, Volume 1*, 187.
54. Baldwin and Clark, *Design Rules,* Kindle loc. 3314.
55. Meyer, "IBM Rises from the Ashes."
56. Cortada, "Change and Continuity at IBM."
57. Baldwin and Clark, *Design Rules, Volume 1*, loc. 4352; "Origins of the IBM System/360 : History of Information."
58. "State of Devops Report 2017."
59. Wouters, McKee, and Luyten, "Estimated Research and Development Investment Needed to Bring a New Medicine to Market, 2009-2018"; Scannell et al., "Diagnosing the Decline in Pharmaceutical R&D Efficiency."
60. Spear, *The High-Velocity Edge*, 140.
61. McChrystal et al., *Team of Teams*; Kim, "The Idealcast: Episode 11"; Kim, "The Idealcast: Episode 13."
62. "David Silverman, Coauthor of 'Team of Teams.'"
63. "David Silverman, Coauthor of 'Team of Teams.'"
64. "David Silverman, Coauthor of 'Team of Teams.'"

Chapter 9

1. "Adapter, Gemini | National Air and Space Museum"; Charles, "The Space Review: Adapter in the Rough."
2. Johnson, *The Secret of Apollo*, 5.
3. Johnson, *The Secret of Apollo*, 12.
4. Johnson, *The Secret of Apollo*, 224.
5. Johnson, *The Secret of Apollo*, 128 & 222.
6. Johnson, *The Secret of Apollo*, 222.
7. Johnson, *The Secret of Apollo*, 223.
8. Johnson, *The Secret of Apollo*, 224.
9. Henderson and Clark, "Architectural Innovation."
10. Baldwin and Clark, *Design Rules, Volume 1.*
11. Spear, "The Essence of Just-in-Time."

Chapter 10

1. Bhattacharya, "A 'Once-in-a-Generation' Winter Storm Is Causing Thousands of Flight Cancellations."
2. NWS Buffalo [@NWSBUFFALO], "A Once-in-a-Generation Storm Will Produce High Winds East of Lake Ontario Thursday Night into Friday Morning, Then over a Larger Coverage of Our Region Friday into Saturday. Winds Could Gust over 65 Mph, Leading to at LEAST Scattered Power Outages, If Not Widespread Outages. Https://T.Co/G5EXx1TVNf."
3. Bushard, "Winter Storm Elliott."
4. Hickey, "How Southwest Failed the Holidays."
5. Not a Blue Check Mark [@FlyingTigress], "Evidently the @SouthwestAir Debacle Is Due to a Software Issue? Holy... @ElShanerino Https://T.Co/3jC-DgHJwJ6."
6. "Executive Session & Hearing."
7. "Executive Session & Hearing."
8. "Executive Session & Hearing."
9. 4Sammich, "I Have Friends in CS...."
10. Trottman, "Vaunted Southwest Slips In On-Time Performance."
11. Hiltzik, "The Real Story behind the Collapse in Southwest's on-Time Performance."
12. Murray, "Strengthening Airline Operations and Consumer Protections."
13. Shannon and Weaver, *The Mathematical Theory of Communication*.
14. Spear, "Frequency Domain Quantification of Manufacturing Process Resolution /."
15. Richards, *Certain to Win*.
16. Kranz, *Failure is Not an Option*, 204.
17. Kranz, *Failure is Not an Option*, 204.
18. Edmondson, *The Fearless Organization*.
19. Westrum, "The Study of Information Flow."
20. Westrum, "The Study of Information Flow."
21. Edmondson, *The Fearless Organization*.
22. "Re:Work Guide: Understanding Team Effectiveness."
23. "Re:Work Guide: Understanding Team Effectiveness."
24. Forsgren, Humble, and Kim, *Accelerate*," Kindle loc. 793.
25. Forsgren, Humble, and Kim, *Accelerate*," 68.
26. Sinek [@simonsinek], "Communication Is Not about Saying What We Think. Communication Is about Ensuring Others Hear What We Mean."
27. McChrystal et al., *Team of Teams*, 177.
28. Risto Siilaasma, interview with Gene Kim, April 20, 2022.

29. Siilasmaa, *Transforming NOKIA*, loc. 1382.

30. Dupor, "Examining Long and Variable Lags in Monetary Policy."

31. Friedman, "The Lag in Effect of Monetary Policy."

32. "Transcript: Fed Chief Powell's Postmeeting Press Conference."

Conclusion

1. Spear, *The High-Velocity Edge*.

2. Kim et al., *The DevOps Handbook*, 184.

3. Womack and Shook, *Gemba Walks Expanded 2nd Edition*, 65.

4. Argyris and Schön, *Organizational Learning*.

5. Kim et al., *The DevOps Handbook*, 25.

6. Kim et al., *The DevOps Handbook*, 43.

7. Ries, *The Lean Startup*; Blank, *The Four Steps to the Epiphany*.

8. "Re:Work Guide: Understanding Team Effectiveness."

9. Forsgren, Humble, and Kim, *Accelerate*, 59.

10. Bernstein, "Characterizing People as Non-Linear, First-Order Components in Software Development, Is Written by Alistair A.R. Cockburn and Published in Humans and Technology, HaT Technical Report 1999.03, Oct 21, 1999."

11. "House of Commons Rebuilding (Hansard, 28 October 1943)."

Appendix A

1. Kahneman, *Thinking, Fast and Slow*.

2. Porter, *The Competitive Strategy*.

3. Jensen and Meckling, "Theory of the Firm."

INDEX

ACKNOWLEDGMENTS

Gene Kim

Thank you to my wife, Margueritte, who makes everything possible for me. And also to my sons, Reid, Parker, and Grant, for putting up with me being in deadline mode for the last three years. And I'm so sorry that I've had to work on our family vacations because of deadlines (again).

Thank you to Anna Noak for going way above and beyond what editors typically do to bring a book into being. Thank you also to Leah Brown: in the final stages of creating this book, almost every aspect of this entire endeavor was in the *danger zone*. I am grateful for their ingenuity and willingness to take unheard of risks to make this book something we are all proud of. Steve and I are very grateful.

I want to thank the following people who helped me understand what effective software architectures are, which inform so much of this book. This was a slowly dawning aha moment that spanned over the last decade: Dr. Carliss Baldwin (Harvard Business School), Adrian Cockcroft, Jeffrey Fredrick (coauthor of *Agile Conversations*), Dr. Nicole Forsgren (Microsoft Research), Scott Havens (Narvar), Elisabeth Hendrickson (Curious Duck Digital Laboratory), Rich Hickey (inventor of Clojure), Jez Humble (Google), Dr. Mik Kersten (Planview), Dr. Gail Murphy (University of British Columbia), Eric Normand (Grokking Simplicity), Mike Nygard (Nubank).

And to the following people who helped me understand the concept of the (socio)technical maestro: David Silverman (CrossLead), Admiral John

Richardson. Dr. Ron Westrum (Eastern Michigan University), and Risto Siilasmaa.

Thank you to Jesse Robbins (Heavybit) for helping me finally understand the amazing Amazon transformation. And to CDR Jeff "Gazer" Pinkerton for helping us better understand coupling and cohesion by explaining the interactions between Landing Signal Officers and naval aviators (and to RDML Seiko Okano for making that possible).

Charles Betz (Forrester), Luke Burton (Apple), Fernando Cornago (Adidas), James Cham (Bloomberg Beta), Jason Cox (The Walt Disney Company), Robbie Daitzman (Vanguard), Andrew Davis (Inside Out), Cornelia Davis (Spectro Cloud), Ian Eslick (Technology/Industry Executive), Jeffrey Fredrick (coauthor of *Agile Conversations*), Adam Furtado (Sagely), Paul Gaffney (Omni Logistics), Jeff Gallimore (Excella), Brendan Hopper (Commonwealth Bank of Australia), Dr. Mik Kersten (Planview CTO), Courtney Kissler (Starbucks), Jerry Kummer (USAF 309th Software Engineering Group), Dean Leffingwell (Scaled Agile), Thomas A. Limoncelli (Stack Overflow), Christopher Little, Ruth Malan (Bredemeyer Consulting), Dave Mangot (Mangoteque), Erica Morrison (Cision), Eric Normand (Author, Grokking Simplicity), Michael Nygard (Nubank), RDML Seiko Okano (US Navy), Manuel Pais, (coauthor of *Team Topologies*), Dr. Jennifer Pierce (Singular XQ), Christopher Porter (Fannie Mae), Lt. Col. Max Reele (USAF), Luke Rettig (Target), ADM John Richardson (USN, ret.), Lt. Col. John Schreiner (USMC), Adrienne Shulman (Tenger Ways), Matthew Skelton (Conflux, coauthor of *Team Topologies*), RADM Doug Small (US Navy), Steve Smith (Equal Experts), Dr. Michael Stone (Wild Health), Phil Venables (Google Cloud), Amy Willard (John Deere), John Willis (Botchagalupe Technologies), Dr. Branden R. Williams (Ping Identity, University of Dallas), Michael Winslow (Amazon Music), Christina Yakomin (Vanguard).

Steve Spear

Many people had a direct impact on the content and form of this book. First, it wouldn't exist without lessons learned from my wife, Miriam. Our offices adjoin, so I get to vicariously learn from her work as an architect. Ideas into plans are only part of that work, which I've come to appreciate. Designing great community buildings that help build great communities (the Layer 1 object in our parlance and the focus of Miriam's work) depends on creating an outstanding Layer 3 social circuitry to draw on and synthesize toward common purpose the contributions of clients, consultants, builders, sub-contractors, inspectors, and suppliers. Seeing how this happens every day helped model each of the mechanisms about which we write.

Several mentors passed while this book was gestating, each of whom left us with unfinished homework.

Clayton Christensen taught that "disruptive innovation" isn't a technological issue; it is a behavioral one. Incumbents get so entwined in their existing mental models of what to sell, to whom, and with what value proposition, that they stop looking for answered problems because they'd lost their empathy for and concerns about the problems of people they didn't know well.

Clay's homework: Go find someone about whom you've given no consideration, learn what their concerns are, and try to develop solutions that fit them and their circumstances.

Hajime Ohba was General Manager for Toyota's supplier support center in North America. Ohba-san taught how tightly aligned the experiences of people doing work were directly with the metrics of the enterprise, showing how to use shop-floor observations to test if the social circuitry that conveyed material, information, tools, skills, and support helped associates to succeed. If not, that was a critique of the conditions leaders had created and premonition of competing poorly.

Ohba's homework: Find someone who is struggling to be consistently creative. Commit time and create the program to build their skills as a problem-solver and create conditions in which they can succeed.

Paul O'Neill led Alcoa, created and championed the Pittsburgh Regional Healthcare Initiative, and was Secretary of the Treasury. Paul led Alcoa during an extraordinary transformation. High-hazard worksites had been high risk, with injuries occurring at rates you would associate with mining, refining, smelting, forging, extrusion, and other heavy industrial processes. Paul championed a dynamic of amplifying little problems so they would be seen and solved before they became big ones. This wasn't just a technical solution of amplifying glitches. It was a social revolution, giving voice to people who'd badged in or punched into work to call out risks they faced, with the expectation that those "higher up than them" would respond immediately by swarming and solving immediate problems and quickly sharing what had been discovered. By this, Alcoa had achieved near-perfect workplace safety, best in the USA, while also improving on quality, yield, time to market, and so forth. He then showed the local healthcare community how the same dynamic would improve patient safety and quality of care while also improving the workforce's experiences too.

Paul's homework: Find people for whom you are responsible and ask them: Are you treated with dignity and respect? Are you given whatever you need to succeed, and does this bring value to your life? Are you recognized for what you do by someone whose opinion matters? Conditions that generate a "no" to any of these merit correction.

Who knows where our understanding of industrial competitiveness would be without Norman Bodek. When American political and corporate leaders were responding to Japanese competitiveness as a Cold War-like nation-state contest, Norman went to Japan, found the expert teachers there, as was his regular practice of finding great teachers for anything that interested him, and created a publisher, Productivity Press, to share their wisdom with English speaking practitioners. It is because of Norman that English readers first knew of Taichi Ohno and Shigeo Shingo. Later in life, Norman shared his own well-earned wisdom, authoring numerous books to remind leaders to focus on the human experience, with machines and materials as supportive of that, rather than getting lost in the costs and quantity of inanimate objects and forgetting those exist only so people can create value for other people.

Norman's homework: Find something you know nothing about. Study it. Teach others what you have learned.

For nearly a hundred years, the Feuerstein family operated Malden Mills, pioneering Polartec, fleece fabrics more generally, and other textile innovations. This is a significant accomplishment. Given their fabrics' performance in unforgiving environments, one can imagine that the company's products did more than make people comfortable. For some, they helped prevent terrible harm in adverse conditions. That the Feuerstein's did this as a New England-based manufacturer, when the industry as a whole was seeking low wages, is also remarkable enough.

However, in December 1995, a catastrophic fire erupted, destroying the factory. Owner Aaron Feuerstein could have done the "normal" thing: collect the insurance money and move on to other things. Instead, he committed to rebuilding, promised to keep the workforce on the payroll in the meantime, and was able to restore employment to nearly the entire workforce, thereby earning the sobriquet "the Mensch of Malden."

Aaron's homework: Ask yourself, with the authority and opportunities you've been given, for whom do you have responsibility?

Many have been unusually generous in letting me see the nitty-gritty of what they do, exposing the difficulty, the detail, and the necessary skill in every creative act. Others have repeatedly shaped and reshaped my thinking by telling me what was wrong. Their contributions are throughout this book.

This includes but is not limited to: Stephen Ashman, John Baldoni, Carliss Baldwin, Joe Barto, Eric Bergamen, Lorraine Bittner, Steve Blank, Chuck Blackledge, Jamie Bonini, Kent Bowen, Rick Breckenridge, Scott Brown, Christopher Brunett, John Carrier, Ellen Chang, BJ Cloutier, Darrell Cook, Ross Csaszer, Karen Davis, Eric Dickson, Christina Dixon, Brian Donnell, Gadi Dvir, Steve Eppinger, Steve Fahey, Alice Fakre, Roberto Fernandez, Jeff Gallimore, Corey Gallo, Brad Garber, Daniel Gordon, Patricia Greco, Bill Green, Jeff Gross, Berto Guerra, Christian Guerra, Bruce Hamilton, Scott Harvey, Peter Hirst, Lucy Holt, Trent Hone, Susann Kazunas, Jeff Jablon, Joel Jergeson, Tami Johnson, Allison Kakmar Richards, Michael Kavanaugh, Steve King, Beth Knapp Read, Tom LaBatt, David Lane, Bill Lescher, Steve Levisohn, David Lewis, Stan McChrystal, Paul McClay, Patricia McDonald, Maria Mentzer, Nicole Morlinaro, Pete Newell, Anna Noak, Jose Olivero, Sam Paparo, Jason Paragas, Vickie Pisowicz, Keith Reitel, John Richardson, Kevin Schilling, Lorin Selby, Dale Shaver, David Silverman, Ezra Sivan Zuckerman, Doug Small, Jason Stack, John Sterman, Michael Stewart, Patrick Stoy, Scott Swift, Michael Tamasi, Keith Terhune, Jeff Trussler, Tim Tyler, Kevin Voelkel, Martin Wallace, Des Walker, Matt Welborne, Steven Wheelwright, Ken Whitesell, Mark Whitney, James Wolfe, Tony Wood, and Ron Wyatt.

In terms of details and nitty-gritty, authors get credit for their work, with editors as the hidden figures. That's just not fair. A book is the Layer 1 "technical object" being created; the authors are working at Layer 2; and the editor works through them by managing Layer 3's processes of text generation, editing, and so forth. We are indebted to and appreciative of Anna Noak, Leah Brown, and their team through this process.

Lastly, in terms of generation to generation, I'm a fourth-generation American whose time is spent in factories, shipyards, laboratories, clinics, and with members of the armed forces, hopefully learning a lot from everyone and sharing back what I can. By coincidence or by design, that continues the family tradition. There, great-grandparents Izzy and Helen Spielman, who had a shoe factory in Punxsutawney, creating good jobs for good people to make good products. My other great-grandparents, Jack and Bessie Wasserman, also immigrants, who'd gone into the clothing business. My one grandfather, Sol Spear, worked in the Brooklyn shipyards during the war, while his wife, Gussie, was raising two boys amidst war-time scarcity and all the anxiety about what was befalling their families, in Europe. My other grandfather, Gene Wasserman, served overseas as did his brother, Bunny, and two brothers-in-law, Len Zoref and Seymour Hirsch, while their wives Anita, Rita, Selma, and Muriel held down the homefront in their absence. There are countless educators, healers, and community servants in the family—my parents, Bernie and Laurie; my brother Jonathan and his wife Lisa; Miriam's parents, Dr. Angel and Matilde Tropp; Miriam's brother Daniel, and many others. Hopefully, this book and the work it represents help continue and sustain the next generations, in at least a small way, such family commitments.

ABOUT THE AUTHORS

G ene Kim is a multi–award-winning CTO, researcher, and author. He is the founder of Tripwire and served as CTO for thirteen years. He is the author of six books, which have sold over one million copies, including *The Unicorn Project* (2019), and coauthor of the Shingo Publication award-winning *Accelerate* (2018), *The DevOps Handbook* (2016), and *The Phoenix Project* (2013). Since 2014, he has been the organizer of DevOps Enterprise Summit, studying the technology transformations of large, complex organizations.

Gene Kim has a Master of Computer Science from the University of Arizona and has been studying high-performing technology organizations since 1999. He was the founder and, for 13 years, CTO of Tripwire, Inc, an enterprise security software company. In 2007, *ComputerWorld* added Gene to the "40 Innovative IT People to Watch Under the Age of 40" list, and he was named a Computer Science Outstanding Alumnus by Purdue University for achievement and leadership in the profession. He lives with his wife and children in Portland, Oregon.

Follow Gene on X @realgenekim and LinkedIn at linkedin.com/in/realgenekim/.

D r. Steven J. Spear, DBA, MS, MS, is a senior lecturer at the MIT Sloan School of Management, a Senior Fellow at the Institute for Healthcare Improvement, and author of influential publications such as *The High-Velocity Edge*, "Decoding the DNA of the Toyota Production System," and "Fixing Healthcare from the Inside, Today." An advisor to corporate and governmental leaders across a range of fields, he is also the founder of See to Solve, a business process software company.

Spear once worked in finance, at a Congressional agency, and at the University of Tokyo. He has a doctorate from Harvard, a masters degrees in mechanical engineering and management from MIT, and a bachelor's degree in economics from Princeton. He and his wife, Miriam, an architect, live in Brookline, Massachusetts, where they volunteer for several community organizations.

Follow Steve on LinkedIn at www.linkedin.com/in/stevespear/.